Edward Riojas's *A Complete Guide to Christian Symbols* is a spiritually enriching guide to the history, meaning, and significance of Christian symbols in religious rituals, liturgical art, and everyday life. From highlighting elements of familiar symbols to identifying intricate details of lesser-used iconography, Riojas uses thoughtful explanations and detailed illustrations to take readers on a fascinating journey through symbolism in Christianity. His expert commentary on liturgical art as it relates to Holy Scripture will inform, inspire, and deepen your understanding of your faith. This book is an essential resource for theologians, artists, and anyone interested in Christianity.

Carrie Roberts, founder, Ecclesiastical Sewing

Ed Riojas has provided us with a comprehensive and interesting guide to understanding the language of symbolism in the church. I plan on using this book as a guide to teach my children about Christian symbols. I appreciate the thoroughness of his research in incorporating several different Christian traditions and the history of the symbols being used. This book is a library of images to aid pastors, laypeople, and families in catechesis. It is a wonderful companion to assist in the understanding of Christian art in museums, churches, and books. This book is a gift to the church!

Kelly Schumacher (Uffenbeck), liturgical artist, Agnus Dei Liturgical Arts

A Christian's life is immersed in beauty. With his brilliantly artistic mind and deep understanding of Lutheran theology, Edward Riojas guides us through the beautiful symbolism that surrounds us in the rhythm of our liturgical lives. He seamlessly weaves church history, traditions, and teachings with the shapes, colors, words, faces, and fabrics of the church, creating a remarkably thorough resource for pastors and laity alike. He describes in detail the tremendous significance of the images and objects we regularly encounter. The curious observer, like me, will no longer wonder what symbols on a vestment represent, what a stained glass window depicts, or what a saint's clothing means. Now, we can recognize and confirm the beautiful symbolism that continually points us to Christ, His promises to us, and the gifts we receive from Him through the church.

Sarah Gulseth, digital media specialist, KFUO Radio

Equally beneficial to the liturgical artist and the curious church member, this book is extremely user friendly as a navigation tool through the world of Christian symbolism. It particularly shines in its attention to the visuals most frequently encountered in the context of congregational worship. The attention given to symbols connected with Reformation history and the theologically informed guidance as to the appropriate use of various symbolic representations make for a unique resource that is as practical as it is visually captivating.

Kelly Klages, artist and illustrator

A COMPLETE GUIDE TO CHRISTIAN SYMBOLS

EDWARD RIOJAS

CONCORDIA PUBLISHING HOUSE · SAINT LOUIS

Published by Concordia Publishing House
3558 S. Jefferson Ave., St. Louis, MO 63118-3968
1-800-325-3040 • cph.org

Library of Congress Cataloging-in-Publication Data

Names: Riojas, Edward, author.

Title: A sign unto you : a primer of Christian symbolism / Edward Riojas.

Description: Saint Louis : Concordia Publishing House, [2023] | Summary: "Christian symbolism condenses narratives, ideas, and themes into concise visuals, thereby communicating and underlining the richness of Scripture and its message. With more than 640 images, A Sign unto You provides a wealth of Christian symbolism in one place, one artistic style, and one format. It briefly explains those symbols, offers a bit of historical use, and provides practical advice on their use. This guidebook of symbolism is a visual source of inspiration for artisans who create banners and other visuals and a teaching tool for those who wish to know more about the vast history of symbols used in the Christian church"-- Provided by publisher.

Identifiers: LCCN 2023030533 (print) | LCCN 2023030534 (ebook) | ISBN 9780758673930 (paperback) | ISBN 9780758673947 (ebook)

Subjects: LCSH: Christian art and symbolism.

Classification: LCC BV150 .R49 2023 (print) | LCC BV150 (ebook) | DDC 246/.55--dc23/eng/20240308

LC record available at https://lccn.loc.gov/2023030533

LC ebook record available at https://lccn.loc.gov/2023030534

---

3 4 5 6 7 8 9 10 11 33 32 31 30 29 28 27 26 25

Contents

Foreword

This volume has a backstory, as do most books. It began decades ago as a rather humble project intended to be a resource for people involved in producing sanctuary art. Artisans create banners, fixtures, furniture, and the like for the sanctuary, whether by commission or through their own inspiration. I have visited enough sanctuaries to know that results vary in quality, inspiration, and—dare I say—correctness. Therefore I hoped to offer a collection of Scripture-based and artistically sound designs as a guide to appropriate Christian symbolism. This book was also intended to be a companion to an existing body of ecclesiastical art that accompanies the historic one-year lectionary and the new three-year lectionary. This book would, in theory, round out what was lacking in that earlier work of mine.

Once that first seed of idea and purpose was sown, it became apparent to me that there were much greater needs. Not only is there a need for Christian symbols of uniform design, there is also a need to correct a lack of understanding among laity and clergy regarding even the most basic of Christian symbols. When one peruses similar books, it quickly becomes obvious that this is not a new problem; it recurs with enough regularity that teaching Christian symbolism is constantly warranted. Without an understanding of the meaning behind sacred symbolism, its beauty and significance quickly fade.

Beyond the commonly recognized symbols, there are mountains of symbols representing scriptural truths and denominational doctrines. And so I began. What was intended to be a crafter's guide for a specific denomination morphed into this visual encyclopedia of symbolism for the broader scope of Christendom, because as soon as I had completed the initial group of symbols, a pastor asked if I could increase the scope by another margin. Eventually the original roster of a few dozen designs swelled to the more than six hundred images you see here. Even with that number, it is impossible to claim this—or any other collection—to be an unabridged volume. Christian symbols are constantly being invented, redesigned, and redefined. Some symbols fall into disuse or complete abandonment, while others are resurrected. Some symbols are usurped by heresy. Others are fought over by the church and the unbelieving world.

In the end, the purpose of this book is multifaceted. *A Complete Guide to Christian Symbols* provides a wealth of Christian symbolism in one place, one artistic style, and one format. It briefly explains these symbols with occasional advice on their use and a bit of history. While this book is not a scholarly tome, it may be used as a teaching tool to support Holy Scripture. It can also act as a sort of guidebook when confronting unfamiliar sanctuaries, denominations, and sacred art. Finally, it is intended to be a visual source of inspiration for the artisans of the church in adorning the house of the Lord.

A great deal of thanks is owed to all those who urged and cajoled and prodded me in completing this endeavor. An even greater debt of thanks is owed to our Lord and Savior, Jesus Christ, who has blessed the labor of my hands, who has blessed Christendom with the visual arts and enough artistic forebears to develop the symbolism that we, through the ages, have inherited, and who has given true meaning and inexpressible beauty to His church in the first place.

Introduction

Not every corner of Christendom uses symbolism. One need only leave an ornate Eastern Orthodox sanctuary, walk down the road, and enter a Baptist church to see opposite ends of the spectrum. The former may dazzle the eyes with an abundance of symbolism and opulent splendor, while the latter may be hard pressed to offer a simple cross somewhere on the premises. The visual difference is jarring. Between those extremes are a plethora of variations, loosely following denominational lines, with even more subtle differences inside each group.

The reason for this isn't simply an appreciation for Christian symbolism or a lack thereof, but rather how artwork in general is viewed by each church body. The topic of art may seem benign enough, but it has been a viciously contended point throughout history and continues to be a source of contention. Grandiose terms like the "Iconoclastic Controversy," for instance, belie the unfortunate shedding of blood among common citizens and clergy for the sake of the much simpler words "graven images."

"You shall not make for yourself a carved image, or any likeness of anything that is in heaven above, or that is in the earth beneath, or that is in the water under the earth" (Exodus 20:4). This verse is always quoted by those who refrain from displaying nearly every visual thing in the sanctuary. Yet they ignore the verse's larger context and fail to reconcile the numerous times in the Old Testament when the Lord commanded His people to fashion various likenesses, including, of all things, a snake on a pole.

The fact is that sacred art follows a parallel path with sacred music. That is, both can point us to the Word by underlining Scripture or illustrating it or repeating it. Christian symbolism takes things another step by condensing narratives and ideas into concise visuals. By pondering them, it is possible to reconstitute the richness of Scripture from a simple design.

Alas, man is a stupid and forgetful creature. A common lament from earlier books on this subject is that we are prone to forget the meaning of symbols and would rather wallow in ignorance than attempt to correct the problem. We look at a dusty tome filled with symbols, inwardly declare that it is no longer relevant, and fail to recognize that its essence is as worthy of our attention now as when first wrought by our ecclesiastical forebears. This collection, therefore, is meant to edify and enrich; it is intended to remind us of the manifold blessings of our Lord and Savior, Jesus Christ; it is meant to be, as it were, frontlets between our eyes.

Among the many subjects taught in seminaries, Christian symbolism is rarely one of them. There are too many other things we would rather have a pastor know. We cannot expect a pastor to be well versed in Christian symbolism if he was never given the chance to learn about it in the first place, yet great opportunities to catechize are lost if even the most fundamental basics of symbolism are ignored.

When Jesus Christ taught, He often used parables—easily-digestible stories filled with imagery—to convey realities in the kingdom of heaven. Mundane objects such as candles and coins and vines unveiled divine truths. In a similar manner, simple shapes and objects have been pressed into service to teach and remind parishioners of those things which we believe. A circle, for example, has come to mean eternity, and a triangle suggests the Holy Trinity. An image of a fish brings to mind Jesus Christ, and an animal's feeding trough reminds us of His holy incarnation. Through the centuries, a collection of images expanded to the point that a sort of visual language emerged. Whole church sanctuaries could be visually broken down and not only explain the life of Christ but also emphasize doctrinal truths and point to related portions of Scripture. Symbols serve as visual shorthand and communicate lessons to the viewer.

A book, however, is a better teaching tool when someone of authority passes on its information. Pastors have both authority and opportunity. They can encourage artisans-in-residence and parishioners to simply observe church surroundings and take an active part in learning about the meaning behind the symbols that appear in the sanctuary.

The Holy Trinity

Central to Christianity is, of course, Christ Jesus, but it is impossible to address the humanity of Jesus without addressing His divinity. Neither can His divinity be addressed without addressing the Father and the Holy Spirit. Thus, a rather large group of symbols has been developed to convey the Holy Trinity as a whole and the Father, Son, and Holy Spirit as individual Persons in that whole. It is an impossible task; no amount of words or pictures can define the boundless and indivisible properties of our Lord. Still, artists try.

Not surprisingly, symbols for the Holy Trinity always contain visuals–often shapes–indicating the number three.

The Tri-radiant Nimbus

FIGURE 1

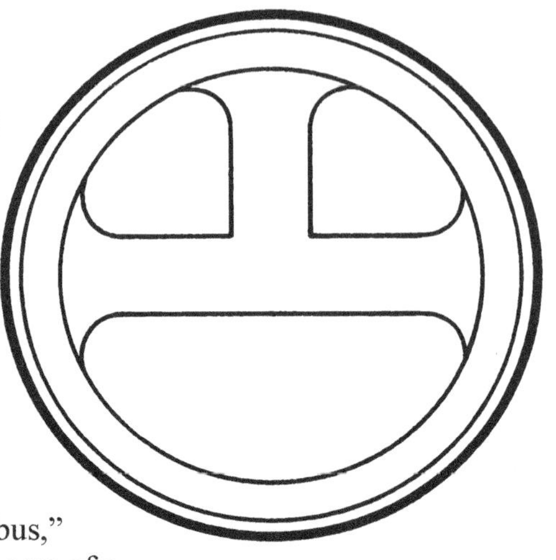

This is one of the oldest, yet by far one of the most misunderstood, symbols of the Holy Trinity. Its origin may be traced to the early church, when artists borrowed the nimbus from other religions. A circle was sometimes placed behind the head of important figures, differentiating them from the common rabble. As artistic expression became more common among the first generation of Christians, a device was used to set Christ apart from His disciples. Thus, the tri-radiant nimbus was created.

Some have called this symbol a "cruciform nimbus," but that is incorrect. This name assumes that the fourth arm of a cross is hidden by the figure itself, but the cross is not part of this symbol at all. This becomes evident when considering images of the Holy Spirit as a dove and the Father as a hand, which bear the same visual device. The Athanasian Creed, in clarifying, admonishes: "Neither confusing the persons nor dividing the substance." The Holy Spirit was not crucified. Neither was the Father. Only the Son was crucified, thus the "cruciform" nimbus is a misnomer.

In fact, the tri-radiant nimbus confesses far more than a simple cross. An image of a crucified Jesus with such a nimbus would be redundant if a cross were behind His head, but a tri-radiant nimbus declares Jesus as a Person of the Holy Trinity, being therefore truly divine and truly human. The same is true of the dove, which is not a simple avian apparition but the indivisible Person of the Holy Trinity. It is also true of symbols of the Father, who did not die on the cross but is also a Person of the Holy Trinity.

Triangle

FIGURE 2

This basic shape does a fair job in defining the Holy Trinity, in that it is one shape with three equal sides and three angles. The triangle has also been used as an alternative to the tri-radiant nimbus.

Circles Encircled

FIGURE 3

Three intertwined circles, often within a fourth circle, give a somewhat better confession than a triangle. The circle—without beginning or end—confesses the eternal quality of God. The three circles intertwined illustrate the indivisible nature of the three Persons of the Trinity.

Entwined Triangle with Circles

FIGURE 4

This symbol makes the tripartite and indivisible nature of the Holy Trinity obvious, if not redundant.

Triquetra, and Triquetra Encircled

FIGURE 5

This design has origins in pagan motifs but was adopted by the medieval church as a symbol for the Holy Trinity. It is generally regarded as a knot construction of three loops, so it doesn't take a huge logical leap to understand the reason for its adoption.

Holy Trinity Shield

FIGURE 6

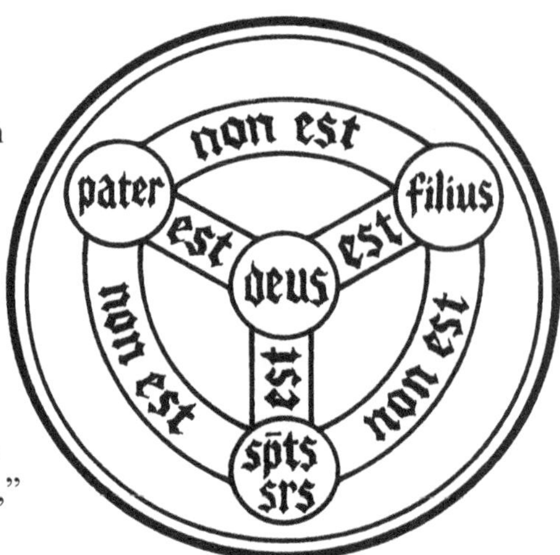

This developed as a condensation of the Athanasian Creed. It explains the unity of Holy Trinity while simultaneously differentiating between the Persons. In particular, it visualizes the Creed's phrase "neither confusing the persons nor dividing the substance." In this Latin version, "God" is in the central circle, while the Persons of the Trinity are represented in outer circles. Bridging those circles are the words *is* and *is not*. Hence, it may be read that "The Father is God," "The Son is God," "The Father is not the Son," and so forth.

Three Angels Supping

FIGURE 7

This image is found in Eastern Orthodox iconography and is one of the more unusual symbols for the Holy Trinity. It is taken from Genesis 18, in which three angels appear to Abraham. Before allowing the angels to state their business, Abraham begs them to eat and goes through the process of preparing a large meal. It is generally understood that the angels are the Persons of the Holy Trinity.

The Father

Depictions of the Father have been problematic from the get-go. Artists have at times tried to depict the Ancient of Days, but the attempts always fall miserably flat; confining omnipresence personified is an exercise in futility. Imagery of the Father has taken the form of an old, bearded man, and it strikes the viewer's eyes as being infinitely insufficient for the majesty and power of that Person. Nevertheless, the Father's attributes, roles, and actions are used in symbolism to help communicate His vast power, presence, and provision since the Creation and unto eternity.

The Father's Hand of Blessing

FIGURE 8

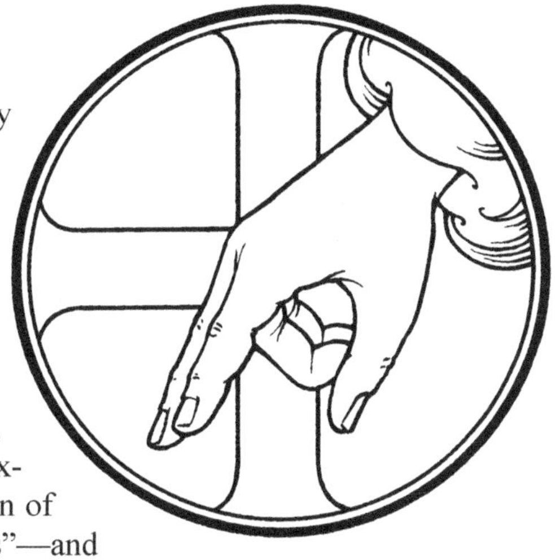

The best approach is to symbolize the Father by showing just His hand. In this way, utmost respect is rendered by avoiding showing His face and by not revealing too much of His scale, both of which are impossible for humans to do or to fathom. This is where symbols best serve us: by indicating through the simplest image that which cannot—and should not—be shown. By showing the Father's hand only, the symbol also plays very well with Holy Scripture, which comes to us through the hand of God, as is expressed in Isaiah 48:13—"My hand laid the foundation of the earth, and My right hand spread out the heavens"—and elsewhere.

Some collections of Christian symbols lump together variations of the hand and claim them all as symbols of the Father. A distinction should be made, however, between some of them. Hands relating to the Father come down from above and often show His hand reaching down from a cloud. Hands that come from below, or that give the impression that the body they are attached to is below or to the side, should be understood as symbols of the Father's Son, Jesus Christ. The fingers are in the same attitude as during the Aaronic blessing given by a pastor at the close of the service, as well as when the pastor acts in the stead and by the command of Jesus Christ. The Orthodox Church takes this symbol a step further in configuring the fingers in such a convoluted way that they spell out the title, Christ.

The Father's Hand of Protection

FIGURE 9

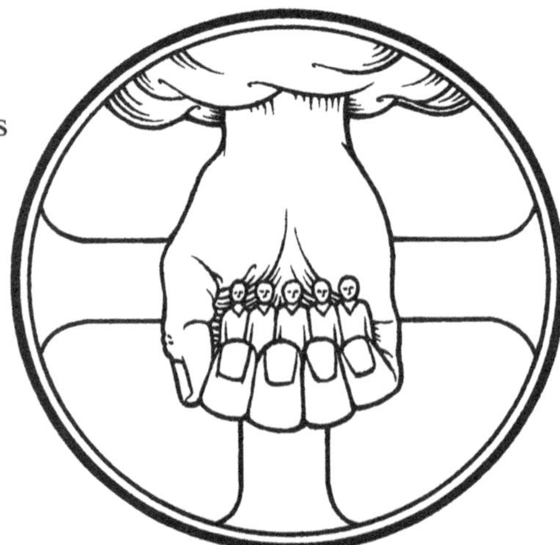

In this lovely reassuring symbol are five figures representing the souls of the faithful. The artist took liberties in assuming the scale of God, but the viewer gets a much better sense of comparison, and the curled fingers indicate that we are His and He will protect us from harm.

The All-Seeing Eye

FIGURE 10

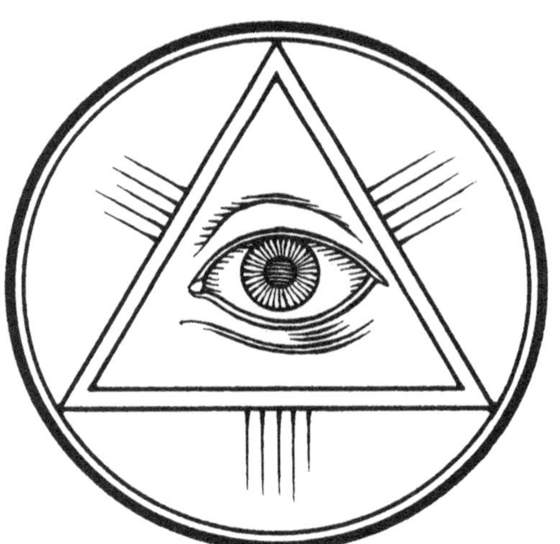

As the hand symbol gives homage without showing the Father's whole form, so does the singular all-seeing eye. It must be shown within a triangle, otherwise the symbol falls headfirst into the realm of secret societies. In fact, it is probably best to avoid using this symbol, if only for the sake of avoiding confusion with groups that have vastly different confessions.

The Yodh

FIGURES 11, 12

This symbol could be included in the Abbreviations section (beginning on page 63), though it is strange enough to our eyes and never stands alone as a symbol, as do most other abbreviations. The yodh is a Hebrew character that is an abbreviation of the identity by which the Lord called Himself in the Old Testament. Such is the reverence given to God that a single character was sufficient to identify Him. Sometimes this character is doubled, giving a nod to the specific name of Adonai. The yodh is shown circumscribed by a triangle, doubled inside David's Star, or set within a stylized sunburst to indicate the cloud of glory. The latter device may hold whole Hebrew words, such as those translated as "Jehovah," "the Lord," or "the Almighty," but these are rarely seen in modern settings.

The Son

The Second Person of the Holy Trinity has the most symbols attributed to Him. This is understandable, for not only do the prophets speak of the Christ through vivid imagery but so also does Jesus speak of Himself through word pictures. Add to this images that the early church developed to describe attributes of Christ, and the list of symbols grows exceedingly long.

Some symbols have been omitted from this collection simply because they have fallen out of use and have either attained worldly meanings or have lost their meanings altogether. The unicorn, for example, was a medieval symbol for Jesus Christ, but now its principal use is as a juvenile motif. Some floral symbols for Jesus Christ have also fallen by the wayside; among them are the gladiolus, the daisy, and the Glastonbury thorn.

The Good Shepherd

FIGURE 13

This is one of the earliest symbols for Jesus Christ adopted by the church. While it may seem to be of limited application—for this term is only found in the Gospel of John—the early church was shrewd enough to take the Hebraic image of David as a shepherd along with Roman imagery of the Greek mythological god Hermes Kriophoros and combine them into use. This allowed believers to supplant ancient but familiar imagery from two cultures with a greater symbol. Newer versions of the Good Shepherd are depictions of Christ Jesus as we know Him from John 10:11 and 10:14, but the earliest images show a young, beardless youth much closer to the Kriophoros ideal. With the lamb over His shoulder, the two are nearly identical.

Agnus Dei

FIGURE 14

It doesn't take much of a leap to move from an image of the Good Shepherd to that of the Lamb of God. Foretold by Abraham, who tells Isaac that "God will provide for Himself the lamb for a burnt offering" (Genesis 22:8) and fulfilled by the proclamation of John the Baptist: "Behold, the Lamb of God, who takes away the sin of the world!" (John 1:29), Jesus as the Lamb of God has been a familiar symbol since the days of Augustine. Jesus Christ is the perfect sacrifice, the sinless one who atoned for our sins. To reinforce this, it is important to include the tri-radiant nimbus to differentiate this Lamb from others.

The Sacrificial Agnus Dei

FIGURE 15

This symbol is appropriate for Passiontide in that it shows Jesus' blood being poured out for us poor, miserable sinners. Most often, a chalice catches the blood, so the symbol is also strongly associated with the Lord's Supper. The Lamb may also be shown holding a cross-topped staff.

The Victorious Agnus Dei

FIGURE 16

This is the Easter counterpart to the Sacrificial Agnus Dei symbol. It is important in this case to show the wound, although blood does not issue from it. The staff is topped with a cross-emblazoned victory banner, which has for centuries been associated with the resurrection. Beginning with the Proto-Renaissance, paintings of Christ's resurrection often place such a banner in His hand. The banner is most often white, indicating Christ's sinlessness, with a red cross, indicating His sacrifice.

Agnus Dei on the Book of Seven Seals

FIGURE 17

Taken from the book of Revelation, this image symbolizes Christ Jesus in the fullness of time. The Lamb is usually shown at rest but still bearing the wound of His sacrifice. It points to the worthiness of our Lord, who alone was able to open the book.

Dayspring

FIGURE 18

A rising sun may be used as a symbol for the coming Christ, especially during Advent. The title for the Christ was uttered by Zechariah when prophesying concerning his own son, John (Luke 1:76–79). It is also referenced in Malachi 4:2 and Luke 1:78: "Through the tender mercy of our God; whereby the dayspring from on high hath visited us" (KJV). And also in Revelation 22:16: "I am the Root and the Offspring of David, the bright Morning Star" (KJV).

Sun of Righteousness

FIGURE 19

This symbol is specifically mentioned in Malachi 4:2: "But for you who fear My name, the sun of righteousness shall rise with healing in its wings." While the prophet speaks of the sun as "rising," it is usually shown fully risen and blazing. In either this symbol or the Dayspring, the monogram for Jesus, IHS or IHC, may be superimposed on the sun.

The Pelican in Her Piety

FIGURE 20

This symbol originated in the Middle Ages to depict the self-sacrificing nature of Christ Jesus. However, the imagery is based on fancy and not on ornithological knowledge. The female pelican is more apt to abandon her brood when food is scarce rather than pierce her own breast to feed them.

The Phoenix

FIGURE 21

This ancient symbol was usurped from pagan mythology by early Christians. The notion of a bird rising to life from its own ashes is used as an analogy for the resurrection of Jesus.

Crucifix

FIGURE 22

The image of the dead or dying Christ on a cross is included in the section on crosses. It is included here as well because it is immediately connected with the Second Person of the Trinity.

Lion of Judah

FIGURE 23

A traditional Jewish symbol for the tribe of Judah and mentioned in the book of Revelation, this is a lesser-used symbol for Jesus Christ.

Butterfly

FIGURE 24

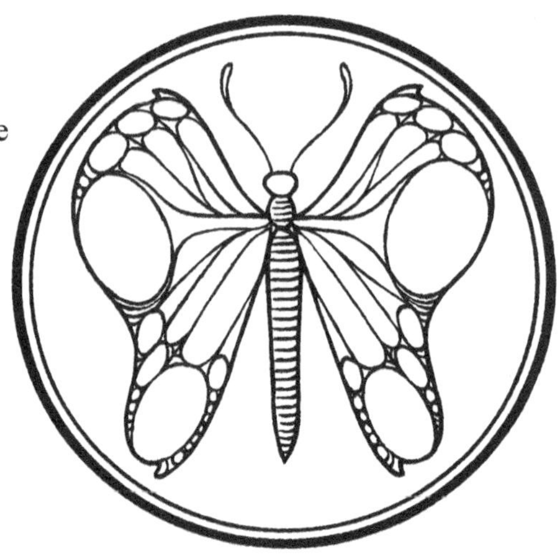

A popular, albeit decidedly weak, analogy for the resurrection, the butterfly is associated with Easter. The reason is that it emerges alive from a cocoon, which seems a sort of death to the casual observer. However, the analogy fails because the insect is alive in its cocoon.

The Pantocrator

FIGURE 25

This Eastern Orthodox image goes beyond simple symbolism when depicting Christ Jesus as the ruler of the universe. Still, it is condensed enough to rank as a symbol unto itself. Jesus is typically shown holding Scripture in one hand while blessing the viewer with the other. A tri-radiant nimbus encircles His head. Textual abbreviations denote Him as "Jesus Christ" and "He Who Is."

The Mystic Rose

FIGURE 26

This symbol gets blurry across denominational lines. Roman Catholics use scriptural mention of the rose in Song of Songs 2:1 as an identifier of the virgin Mary. Lutherans, however, reference Isaiah 11:1 to lay it at our Lord's feet: "Then a shoot will spring from the stem of Jesse, and a Branch from his roots will bear fruit" (NASB). This imagery is the inspiration for the beloved Christmas hymn "Lo, How a Rose E'er Blooming."

The Gate

FIGURE 27

Taken from Jesus' own words in John 10:7 to describe Himself as the way to the Father and eternity, this symbol communicates that best when given the addition of a cross, Alpha-Omega, or some other monogram of our Lord.

The Capstone

FIGURE 28

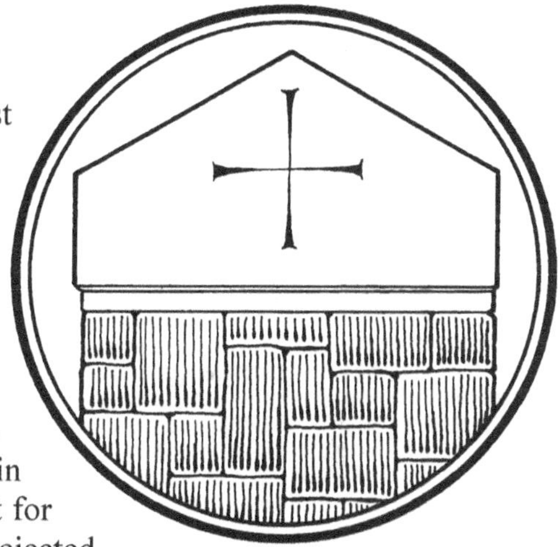

This symbol is another analogy of Jesus Christ showing His immeasurable importance in the structure of Christendom. In architecture, the capstone is the top stone in the building, so it is a fitting metaphor for Christ Jesus as the head of the church. Jesus Himself used the term. In the King James Version, Jesus says, "Did ye never read in the scriptures, The stone which the builders rejected, the same is become the head of the corner: this is the Lord's doing, and it is marvelous in our eyes?"(Matthew 21:42). And quoted in 1 Peter 2:7: "So the honor is for you who believe, but for those who do not believe, 'The stone that the builders rejected has become the cornerstone'" (ESV).

The Cornerstone

FIGURE 29

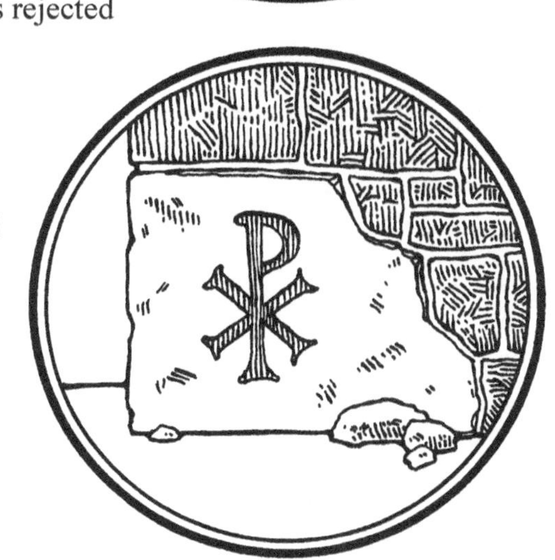

This symbol is so entrenched in Christological thinking that we include it in virtually every church and institutional structure, even though modern building techniques render it unnecessary. It symbolizes that Jesus Christ is the singular Person upon which leans the weight of the whole church.

The Vine

FIGURE 30

This familiar imagery is drawn from Jesus' words in John 15:5.When depicting this, it is important to go beyond a simple plant and embellish the symbol with a cross and some evidence of fruit. This example fuses a cross with a Chi-Rho to get the point across.

The Light of the World

FIGURE 31

Lanterns and candles are often used to symbolize Jesus' description of Himself (see John 8:12; John 9:5; 1 John 1:5–9). Interestingly, this symbol often shows up in the hands of His earthly father, Joseph, who literally carried the Light of the world. It is important to show strong light radiating from either variation.

Key of David

FIGURE 32

This prophetic image is often used during the Advent season because it is specific to Jesus opening heaven to those who believe in Him as the Savior. The imagery comes from Isaiah 22:22: "And I will place on His shoulder the key of the house of David. He shall open, and none shall shut; and He shall shut, and none shall open." And also from Revelation 3:7: "And to the angel of the church in Philadelphia write: 'The words of the holy one, the true one, who has the key of David, who opens and no one will shut, who shuts and no one opens.'" I prefer to show it with both a Star of David and a cross to link the prophetic Old Testament with its fulfillment in the New Testament.

Stump of Jesse

FIGURE 33

This is another prophetic image from Isaiah 11:1 that points to Christ Jesus. It's important to show a truly dead stump, so it's okay to lose some bark and give it substantial cracks. The shoot, on the other hand, should be full of new life, to the point of bearing a bud or blossoming.

The Ram Caught in a Thicket

FIGURE 34

Pulled from the narrative of the near-sacrifice of Isaac, this prophetic symbol points to our Savior. When pondering the Lord's command, "Take your son, your only son" and Abraham's simple statement that "God will provide for Himself a lamb," (Genesis 22:2, 8) recall that John the Baptist pointed to Jesus and said, "Behold, the Lamb of God, who takes away the sin of the world" (John 1:29).

The Wellspring, or Living Water

FIGURE 35

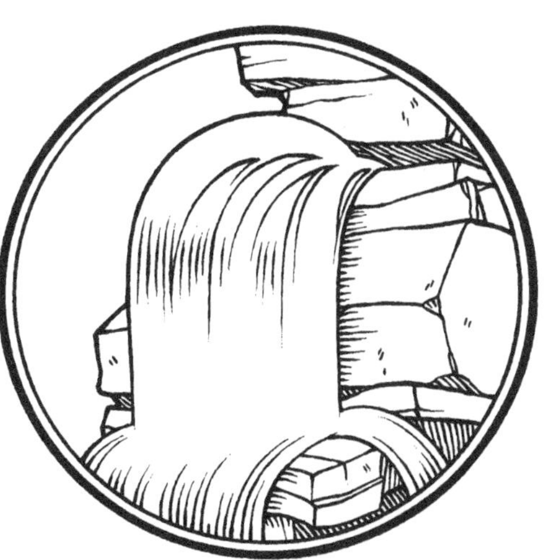

Our Lord Jesus Christ, spoke of Himself with this imagery in His encounter with the Samaritan woman at the well and elsewhere, but it also prophetically showed up during the wanderings of the children of Israel in the wilderness and was repeated in the Revelation of St. John. Symbolically, it can appear as water flowing from a rock, as a fountain in a garden, or as simple waves below other imagery.

The Rock

FIGURE 36

The foundation on which we build our lives (see Matthew 7:26; Luke 6:48), Jesus is the rock of our salvation. He is also the stumbling block that causes the fall of unbelievers (Matthew 21:44). This imagery appears in the Old Testament in the form of the stone that was struck, as Jesus was, and from which springs living water (Exodus 17:6). In our symbol here, Christ is shown as immovable and steadfast by surrounding a large rock with weather-beaten water. A symbolic cousin of this idea is that of the church on a rock, though in that case it is necessary that a church-like structure be placed atop the rock.

The Trap for Satan

FIGURE 37

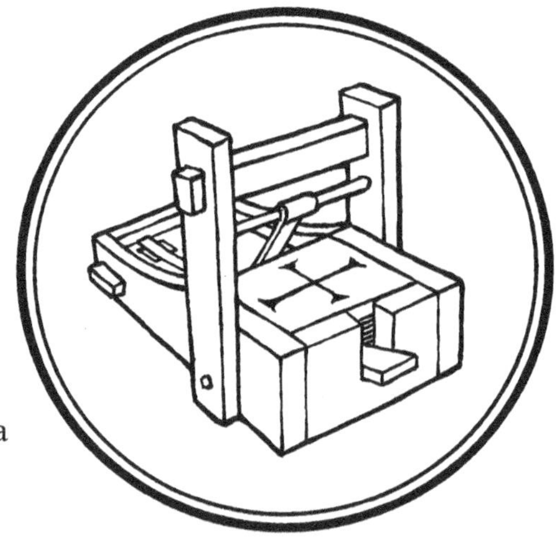

This odd little symbol shows up in the Merode Altarpiece, a triptych by fifteenth-century painter Robert Campin of the Netherlands; that alone makes it worthy of mention. In one panel, Joseph is shown working in his woodshop. A finished wooden rat trap sits nearby on his workbench, signifying that Christ will eventually trap Satan. The imagery also appears in a sermon series by St. Augustine, where it is called a trap for the devil.

The Word

FIGURE 38

At first glance, we may wonder why a random scroll is depicted in a sacred image, but this is a reference to our Savior, especially if it bears other symbols associated with Him. Referencing John 1:1, we know that our heavenly Father created language and comes to us in His Word, the Bible, and in His Son, Christ Jesus.

Hand of Blessing, Eastern and Western Churches

FIGURES 39, 40

A hand in an attitude of blessing with a tri-radiant nimbus can be used to symbolize Jesus Christ, especially if it is visually understood that the Person is below the hand and not above it. If the Person is below the hand, it points to His humanity. The Eastern Orthodox version of this symbol has Jesus' third finger bent under His thumb. By their position, the fingers then spell out in Greek the word *Christ*.

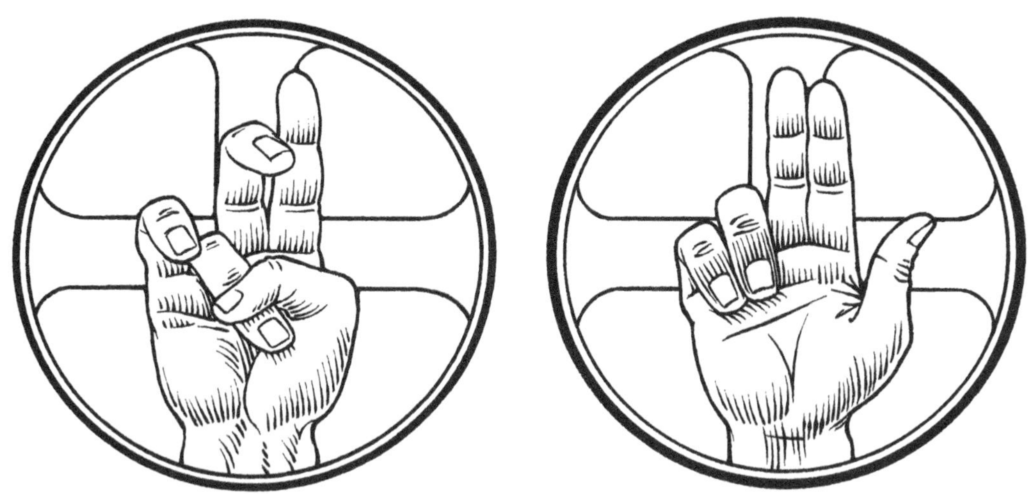

The Holy Spirit

Symbols for the Third Person of the Holy Trinity are typically a dove, flame, wind, water, and oil. The most familiar to us is the dove, and there is one important thing to note when it is shown: it must have the tri-radiant nimbus behind its head. This isn't just a formality. By confessing the dove as an image of the Spirit of God, it is differentiated from another dove in Christian symbolism that relates to the promise of peace and is a symbol of hope and reconciliation from the narrative of the flood described in Genesis 8:11. Therefore, when using a dove to represent Peace Lutheran Church, for example, it's important to leave the tri-radiant nimbus off.

The Dove

FIGURE 41

The dove's attitude, or pose, should be considered. It is often shown descending from heaven as in the Gospel account of Christ's Baptism in the Jordan River, from which the image originates. Consider as well references to the Spirit in Isaiah 11:2, "The Spirit of the Lord shall rest upon Him" and 42:1, "I have put My Spirit on Him." We may also see the dove ascending or alighting, which indicates our prayers, hope, and peace.

Gifts of the Spirit

FIGURES 42, 43

Sometimes the dove is shown with seven flames or seven lamps. These represent the gifts of the Holy Spirit according to Isaiah 11:1–2. At times, the dove is omitted and the seven flames or lamps, still representing the gifts of the Spirit, stand alone. It should be noted here that the nine fruits of the Spirit, listed in 1 Corinthians 12:8–10, are never depicted as flames. Instead, they may appear as abbreviated letters on a nine-pointed star. Alternately, they may be written out on some sort of scroll in English, Latin, or some other language.

Crosses

By far, the most familiar Christian symbol is the cross, but it was not always so. Despite the ubiquitous cross showing up on Christian church pinnacles, hymnal covers, and fashion accessories from jewelry to apparel, the symbol was decidedly unpopular with the early church. In fact, it was unpopular with everyone. Since a cross represented an especially cruel Roman execution device, it was considered rude to even mention the thing in conversation, much less emblazon it on a coffee mug or t-shirt. Images of other forms of capital punishment don't sit well with us, so we shouldn't be surprised that its ancient counterpart lacked fans. So how did this change?

The short answer is: slowly. While the image of an empty cross began showing up decades after Christ's ascension, it took hundreds of years for an image of the dead or dying Christ on the cross to surface.

Holy Scripture gives evidence of the impetus behind the change in attitude from horror to honor where the cross was concerned. There is a subtle hint in St. Paul's scathing admonition to the Galatians in the third chapter of his letter: "O foolish Galatians! Who has bewitched you? It was before your eyes that Jesus Christ was publicly portrayed as crucified" (Galatians 3:1). One must note that Galatia is far from Jerusalem, and it is therefore unlikely that the Galatians witnessed firsthand the crucifixion of Jesus. While we cannot know for certain, that "public portrayal" could hint at the early existence of an image of the crucifixion to which the Galatians were indeed witnesses.

Later in the same letter to the Galatians, Paul pulls no punches when he declares: "But far be it from me to boast except in the cross of our Lord Jesus Christ" (Galatians 6:14a).

For those who might take umbrage at the "least of the apostles" and his view of the cross, it is wise to consider the words of Christ Jesus Himself, "And I, when I am lifted up from the earth, will draw all people to Myself" (1 Corinthians 15:9; John 12:32). It is impossible, even knowing the horror of a crucifixion, to deny the magnitude of Christ's salvific act on that cross. Nor is it possible to avoid that which the prophet Zechariah foretold, "When they look on Me, on Him whom they have pierced" (Zechariah 12:10). It may indeed be true that man is slow to understand, but, thanks be to God, when we finally grasp the truths of Holy Scripture, we cling to them tightly. Now it is impossible to dislodge the once disdainful device from the heart of Christendom.

Not all crosses are created equal, however. Scrutiny must be given to a cross's meaning and origin before incorporating one into a design. This is extremely important for those desiring to make appointments for the sanctuary, whether it is simple banners or permanent chancel installations.

A few crosses have denominational applications, as in the case of the papal cross. Some crosses have seasonal or topical uses or have ethnic origins. Others have been adopted by fringe groups or societies. And more than one style of cross has had the dubious distinction of bearing the brunt of history's ugliness and has not only gone out of use in Christendom but has also been purged by society as a whole. The rebated cross, cross cramponée, and cross voided all fell, along with the Nazis, who used those crosses as identification within the regime.

Heraldic use of the cross figured prominently when ancestral identification at home and on the battlefield was of utmost importance. Associated with the Crusades and Middle Ages, heraldry relates to armor and accoutrements related to the pageantry of military might and social rank. We correctly think of shields, banners and standards, and tunics and capes. Most of those symbols can be identified by French nomenclature—the language of heraldry. The number of such variations is too great to include them all here, but this collection is a good representation.

The bulk of cross designs are Latin, Greek, or Tau. The Latin cross has unequal arms, while the Greek cross has equal arms and looks like a plus sign. The Tau cross resembles the letter *T*.

Although one of the simplest of crosses, the Latin cross was not the earliest design, not even among crosses in general. Early Christians were keen to adopt existing images from the Hebraic culture, from the surrounding Goyim, and from everyday life and adjust them into new service. Fishing and seafaring imagery were used as well, including the anchor, with its subtle nod to a cross. Variations of anchor crosses can be found engraved on early Christian funerary monuments. Early Christians knew the images not only symbolized the cross of Christ and the steadfast love of the Lord but also the spreading of the Gospel through becoming "fishers of men."

Adorned Cross

FIGURE 44

Our survey is conducted alphabetically, so we begin with the adorned cross, which encompasses a great many styles, including heraldic variations. An adorned cross has decorative embellishment and usually bears little resemblance to the type of cross on which Christ died. Our example has lilies, but just about anything can adorn such a cross.

Aiguisée Cross

FIGURE 45

This heraldic cross is somewhat like the Passion Cross. Its name originates from the French word for "pointed" or "edged."

Alisée Patée Cross

FIGURE 46

Following the heraldic French nomenclature, this variation of the so-called Iron Cross has rounded "feet." A version of this design is often used in small details on vestments.

Anchor Cross

FIGURE 47

There are many variations on this ancient style of cross. The early church embraced this symbol because it was familiar to fishermen and, in an era when Christians were often threatened, this design was popular because it was less conspicuous than a Latin cross. This example is modeled after one inscribed on a Christian stone sarcophagus.

Anchor Cross, Inverted Grapnel

FIGURE 48

One must squint a little to see the cross in some designs. This one throws a curve because it was displayed upside down.

Anchor Cross, Peaked Arm

FIGURE 49

This variation clearly shows that nautical design was in its infancy during the early church period, with forms varying regionally.

Anchor Cross, Recurve Arm

FIGURE 50

This is yet another variation on the theme. There is no correct anchor to use, for all symbolize the steadfastness of our Lord amid the storms of this life.

Armenian Cross

FIGURE 51

One of several ethnic- or nationality-based crosses in this collection, the peculiar floral embellishment distinguishes the Armenian cross from others in Christendom. It is likely that the underlying motif borrows from nearby pagan religions.

Avellaine Cross

FIGURE 52

This heraldic cross incorporates aspects that resemble the flowers of the *Corylus avelana*, or common hazelnut.

Barbée Cross

FIGURE 53

One should think twice before using this particular design, sometimes called the "arrow cross" for obvious reasons. Originally, the heraldic device representing barbs on a fishing hook symbolized "fishers of men." However, it was adopted by extremist groups in both the United States and Hungary beginning in the 1930s and '40s; Hungary has since outlawed use of the symbol.

Bezant Cross

FIGURE 54

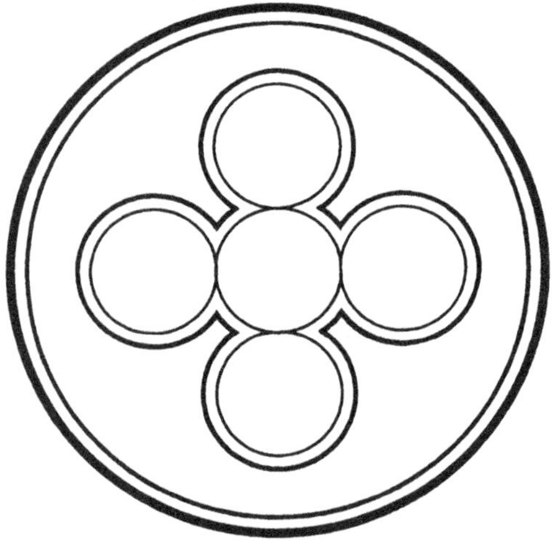

Composed of circles, this heraldic cross originated during the Crusades but references an earlier time. Its name comes from an old French word for "coin." It is likely that crusading knights found many coins when they invaded Constantinople and the regions around it.

Bottonnée Cross

FIGURE 55

Also known as the "budded cross," this heraldic design has been used for centuries in Christendom though it is often seen on altars today. Its design is not only attractive, but its buds hint at new life while echoing Aaron's budded staff, a piece of dead wood that sprouted buds, blossoms, and almonds (see Numbers 17:8).

Bottonnée Fitchée Cross

FIGURE 56

The French nomenclature of heraldry can get a bit cumbersome to our ears. This variation of the budded cross is fitched, meaning that its base has been formed into a point. Within the church, a pointed base or pointed arms of a cross remind us of the sharp point of nails and therefore carry an association with our Lord's Passion.

Canterbury Cross

FIGURE 57

Some peculiar designs have become site-specific. This cross was designed after a Saxon brooch dating from the ninth century that was found in Canterbury, England. Said to represent the Anglican Communion, the design has been swept up in local lore and refuses to relinquish its place in gift shops. The arms are narrow where they meet in the center and wider at the outer ends and are said to resemble the triangular shape we associate with the Trinity.

Capital Cross

FIGURE 58

Heraldic design does not always follow visual logic. Just because two objects can form a cross does not mean they should be used. This cross is formed by intersecting architectural columns and might be seen as part of chapel or church décor.

Celtic Cross

FIGURE 59

Like the Armenian cross, this example has strong links with an ethnic group—from the British Isles in this case. Also known as the cross of Iona, it commemorates the landing of missionaries at Iona in Scotland and at Ahenny in Ireland. The cross itself dates to the Middle Ages, but its name dates to only the 1800s. Its conspicuous circle (the nimbus) represents eternity. This version has a flaring base typical of many funerary monuments in the British Isles.

Cercelée Cross

FIGURE 60

The number of variations of decorative crosses in heraldic design is owed to the fact that knights not only desired to be associated with the church but also needed to be easily identified while fighting on the field. The name of this cross comes from an Old French word for "curl."

Christ the Victor Cross

FIGURE 61

This form has been used for centuries in the church. Its Greek abbreviation for Jesus Christ, along with the word *victory*, echoes what is proclaimed in 1 Corinthians 15:50–58 and other passages in Scripture: that Christ Jesus is indeed the victor in spite of and because of the cross.

Christus Rex Cross

FIGURE 62

The distinctiveness of this design is easy to spot in the sanctuary. It confesses Christ as King of all creation, even as He is crucified. Thus, the figure of Jesus is robed, either in royal robes or in a chasuble of the celebrant, and His head is royally crowned. *Christus Rex* is the title for Jesus Christ and indicates His office as King of kings (see 1 Timothy 6:14–15).

Clechée Cross

FIGURE 63

A decorative heraldic design, this cross apparently has some semblance to a type of old French key, to which the name alludes. The form dates to twelfth-century France and is sometimes called the Occitan cross.

Coptic Crosses

FIGURES 64, 65, 66

In use since the fourth century, one form represents the Holy Trinity and the twelve apostles because it has a total of twelve points. Developed by the Coptic Church, this symbol is also used by the Ethiopian Church. The Coptic Church was based in Egypt and spread in Africa and the Middle East. It is thought to have been established by Mark. The church likely borrowed motifs from cultures surrounding the region. Some of their distinctive crosses have a decided Arabic flavor, while others use circles and crosses in curious combinations.

Cordée Cross

FIGURE 67

The cross cordée is a somewhat rare variation of the Passion Cross in that its rope represents the binding of Jesus before His crucifixion.

Crenellée Cross

FIGURE 68

Also called the cross embattled, this heraldic cross brings to mind the crenellations seen atop castle walls used by soldiers to defend the stronghold. The name comes from a Latin word meaning "notch." Its design symbolizes strength; therefore, it can be used to symbolize the Church Militant.

Croissant Cross

FIGURE 69

With pagan associations, this symbol has been adopted by faith traditions outside of Christianity. There is so much possible confusion and probable heresy contained in this heraldic device that it's a very good idea to avoid using it at all costs.

Cross Crosslet

FIGURE 70

This design has several cousins in which each successive cross is multiplied so that even the nomenclature becomes convoluted (for example, the cross crosslet double-crossed). It dates to around 1400 and is associated with Poland, Serbia, and Romania. The symbol's basic meaning is that the Gospel of Christ is to be spread to the four corners of the world. It is sometimes called the Mission Cross.

Cross Crosslet Fitched

FIGURE 71

Consider this a reminder that every heraldic cross may be given a variation with a pointed "foot," because one can never have too many heraldic devices. In this example, the lower arm can represent the long point of a sword or spike. *Fitch* comes from a French word for "ground." Therefore, a fitched cross may be stuck into the ground.

Crowned Cross

FIGURE 72

The Christus Rex is greatly condensed in this symbol. The crown may be displayed below or above the arms of the cross, but it is best when the crown surrounds the cross. Variations point to Christ as the victorious King through His crucifixion.

Crucifix

FIGURE 73

A Latin cross with the dead or dying body of Christ (called the corpus) affixed to it emphasizes Jesus' death on the cross. While there are those who would rather dwell on the empty cross of Easter instead of the specter of sin and death and the reason for which Jesus Christ had to die, we must always echo St. Paul in declaring, "We preach Christ crucified" (1 Corinthians 1:23). *Crucifix* comes from the Latin *crucifixus,* meaning "one fixed to a cross." Martin Luther approved of the crucifix as a focal point for worship, but some Lutheran churches in the United States have adopted the empty cross as a symbol of the resurrection instead as a symbol of the foundation of our faith—Christ's sacrifice for our sins.

Crux Ansata

FIGURE 74

This cross is associated with the Coptic Church. Unlike other Coptic crosses, however, this example is more overt in borrowing from surrounding cultures by simply copying the Egyptian ankh symbol. It's easy to make the logical jump from the ancient pagan symbol for life to the cross, through which Christendom inherits eternal life. Still, it is difficult to disassociate the Crux Ansata from its pagan origins, so it is a good idea to avoid using it in the church setting.

Degraded Cross

FIGURE 75

This heraldic cross multiplies the base seen in the so-called cross of Calvary. This stepped style of cross dates to the thirteenth century. Because it convolutes that symbol's meaning, it's best to avoid this decorative variation.

Demi-Sarcelled Cross

FIGURE 76

This somewhat exaggerated symbol may draw inspiration from the outer feathers of a bird's wing, which should cause us pause when considering it for the Lord's house. The word *sarcelle* is drawn from an old French word for a kind of duck. The symbol dates to the 1200s.

Double Fitchée Cross

FIGURE 77

This heraldic cross, dating to the 1300s, may be familiar as a popular pattern for quilts. The word *fitchée* is often used to mean "pointed," but its correct interpretation is from a French word for "fixed"; that is, a cross with a fitchée end would have been stuck, or fixed, into the ground.

Easter Cross

FIGURES 78, 79

The empty cross reminds us of Jesus' resurrection and symbolizes our faith in the risen Lord while the rays emanating from the center symbolize the spread of the Gospel throughout the world. These variations are often used on more elaborate fixtures.

Eastern Orthodox Cross

FIGURE 80

Dating to the sixth century, use of this cross began when the Catholic Church was unified. Following the Great Schism, the split into Roman Catholic and Eastern Orthodox Churches in 1054, this particular style of cross has been associated with the Russian Orthodox, Polish Orthodox, and the Czech and Slovak Orthodox Churches. It is not used by the Roman Catholic Church or Western Protestant traditions. The distinctive lower, slanted cross member is simply intended to show a footrest for the feet of the crucified Christ, while the top cross member indicates the Roman titulus.

Engrailed Cross

FIGURE 81

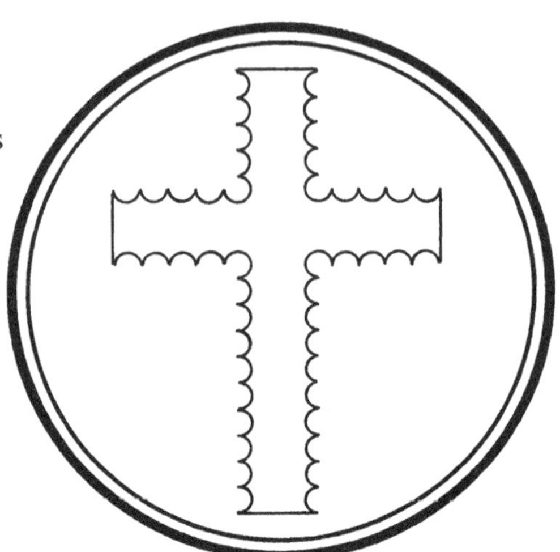

Meaning simply "dimpled" or "scalloped," this cross is associated with Celtic, Gnostic, and Templar traditions in England and Scotland. The pointed edges of this heraldic cross are meant to convey the suffering of Christ as He was crowned with thorns.

Erminée Cross

FIGURE 82

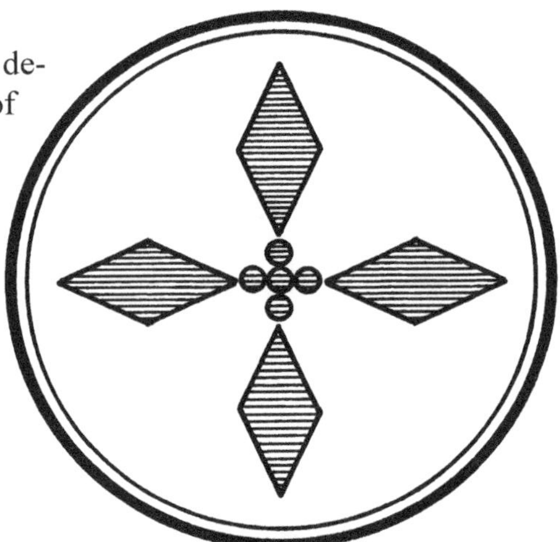

In their efforts to generate ever new and different designs, heraldic artists began incorporating any number of graphic shapes, as is evident with this cross formed by stylized spots peculiar to regal garments made of ermine fur. This one is based on an English cross from the late 1400s.

Evangelists' Cross

FIGURE 83

This is very similar to the Calvary cross, except it has four steps at its base representing the four Gospel writers.

Fer-de-fourchette Cross

FIGURE 84

There are several variations on this heraldic "forked" cross, from which it derives its name, but all are decorative forms.

Fleur-de-lys Cross

FIGURE 85

The fleur-de-lys as a symbol has been in use since at least 1300, and variations of crosses terminating in lilies can usually be traced to either French or Marian roots, though it was also adopted for use in England and Scotland. They are now so prevalent within the church that one would be hard-pressed to declare them unfit for use. They are, in fact, sometimes argued to symbolize the Holy Trinity through the three floral parts.

Fleurée Cross

FIGURE 86

This subtle variation of the more overt fleur-de-lys cross shows how forms can be stripped of ornamentation and still be recognized.

Fleurettée Cross

FIGURE 87

Further streamlining of an original design eventually creates something altogether different. Because such tweaking can be applied to any symbol, it quickly becomes obvious that no collection of Christian images can ever be all-inclusive or complete.

Four Pheons Cross

FIGURE 88

While a heraldic cross, it nonetheless points to Holy Scripture. A knight's shield charged with this symbol would carry deep meaning, for it alludes to Ephesians 6:16, "In all circumstances take up the shield of faith, with which you can extinguish all the flaming darts of the evil one."

Fretée Cross

FIGURE 89

This heraldic cross is simply a decorative pattern. A fretted design is composed of overlapping strips that create a lattice-like pattern.

Fusilée Cross

FIGURE 90

Names of heraldic devices sometimes have meandering roots. The name of this particular design traces to Old French and Middle English words for a lozenge or diamond shape, and that, in turn, traces back even further to a diminutive Latin word for "spindle."

Greek Cross

FIGURE 91

This version simply has arms of equal length. It tends to find its way into Eastern Orthodox applications but needs not be limited to that. In fact, one of its cousins is distinctly Lutheran. You can try and impress friends by referring to it by its proper name, the *Crux Quadrata*. There is no protocol for using a Greek cross over a Latin cross. The architectural footprint of Greek [Orthodox] churches seems to be the only instance in which the Greek cross is used as a rule. Western churches, on the other hand, tend to use the Latin cross, with its longer descending arm, for a floor plan.

Greek Cross Encircled

FIGURE 92

On occasion, the Greek cross is circumscribed by a circle to add eternity to the symbol's meaning. The circle may represent the nimbus of Christ, indicating the eternal life He provides. Use of this form is traced as far back as the 400s; the Coptic Church also uses a variation of this symbol.

Greek Cross, or Encircled Tau

FIGURE 93

This variation of the encircled Greek cross makes use of a more antiquated form. The Greek cross is reduced in size and placed on top of a tau, which is often used to suggest the prophecy of Christ and the season of Advent.

Ionic Cross

FIGURE 94

A variation of the Celtic cross, this symbol commemorates the landing of missionaries at Iona in Scotland. Its conspicuous circle represents eternity.

Jerusalem Cross

FIGURE 95

Also known as the Crusader's cross, or heraldically as the cross cantonnée, this symbol was used by the Kingdom of Jerusalem (1099–1203). While variations showing five crosses have been traced to Normandy around the time of the invasion of Britain in the early eleventh century, its original meaning has been clouded through the centuries. Some have attributed the four crosses to the four Gospels. Others have counted the central cross along with the four and conclude it represents the five wounds of Christ. Yet others have suggested it represents the four corners of the world, the four nations that united to fight during the Crusades, or simply the old four quarters of the city of Jerusalem itself.

Latin Cross

FIGURE 96

Most people would recognize this as the most basic of crosses, and it has been in use as a symbol of Christianity since the second century after Christ. Older art books give proportional rules that govern its design, but these have been bent so often that one needn't fret if the arms, for example, are not equal to the vertical above the intersection. Christian churches often use the Latin cross as the shape of the floor plan. For those keeping score, it is also known as the *Crux Imissa*.

Maltese Cross

FIGURE 97

This is another cross closely associated with the Crusades. The Knights Hospitallers, based on the Island of Malta, adopted the cross as their symbol. Their role was to protect pilgrims as they made their way to Jerusalem. Its eight points suggest regeneration or the resurrection. Because variations of it have been adopted by numerous civil and military orders, it's probably best to avoid using it in the Church.

Millrine Cross

FIGURE 98

This heraldic cross takes its imagery from the metal bracket used to keep a millstone in place. Apparently, folks were running out of inspiration. There are plenty of other confessional crosses to use before this decorative device.

Moline Cross

FIGURE 99

The eight points of this heraldic cross, also known as the cross ancrée, designate its bearer as the eighth son within the family. Note that it is different from the Fer-de-fourchette (Figure 84) in that the arms of that cross are equal in length.

NIKA Cross

FIGURE 100

This Greek cross has characters in each quadrant that spell out the Greek word for "victory" or "victor," thereby confessing the crucified Christ Jesus as being victorious over death. It is popular in Eastern religious traditions and often found on icons. We might also see it stamped on communion wafers.

Orb and Cross

FIGURE 101

This combination of images, also called the Globus Cruciger, confesses the triumph of Christianity over the entire world. It is a common thing among the bejeweled regalia of earthly kings and in eastern European religious art. The orb is most appropriately used when placed in the hand of our enthroned Lord, who rules over heaven and earth.

Papal Cross

FIGURE 102

The cross bearing three parallel arms that diminish in size toward the top is reserved for the pope of the Roman Catholic Church.

Parted and Fretty Cross

FIGURE 103

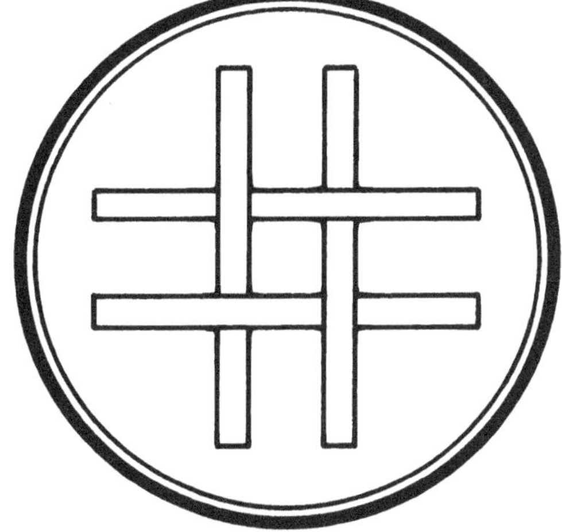

A simple heraldic device with interlacing bands that overlap, the root word of *fret* used here comes from Middle English and Old French, meaning “to decorate with an interlacing pattern.”

Passion Cross, Graded

FIGURE 104

Also known as the Calvary cross or graded cross, this is one of several crosses used to symbolize the Passion of our Lord. Its three-stepped base represents the three theological virtues: charity, hope, and faith. An ancient symbol, its use can be traced to fifth-century Byzantium.

Passion Cross

FIGURE 105

Heraldically known as a cross urdée or urdy, this cross is most closely identified with the Passion of our Lord, as the sharp points represent Christ's suffering. It may be shown sitting in a chalice, in which case it signifies either the Garden of Gethsemane or Maundy Thursday. Multiple variations of the Passion Cross have been developed for specific venues and purposes.

Passion Cross with Thorns

FIGURE 106

Any number of items associated with the Passion of Jesus may be shown with the cross. This variation is common, and it mirrors the somewhat similar crowned cross. In this case, the crown of thorns also hints at a circle, which symbolizes eternity and slaps death in the face.

Passion Cross Pomée

FIGURE 107

This variation of the Passion Cross has a conspicuous rounded knob at the top, somewhat suggesting a human body. With its variety of spellings (pommy, pomme), it's possible that the word *pomée* is derived from the French word for "apple" and pertains to something valuable, as in the "apple of His eye."

Passion Cross with Shroud

FIGURE 108

Color plays an important role in symbolism, as in this case. The shroud should be black to properly symbolize Christ's Passion or Good Friday. Otherwise, the shroud should be white for Easter.

Patée Fitched Cross

FIGURE 109

As stated earlier, a heraldic cross is said to be "fitched" when the bottom arm of the cross comes to a point. *Patée* comes from a French word that means the arms of the cross are narrower at the center and wider at the outside.

Patée Fitched Equilateral Cross

FIGURE 110

Occasionally, heraldic rules are bent a bit. This variation of the patée fitched cross has points emanating from each of its arms.

Patée Fitched Foot Cross

FIGURE 111

This is another variation of a fitched cross with a point issuing from the otherwise normal foot of the cross.

Patée Formée Cross

FIGURE 112

This style of cross is used in numerous applications, from royal crowns to military insignia. It was adopted by the Teutonic Knights and other crusaders and first appeared in early medieval art around 600. Because of its overwhelming usage outside the church, particularly for military valor and as a symbol of nationality, it's probably best to avoid overt use of this symbol in today's Christian settings.

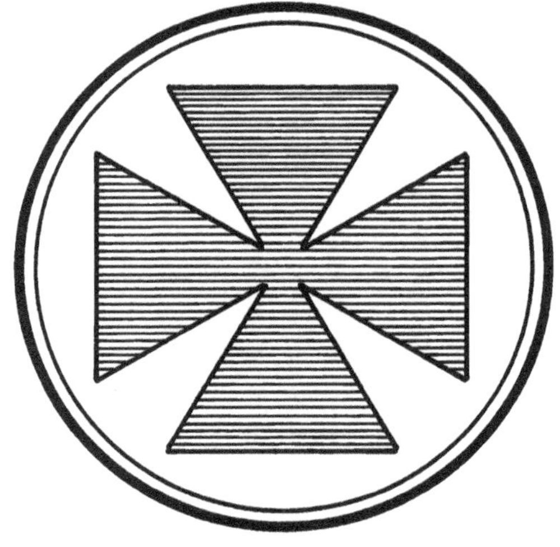

Patée Cross

FIGURE 113

Unlike the formée variation, the inward edges of this cross are curved. Again, for the reasons stated above, it's best to avoid this one beyond diminutive applications such as dividing pieces of text or marginal decoration.

Patonce Cross

FIGURE 114

The elegance of this decorative cross has earned it a reputation of being a favorite among designers of churchly accoutrements, particularly in thirteenth-century France. It is essentially a fusion of a cross patée and a cross fleurée.

Patriarchal Cross

FIGURE 115

A cross with two parallel arms that diminish in size toward the top is called the patriarchal cross (or in some instances, the Cross of Lorraine). It is obviously associated with various patriarchs. While it tends to be found in Roman Catholic art, Russian Orthodox art, and European heraldry, it may, with care, be considered for non-Roman uses.

Pommée Cross

FIGURE 116

This heraldic cross has round knobs, or "apples," as the name suggests, at the ends of its arms and symbolizes the rewards of Christian service.

Potent Cross

FIGURE 117

The name of this cross originates from an old word for crutch, and as such its four crutch-like arms suggest our Lord's power to heal. It is often combined with other symbols, such as the Jerusalem Cross, or is slightly modified.

Quadrate Cross

FIGURE 118

A square, or "boss," is superimposed on the center of this cross design.

Ragulée Cross

FIGURE 119

This decorative cross is said to resemble the rugged branches of a pruned tree.

Shepherd's Cross

FIGURE 120

This cross may be used either in reference to Christ as the Good Shepherd or, more often, as a symbol for the Holy Ministry in which pastors serve as under-shepherds. The symbol may be either a crossed rod and staff or a fusion of the two. Sometimes the horizontal member is smaller and much nearer the crook of the staff.

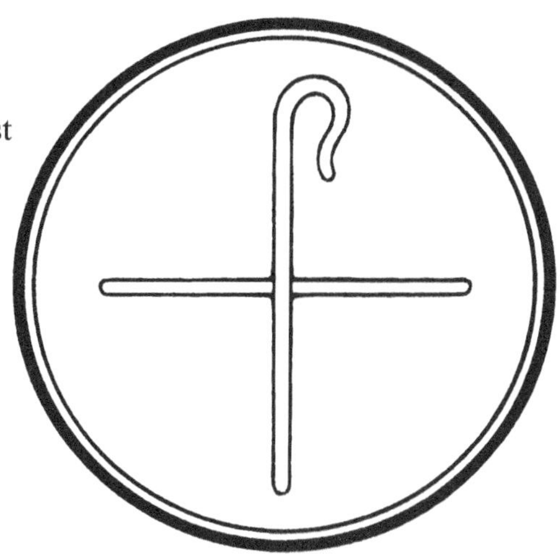

Spatulate Cross

FIGURE 121

Crosses of this general type have flaring arms with serif-like appendages that work well in applications where serif typefaces are also used.

Tau Cross

FIGURE 122

Shaped like the Greek letter *tau*, this cross has been used from antiquity. However, its convoluted origin can be found in the Old Testament and has little to do with Greek. Ezekiel 9:4 relates that the faithful were given "a mark on the forehead." Literally, it says "mark with a taw." The taw and tau share the same sound, but one has to sidestep modern Hebrew and look further back in time. Their foreheads were more likely marked with an early Hebrew taw—which is a cross shape. Still, this cross is used in its Greek form to symbolize Advent and the promise of the Messiah.

Tree of Life Cross

FIGURE 123

This is a branch (pardon the pun) of the adorned cross. It shows up in theologically varied groups, from Judaism to Shakerism. It is best used, however, in a cruciform design, to confess that we have life through the cross.

Tree of Life, or Vine Cross

FIGURE 124

While our example bears tendrils and leaves of a grape vine, it is even better when festooned with clusters of grapes, showing that we bear fruit when acting as productive branches.

VDMA Cross

FIGURE 125

With origins in the early years of Lutheranism, the VDMA cross has become extremely popular in recent years among Lutherans. Frederick the Wise first used this symbol, having it embroidered on the sleeves of his house servants' uniforms in 1522. It later spread from domestic use to armor and weaponry; the symbol was a general rallying cry for the staunchest supporters of the Lutheran faith. VDMA is an abbreviation of the Latin phrase *Verbum Domini Manet in Aeternum.* Translated, it means "the Word of the Lord endures forever" and is based on 1 Peter 1:24–25. It is best reserved for confessional Lutheran applications and is especially meaningful for Reformation Day.

Viking Hammerhead Cross

FIGURE 126

This oddity is worth including in our collection if only because it is an example of early cultural absorption into Christianity. This is taken from a monument at St. Michael and All Angels Church in Addington, England, and shows the transition from a hammer symbol of the pagan god Thor in Norse mythology to a variation of a Celtic cross.

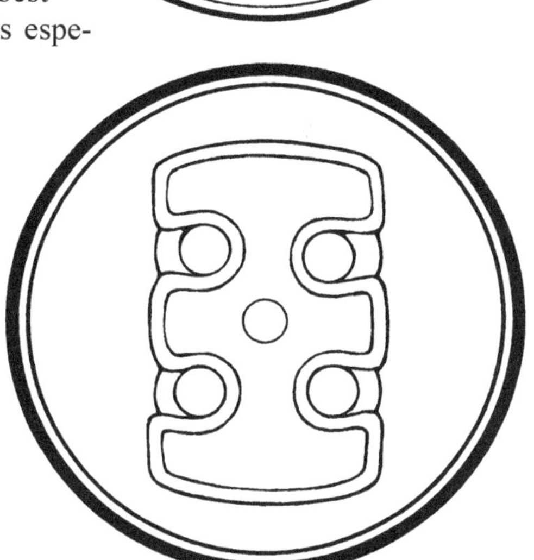

Abbreviations and Words

Because symbols are condensed visuals, it should come as no surprise that abbreviations of words play a tandem role and are often used as symbols in and of themselves. Some of these are so common that we understand their meaning without recognizing the full word they represent. We see a Chi-Rho, for example, and know it is a monogram for *Jesus Christ* without spelling out "Christos," much less the Greek characters from which the word is transliterated. There are so many abbreviations of various words that the few included here are representative of those the parishioner is most likely to see in a sanctuary of the Western Church.

One aspect that is peculiar to symbolic abbreviations is that they often have a line passing over the top of the characters. That line may be straight, or it may be decorative and curvy. This is the antiquated equivalent of the period in modern abbreviations. It was understood that a character or characters were missing beneath the line.

A+D

FIGURE 127

Church visitors might see this abbreviation before setting foot inside. Search for the cornerstone on a church building, and on many old secular buildings, and chances are it will be engraved with a date of dedication. Written fully as *Anno Domini*, this translates into English as "the year of our Lord." A cross should always be placed between the two characters. This abbreviation was used from the time of the early church to indicate the years succeeding the birth of Christ. The recent secular denotation of CE (Common Era) has pushed Christ out of the picture, even though the numbering of years is still based on the date of His birth.

Chi-Rho

FIGURES 128, 129

Although several Christograms (abbreviated names of Jesus Christ) have been handed down to us as symbols, the Chi-Rho is one of the most recognized and one of the earliest, being implemented as a royal standard by Constantine I in the early part of the fourth century. The symbol is comprised of the first two Greek letters of the title *Christos* (Christ). The characters are often superimposed, often in such a way as to create a conspicuous cross. It's interesting that before the birth of Christ, the symbol was used as a marginal notation in writing to denote an especially significant passage, much in the same way that we use an asterisk.

Iota-Chi

FIGURE 130

Speaking of asterisks, this symbol looks very much like one but is a Greek symbol representing the first letters of *Jesus* and *Christ* and is used to mean "Christ the King." Sometimes it is circumscribed by a circle and looks rather like a wheel with six spokes.

Alpha-Omega

FIGURE 131

This pairing of characters, the first and last in the Greek alphabet, is often included with a Chi-Rho symbol, thus compounding the symbol to mean "Christ, the beginning and the end" and references the eternal nature of the Lord. It is taken from the book of Revelation, notably 1:8, and is a reference to Isaiah 44:6. The symbols have been used in Christian imagery since the time of the early church.

IC XC

FIGURE 132

This abbreviation is seen on, but not limited to, Orthodox icons. It is the Greek shorthand for *Jesus Christ*, using the first and last character of each name.

Ichthus

FIGURES 133, 134

Known by its English transliteration, this is not an abbreviation but an acrostic based on the Greek word for "fish." The acrostic roughly translates as "Jesus Christ, Son of God, Savior." The Christian Church has used the symbol since the second century. Some claim the symbol was used to identify Christians during times when they were persecuted for the faith. The fish may have been chosen to reference Jesus' miraculous feeding of the five thousand or to indicate Jesus commissioning His followers as "fishers of men." The examples shown make use of an alternate combination of characters—IXΘYC.

OWN

FIGURE 135

These Greek characters are often found in the three rays of the tri-radiant nimbus behind the head of Jesus. Roughly translated, it means "He Who Is."

IHC or IHS

FIGURES 136, 137

Much has been read into this abbreviation. At one time, just about every brass altar cross in America bore this abbreviation, and many examples can still be found. It is simply an abbreviation of IHCOYC, the Greek word for *Jesus*, but the abbreviation has been bent and twisted in directions other than its original intent. St. Bernardine of Sienna, an Italian priest who lived in the first part of the fifteenth century, supposedly started an alternate—and inferior—Latin definition as *Iesus Hominum Salvator* ("Jesus, Savior of Mankind"). To make matters worse, some parament manufacturers thought the *I* was incorrect and inserted a *J* in its place, rendering the abbreviation meaningless. Fringe groups have also tried to force inferior meanings on the original symbol, for example, to read, in English, "In His Service."

To improve on the symbol, however, a horizontal line may be added over the lowercase letters to indicate an abbreviation. This may seem a simple matter, but doing so may be an opportunity to create a fused cross. A Latin cross may be attached to the *H* when using uppercase initials. It may be noted here that extreme care should be used when fusing uppercase characters in the "IHS" version—it often creates an unfortunate dollar sign that is hard to unsee.

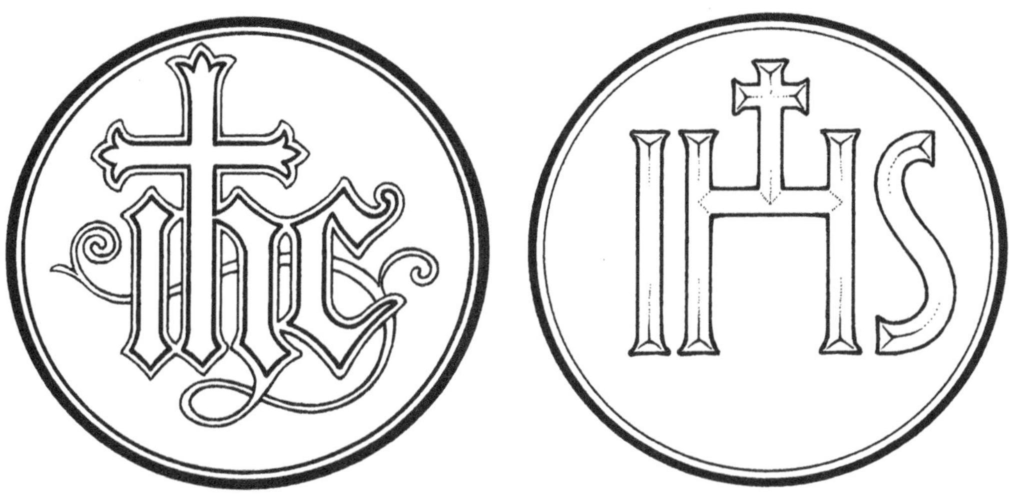

INRI

FIGURE 138

The abbreviation stands for *Iesus Nazarinus Rex Judaeorum* ("Jesus of Nazareth, the King of the Jews"), the Latin inscription that Pilate had written above Jesus at His crucifixion, according to John 19:20. This simple abbreviation totally ignores the Greek and Aramaic translations, also inscribed on the titulus, that were intended to be understood by all who saw the words as mockery of the one they referred to. It is likely that Pilate also intended the words to annoy the Jewish leaders (see John 19:21).

Ἰησοῦς

FIGURE 139

This is the name *Jesus* spelled out in upper and lowercase Greek letters.

OBCLDXC

FIGURE 140

This is a curious abbreviation that sometimes shows up in Orthodox icons of the crucifixion. It may appear on the titulus above Jesus' head instead of INRI, or it may be found elsewhere in the image. It is a twisting of Pilate's charge in naming Jesus "King of the Jews." Instead, this symbol translates as "King of Glory."

M

FIGURE 141

Wherever an *M* is placed in sacred art, it usually points to Mary, the mother of our Lord. Most often it is associated with Roman Catholicism and Marianists in particular, however, it can be used with care in other applications. One non-Roman example is a visual device containing a fused *M*, cross, and triangle. This is a symbol for the dual natures of Christ, showing His divinity by means of the Holy Trinity and showing His humanity by means of His birth of the virgin Mary and His death on the cross.

Ma Di

FIGURE 142

Often written with lowercase letters, this is a Latin abbreviation for *Mater Dei,* or "mother of God."

MP ΘY

FIGURE 143

This Greek abbreviation for "mother of God" shows up in Eastern Orthodox icons of Mary.

MR

FIGURE 144

This is a more formal application representing Mary, the mother of our Lord. The symbol may be interpreted as an abbreviation of "Maria Regina," (Mary, Queen). Alternately, if one squints at the fused characters, the individual letters of *Maria* can be untangled.

ECCE AGNUS DEI

The Church Year

There is an abundance of symbols relating to the Church Year and its various commemorations. These are perhaps most often seen in a sanctuary when paraments and vestments change in accordance with the church seasons. While there are typical symbols and colors used for each season, alternatives are available. Some variations may be a bit obscure, but they are meaningful nonetheless. Included in this section are other symbols, such as an adaptation of the Stations of the Cross. The Stations have been edited for Lutheran consumption because the Roman version includes a couple of events that are not found in Scripture.

In this section, the Church Year relates only to the life, death, resurrection, and ascension of our Lord Jesus Christ, and the sending of the Holy Spirit on Pentecost. Minor festivals and commemorations relating to the church are found elsewhere in this collection.

The Annunciation

FIGURE 145

The profound miraculous nature of this event, celebrated on March 25, is such that no one single visual device can fully represent it. The example here represents each of the characters in the narrative: a star and wings portrays the angel Gabriel; the Dove with a tri-radiant nimbus portrays the Holy Spirit; and an *M* monogram in the shape of a lily portrays the virgin Mary. Interestingly, a single lily may also represent the annunciation, provided it does not have stamens, the male parts of the flower.

The Visitation

FIGURE 146

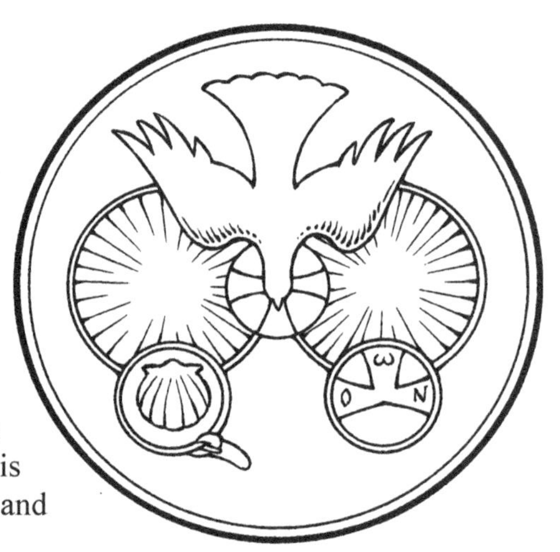

This symbol, though admittedly contrived, attempts to condense the meeting of Mary and her cousin Elizabeth. The overarching image of the Holy Spirit connects the two saints, symbolized by twin halos. Each saint, in turn, is connected to their progeny—St. John the Forerunner is symbolized by a leather belt and a scallop shell (at lower left) and Jesus Christ is symbolized by a tri-radiant nimbus with an acrostic representing "He Who Is." The Visitation is celebrated on July 2 in the historic one-year lectionary and on May 31 in the new three-year lectionary.

The Nativity of John the Baptist

FIGURE 147

The Forerunner is here represented by a newborn or toddler holding a cross-topped staff with a banner which reads, "Behold the Lamb of God." In this example, the child also points up, to underscore his lesser role. The Nativity of John the Baptist is celebrated on June 24.

Advent

FIGURE 148

While there are a few symbols associated with Advent—primarily those prophetic symbols for Christ that are mentioned in the O Antiphons—a crown is our sole example. A star is sometimes used, but because it has a closer association with Epiphany, it's best to relinquish its role during this season. The crown simply communicates "Our King comes."

Christmas, or The Nativity of Our Lord

FIGURE 149

It is nearly impossible to avoid an image of a European-style manger, so our example follows that old, though inaccurate, image. A tri-radiant nimbus is placed behind the head of the Child, and for emphasis, a Chi-Rho fused with a cross tops a crown to show that our King and promised Savior did indeed arrive.

The Name of Jesus and the Circumcision of Jesus

FIGURE 150

Today's Christians may get squeamish about some Levitical details in Holy Scripture, but they are still celebrated on January 1 to show that the fulfillment of the Law was made perfect in Jesus. In this example, an elaborate circumcision knife is shown with the Hebraic name *Jesus*.

Epiphany

FIGURE 151

A bright star is used to connect the revealing of Jesus Christ to the Gentiles, via the Magi, and to the whole world by the brightness of His light. I avoid the five-pointed star, which is overwhelmingly used by civic and national entities, in preference to a properly designed, eight-pointed star, which can indicate not only Jesus' birth and Epiphany but also His death and resurrection. Epiphany is observed on January 6.

The Purification of Mary and the Presentation of Our Lord

FIGURE 152

This symbol finds its way into hidden corners of paintings of the Nativity and into some Christmas carols. Two turtle doves were the minimum sacrifice for such an event, pointing to the humility of Jesus and the "lowly estate" of His mother, Mary. The event is celebrated on February 2.

Palm Sunday

FIGURE 153

This needs no explanation. Palm fronds may be crossed diagonally, or in cruciform fashion, or in just about any other configuration.

Maundy Thursday

FIGURE 154

While a bejeweled chalice may be used to represent the event, it's fitting to show a more probable vessel. Make sure to show unleavened bread, and not a fluffy loaf of sandwich bread. A monogram for Christ makes an important addition, confessing that this *is* Christ's body and blood.

Good Friday

FIGURE 155

There are plenty of symbols that may be used for Good Friday, including most from the Passion or the Stations of the Cross. This is one instance where it's best to reserve use of glorious rays—those will be used in three days with abandon—and stick with imagery that communicates the gravity of the sacrificial death of our Lord.

Stations of the Cross: The Betrayal

FIGURE 156

Thirty pieces of silver—yes, count them—and a coin purse represent the betrayal of Jesus.

Stations of the Cross: The Arrest

FIGURE 157

Among the things that may be represented in this symbol are a sword, club, torch, lantern, and rope.

Stations of the Cross: Peter's Defense

FIGURE 158

A sword and a human ear can be used for this, though avoid showing a Roman gladius, for Peter would have likely been arrested for carrying such a weapon.

Stations of the Cross: The Scourging

FIGURE 159

It quickly becomes obvious why such symbols evolved for Christ and His martyred saints. It is much more palatable to look on the implement itself rather than the wounds it caused.

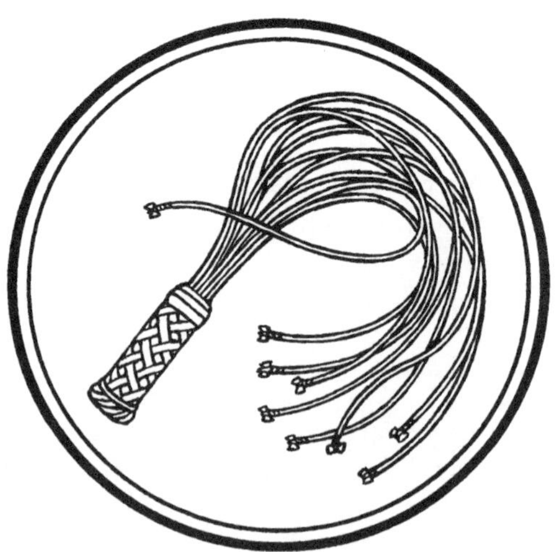

Stations of the Cross: Pilate Washes His Hands

FIGURE 160

Again, it is good practice to attempt to create some semblance of specific historical objects, so the imagery here is of a simple basin.

Stations of the Cross: The Denial

FIGURE 161

The crowing rooster has long been a symbol of Peter's denial of Christ. It has even been placed atop church spires, if only to give parishioners an extra helping of humble pie while en route to church.

Stations of the Cross: The Mockery

FIGURE 162

A reed staff, a crown of thorns, and a cast-off robe were used to humiliate an already-beaten Jesus.

Stations of the Cross: The Crucifixion

FIGURE 163

There are variations on this theme, all of which use nails. Sometimes three nails are represented, and at other times, four. They may be placed in a cruciform arrangement, with or without a hammer.

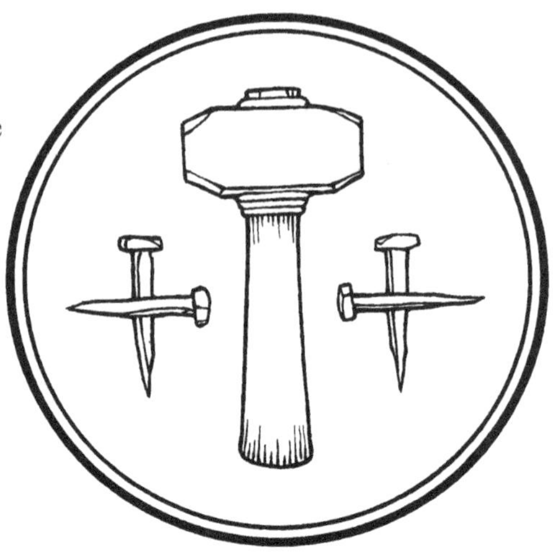

Stations of the Cross: The Titulus

FIGURE 164

Pilate's inscription may be shown in a variety of ways, from the full Latin, Greek, and Aramaic translations to the heavily condensed "INRI." A simple scroll may be used or, as in this example, a tabula ansata shape.

Stations of the Cross: The Division of Garments

FIGURE 165

Dice, to indicate the casting of lots, are usually included in this symbol, along with a single, undivided outer garment.

Stations of the Cross: Gall and Sour Wine

FIGURE 166

While representing separate events in the Passion of our Lord, a single symbol is used interchangeably for the gall, which Jesus refused, and the sour wine, which He drank. A sponge on a reed and a vessel are included in this image.

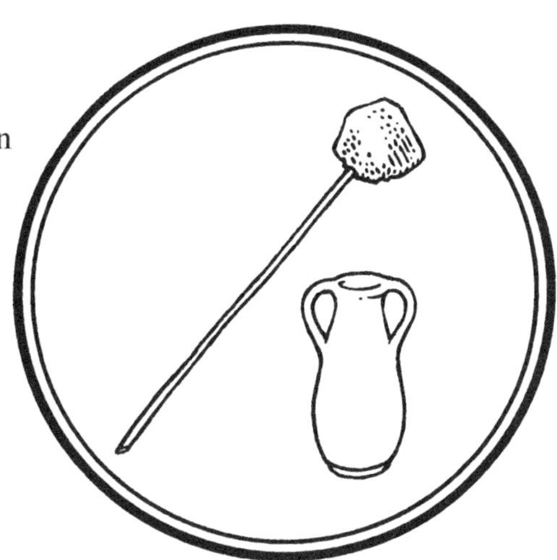

Stations of the Cross: The Piercing

FIGURE 167

A Roman pilum spear is used in this symbol, along with a heart. While not specified in Holy Scripture, Christ's heart is usually included by default in Roman Catholic legends.

Stations of the Cross: Rending of the Temple Curtain

FIGURE 168

The addition of a cloud of glory helps underscore the fact that it was God Himself who tore the curtain in two, from the top to the bottom, ending our separation from the Holy of Holies.

Stations of the Cross: The Sealed Tomb

FIGURE 169

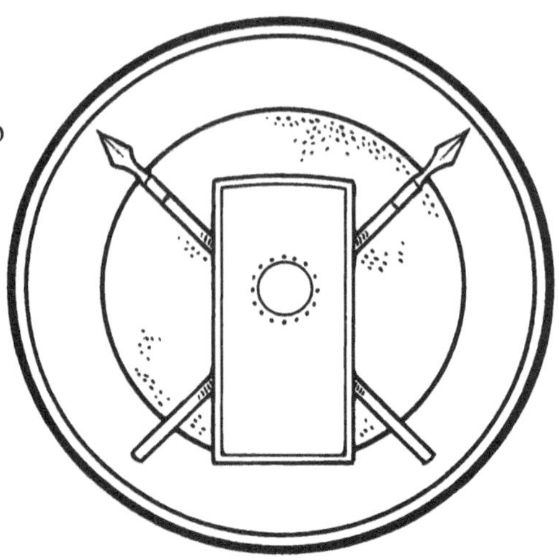

Any number of Roman weapons may be used atop the round stone that covered the tomb. While not included in this example, the wax seal may also be included, along with its cords.

Easter

FIGURE 170

Several items may be used to symbolize the resurrection of our Lord. Two Easter symbols have been combined in this one example—the cross draped with a white linen cloth, and the cross with rays emanating from its crooks.

Pentecost

FIGURE 171

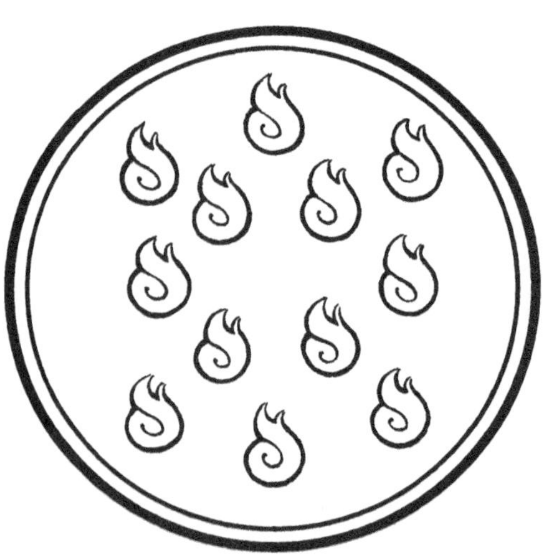

Various symbols representing the Holy Spirit may be used for this holy day, but in this case twelve tongues of flame indicate the twelve apostles, the twelve tribes, and the flames from the event itself.

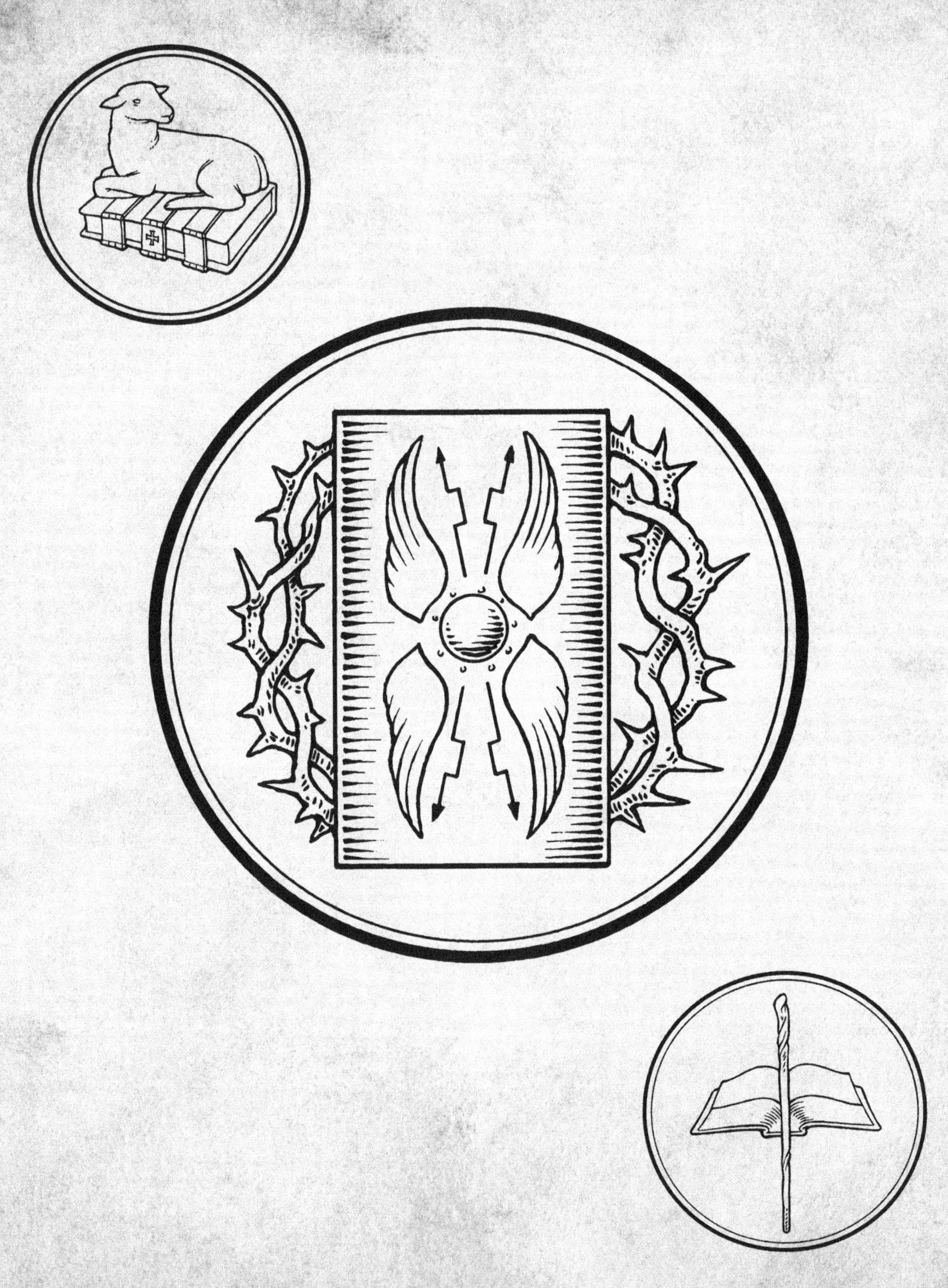

Saints and Sinners

The men and women of biblical accounts have been depicted in sacred art from the time of the early church. The apostles, Mary (the mother of our Lord), and various other figures from Scripture were the first to show up in mosaics and frescoes. It soon became clear, however, that some sort of visual aid needed to be used to differentiate those figures from average citizens. The halo (nimbus) was introduced, but folks needed clues as to which figure was Peter and which was Paul, for instance. It didn't help that there were several Marys.

The Church of Rome developed criteria for determining who received the formal title of saint, including, but not limited to, the performance of two verifiable miracles and leading an exemplary life. The criteria were susceptible to change throughout history, but it has always been the pope who has the final say about sainthood. And it may be noted that not all "saints" thus labeled by the Roman Church led saintly lives. Their notoriety, however, has been so embedded in the history of the church that it would be unfair to omit them and foolish to ignore their existence.

All this was, of course, approached long after the death of the candidate, who was already enjoying the bliss of heaven. Lutherans eschewed such practice of openly declaring who deserved the title, preferring to defer judgment on those who did or did not meet these standards to the Lord God.

What did come out of all this was a vast trove of symbols used to identify historical figures of Christendom, some labeled as traditional standbys, others as regional favorites associated with specific cultures. Because of legends or attributes associated with individual saints, most became "patron saints," to whom the masses would pray in a given situation. Some of these patron saints were reduced to ridiculous status, such as St. Roch, with his title as patron saint of bachelors, diseased cattle, dogs, falsely accused people, invalids, Istanbul, surgeons, tile-makers, gravediggers, second-hand dealers, pilgrims, and apothecaries.

What is also strange is the fact that Old Testament patriarchs, prophets, and distinguished figures do not bear the title saint. There is no St. Abraham; he is simply Abraham. For that reason alone, the symbols in this section exclude those Old Testament personalities.

Another oddity is Judas Iscariot. For obvious reasons, he does not bear the title of saint. He is, however, always included in the company of the apostles, if only as a warning to the viewer.

This collection is only a fraction of any official roster of saints. Of course, we know the list is much longer than any that mankind has deemed worthy, and we look forward to the day when the veil is lifted and we see with our own eyes not only the entire host of heaven but our Lord's face as well.

Commemoration dates are given for saints and generally coincide with their deaths, but those dates vary greatly between denominations. This is because Orthodox, Coptic, and Western Churches follow completely different calendars, and varying traditions surround each saint.

St. Acacius

FIGURE 172

There are several saints bearing this name. The one represented here, also known as Agathus, was a Cappadocian of the fourth century who joined the Roman army and later became a centurion. For his confession, he was martyred in Byzantium on May 8, 303, the date on which he is commemorated.

St. Adalbert of Prague

FIGURE 173

St. Adalbert was a Bohemian bishop who became a missionary to the Poles, Hungarians, and Prussians. Born into a wealthy and powerful family, he was well educated and somewhat worldly, though he lived an austere life. He was martyred in the late tenth century as he attempted to convert the Baltic Prussians. His commemoration is celebrated on April 23.

St. Agatha of Sicily

FIGURE 174

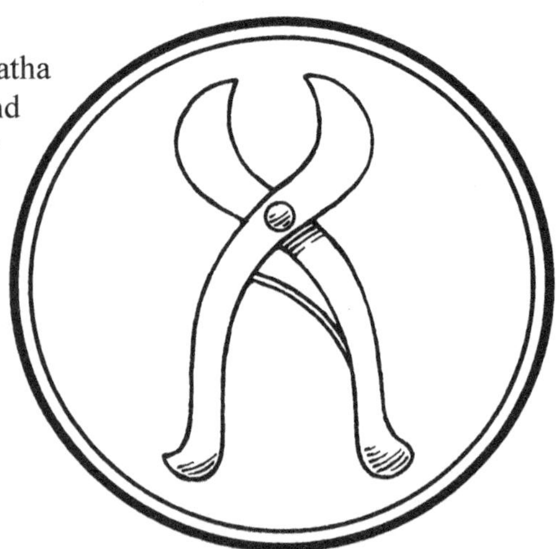

Known for her beauty and unshakable faith, Agatha dedicated herself to God and chose a life of service and prayer. She was tortured and died in the third century during the Decian persecution. As with many martyrs, her symbol points to the manner in which she was tortured. Among her many patronages is breast cancer. Her commemoration is February 5.

St. Agnes of Rome

FIGURE 175

Daughter of a Roman nobleman and raised in a Christian home, Agnes is the subject of several legends. What is known with some certainty is that this fourth-century martyr was a just 12 or 13 when her Christian confession caused the forfeiture of her life. She is remembered on January 21.

St. Aidan of Lindisfarne

FIGURE 176

This seventh-century monk evangelized in northern England and is credited with converting the Anglo-Saxons. Born in Ireland, he was known for his knowledge of the Bible and was regarded as an eloquent preacher. He founded a monastery that became a center of learning and mission work. His symbol—a torch—signifies the Gospel with which he illuminated the people. He is remembered by most church bodies on August 31 and on June 9 by some Lutherans.

St. Alban

FIGURE 177

Considered the protomartyr of the British people, this pagan-turned-Christian of the third or fourth century is often depicted as an armored soldier holding a large cross, symbolizing that he gave his life while defending the priest who converted him. He is first mentioned in a work called *The Praise of Saints* by Victricius, written in 396. St. Alban is commemorated on June 20.

St. Alphege

FIGURE 178

Sometimes called Ælfeah of Canterbury, St. Alphege was an Anglo-Saxon bishop and later archbishop. Regarded for his care of the poor, he was a mediator with the Danes and is said to have inspired the Danish chief to convert to Christianity. After a visit to Rome, he returned to Canterbury, was captured by Viking raiders, and was killed in 1012. St. Alphege is a patron saint of kidnap victims and is commemorated on April 19.

St. Alphonsus

FIGURE 179

Considerably more contemporary than most saints, this Roman Catholic bishop lived during the eighteenth century in Italy. His first profession was in law, but he was ordained as a priest and was known as a moral theologian and doctor of the church. His writings on moral theology, prayer, and dogmatics, along with devotions and works about Mary, have been translated into over sixty languages. He is commemorated on August 1.

St. Ambrose of Milan

FIGURE 180

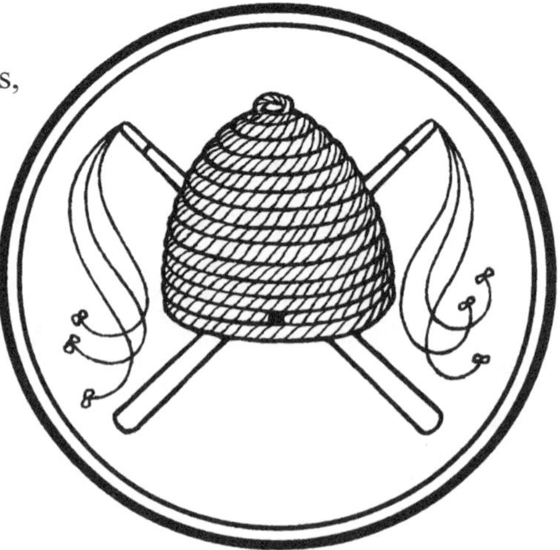

An accomplished author of Bible scholarship, hymns, and sermons, Ambrose was an influential public figure who is held up as the model of a Christian bishop. One of the four original doctors of the church, Ambrose is remembered for many things, including his fight against Arianism and his influence on the younger Augustine of Hippo. Ambrose, in fact, baptized Augustine. St. Ambrose is remembered on August 28.

St. Anastasia of Sirmium

FIGURE 181

A medicine pot is the symbol of this late-third-century martyr who was a healer and exorcist. Most legends about her were written many years after her death, so there is little fact to go on, but it is believed she ministered to Christians in prison and used potions to help heal them. She died during the Diocletian persecution in what is now Serbia and is commemorated on May 2.

St. Andrew

FIGURE 182

One of the Twelve, Andrew, along with his brother Peter, was called from his work as a fisherman to be a fisher of men. A disciple of John the Baptizer, Andrew is considered to be the first of the apostles to be called to follow Jesus and knew in an instant that Jesus was the Messiah (John 1:41). According to tradition, this apostle was crucified on an X-shaped cross. The symbol has also long been used as the national flag of Scotland, of which he is the patron saint. His feast day is November 30.

St. Anne

FIGURE 183

According to apocryphal tradition, but not mentioned in the New Testament at all, St. Anne was believed to be the mother of the virgin Mary and served as midwife at Jesus' birth. Some traditions hold that she was the grandmother of apostles John, James, Simon, Jude, and James the Less. It should come as little surprise that St. Anne's symbol—a three-blossomed lily—is a reflection of her daughter's symbol. She is remembered on July 26 among Roman Catholics.

St. Anselm of Aosta

FIGURE 184

This twelfth-century saint was appointed archbishop of Canterbury by the son of William the Conqueror. He was born in Italy to a landed family and was well educated in classical traditions. Anselm defended the Nicene Creed, the two natures of Christ, and atonement by Christ's death on the cross. He advocated for the independence of the church against secular intrusion, hence the ancient symbol of the church—a ship—has been updated to reflect the period. April 21 is St. Anselm's commemoration day.

St. Anthony of Egypt

FIGURE 185

Considered the father of all monks, this fourth-century Christian left his wealth to become an ascetic, eventually leading a hermit's life in the Egyptian desert. His desire to follow the example of the apostles instilled in him a devotion to prayer. His symbol is a tau cross, and his commemoration day is January 17.

St. Anthony of Padua

FIGURE 186

Often the patronage of saints goes in odd directions. Born in Portugal, St. Anthony of Padua began religious studies as a teenager and joined the Franciscans. From an assignment in Africa, he was returning home to Portugal when his ship was blown off course and he ended up in Italy, where his gift of preaching was discovered. This thirteenth-century Franciscan monk is known as the patron saint of lost things. He died on June 13, 1231, and was commemorated as a saint less than a year later.

St. Apollinaris of Ravenna

FIGURE 187

Thought to have been born in Antioch, according to tradition this saint was made the first bishop of Ravenna by St. Peter himself, although the dating of his tenure as bishop is strongly debated. Known for his preaching and evangelism, his martyrdom is commemorated on July 20.

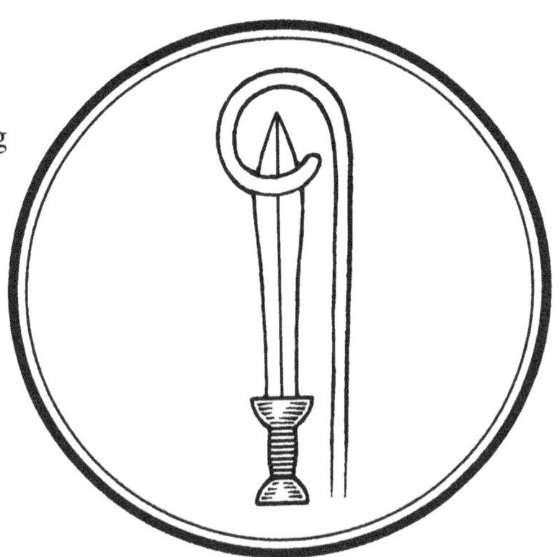

SS Aquila, Priscilla, and Apollos

FIGURE 188

These three are recorded in Acts 18:18–28 and in Romans 16:3–4. Aquila and Priscilla were husband and wife who lodged St. Paul in Corinth and worked as tentmakers. Later, Aquila and Priscilla traveled to Greece, where they met Paul and tutored Apollos. While Apollos was eloquent and competent in the Scriptures, Aquila and Priscilla taught him more accurately the way of God. The three are commemorated on February 13.

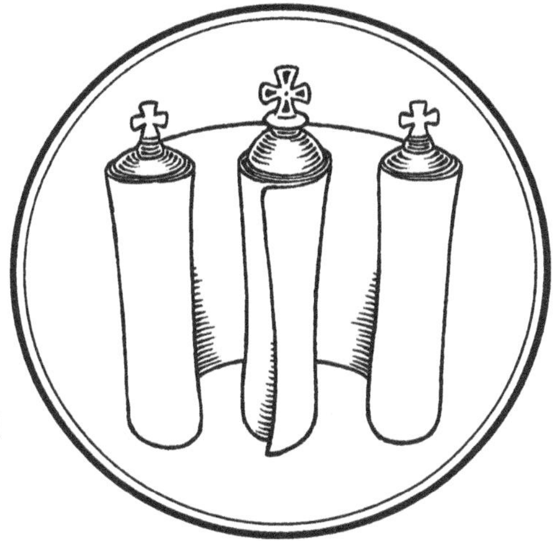

St. Asaph

FIGURE 189

Little is known about this sixth-century bishop, but the plethora of Welsh-named places attributed to him gives little doubt to his existence and veneration. Although by tradition he is commemorated on May 1, the Welsh often nudge that to May 5.

St. Athanasius

FIGURE 190

This pastor and confessor of the church is known, among other things, as a key figure at the First Council of Nicaea and also, by medieval attribution, the author of the Athanasian Creed. Born in Egypt, he traveled throughout that nation and Libya to defend the faith among schismatic groups. He wrote extensively on the divinity of Christ, as well as letters to his followers, Bible commentaries, and apologetics. Hence his symbol contains a triangle, which represents the Holy Trinity. The saint is commemorated on May 2.

St. Augustine of Canterbury

FIGURE 191

Along with forty or so others, Augustine was sent by Pope Gregory I to teach the Christian faith in pagan England. This Benedictine monk became the first archbishop of Canterbury, founded Christ Church, and converted King Ethelbert and many of his subjects to Christianity. This saint is sometimes (incorrectly) referred to as the "apostle to the English." He is commemorated on May 26.

St. Augustine of Hippo

FIGURE 192

This early church father had such influence that he is venerated in virtually every Christian denomination that commemorates saints. Still, he managed to become the patron of some rather random causes, including brewing, printing, and sore eyes. Born in northern Africa, he proved to be a brilliant theologian and prolific author. His writings became foundational documents of the Christian faith, heavily influencing Martin Luther, among others. The saint is commemorated on August 28.

St. Barbara of Heliopolis

FIGURE 193

This third-century Lebanese woman was, according to legend, kept in a tower by her father until lightning broke it open. Her symbol points to this legend, and because of her experience, she has become the patron saint of dangerous occupations, including artillerymen, miners, firemen, and the Russian Missile Strategic Forces. That said, her existence is questionable and stories about her can be traced only to the seventh century; there is no mention of her in earlier writings. St. Barbara is commemorated on December 4.

St. Barnabas

FIGURE 194

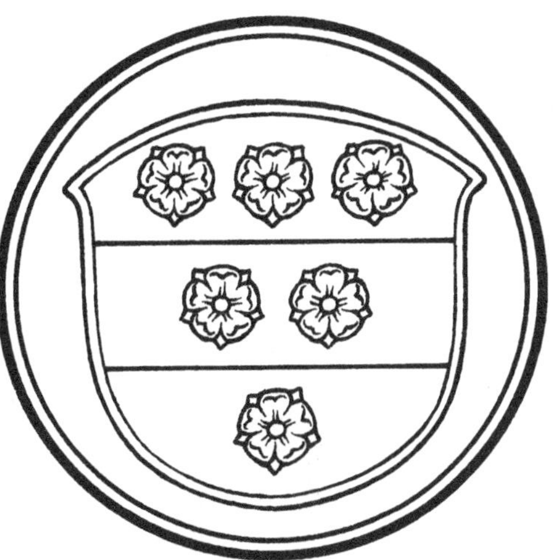

A Cypriot Jew and a Levite, St. Barnabas was an apostle as recorded in Acts and referenced in some of the epistles, and was a missionary companion of St. Paul and John Mark. These three apostles preached to and baptized pagans in Cyprus. Although his death is not recorded in the New Testament, tradition holds that Barnabas was tortured before being martyred. It is because of an old tradition of young men festooning themselves with roses on the saint's feast day on June 11 that roses adorn his symbol.

St. Bartholomew

FIGURE 195

One of the Twelve called by Jesus as apostles, Bartholomew is believed to have preached in Ethiopia (though some say India), Armenia, Persia, Mesopotamia, and Egypt. Because he was martyred by having his skin flayed, three flaying knives are used to symbolize the saint. St. Bartholomew can also be depicted holding his own skin. August 24 is his feast day in the Western Church.

St. Basil the Great of Caesarea

FIGURE 196

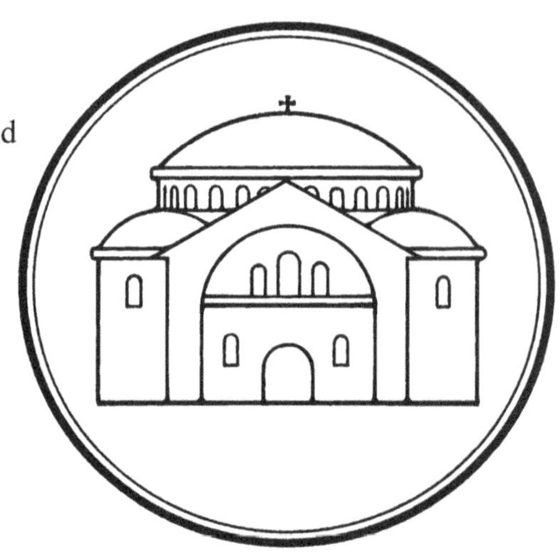

Together with his brother, Gregory of Nyssa, and friend, Gregory of Nazianzus, St. Basil is commemorated on January 10 in the Lutheran Church. He is known for his theological writings and his philanthropy. Because of his confessional work in building up the church, his symbol is an ancient church building.

St. Bavo of Ghent, or St. Bavon

FIGURES 197, 198

In his youth, Bavo was an undisciplined aristocratic soldier. After his wife died, the man gave his wealth to the poor and eventually became a monk. An aristocrat's hawk is his symbol. An alternate symbol is a hollow tree, representing his first dwelling as a recluse before moving into a cell near the Abby of Ghent. He is commemorated on October 1.

St. Bede

FIGURE 199

Living in the seventh and eighth century in Northumbria, Bede was a gifted theologian and scholar and has been given the titles doctor of the church and father of English history, along with the more beloved epithet Bede the Venerable. Among his enduring accomplishments was influencing the Julian calendar by adopting the Anno Domini method of dating and the Easter table. Bede is commemorated on May 25.

St. Benedict of Nursia

FIGURE 200

This father of Western monasticism has a symbol with the inscription "The cross of the holy father," which makes a play on words using his own name. His commemoration day is July 11.

St. Benno of Meissen

FIGURE 201

This saint became Bishop of Meissen, Saxony, in 1066. Despite getting caught up in various political and religious fights within the Germanic lands, and even being excommunicated at one point, he was eventually canonized and is remembered for his work among the Saxons. St. Benno is commemorated on June 16.

St. Bernard of Clairvaux

FIGURE 202

The names of some saints slide off the tongue with an ease of recognition. St. Bernard penned the beloved hymn "O Sacred Head, Now Wounded." The fact that he was offered a bishopric three times (without accepting) is reflected in his symbol. He is remembered on August 20.

St. Bernardino of Siena

FIGURE 203

Credited with influencing the use of IHS (superimposed on a sun) as a symbol for Jesus Christ, Bernardino attempted to revive Catholicism in Italy during the fifteenth century by, in part, denouncing witchcraft, homosexuality, and high interest rates (usury). Because he was also a scholar of systematic economics, he is the patron saint of advertising and public relations. He is also the patron saint of gambling addictions and San Bernardino, California. He is commemorated on May 20.

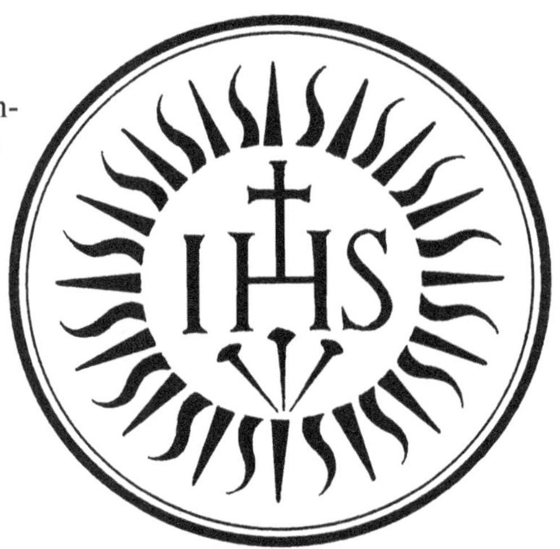

St. Blasius of Sebaste, or St. Blaise

FIGURE 204

Popular in medieval Catholic and Orthodox churches, his symbol is a wool comb, which apparently was used to torture the fourth-century Armenian bishop. St. Blasius is commemorated on February 3.

St. Bonaventure

FIGURE 205

A minister general of the Franciscan Order and cardinal bishop of Albano, this thirteenth-century Italian was known for his scholarly abilities, which earned him the title of doctor of the church. His commemoration date is July 15.

St. Boniface of Mainz

FIGURE 206

Martyred in Frisia in 754 while preaching the Gospel to converts, this missionary helped lay the foundations of Christianity in Germany. Boniface is said to have chopped down Donar's Oak (also called Thor's Oak), a tree that was held as sacred by pagans in Germany. The legend is that he used the wood from the tree to build a church. He is commemorated on June 5.

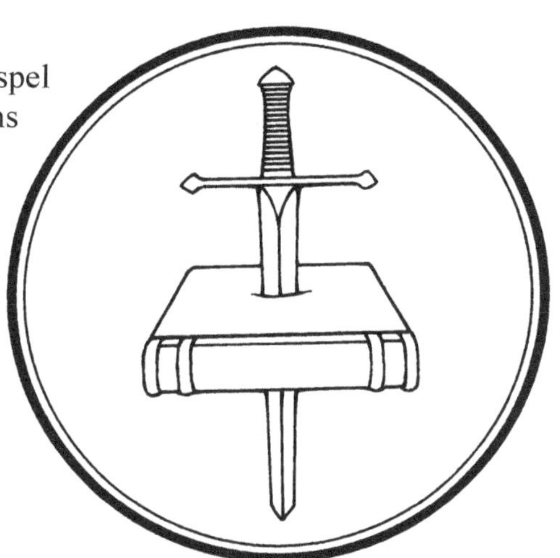

St. Botwulf of Thorney, or St. Botwulph

FIGURE 207

Little is known about this seventh-century English abbot, though there were as many as seventy churches dedicated to him, including the first Augustinian monastery in England. His symbol represents the roofline of the abbey at Icanho, which he purportedly built, and its surrounding water. He is commemorated on either June 17 or 25, depending on whether you live in England or Scotland.

St. Bridget of Sweden

FIGURE 208

Born in 1303, Bridget is known for her acts of charity, for her visions, and for founding the Order of the Most Holy Saviour in Sweden. She is considered one of the six patron saints of Europe, along with her daughter, St. Catherine. Her symbol of a pilgrim's hat, staff, and purse reflects her pilgrimage to Santiago de Compostela, Spain—what was then referred to as "the Way of St. James"—as well as pilgrimages to Rome, Jerusalem, and Bethlehem. She is remembered on July 23.

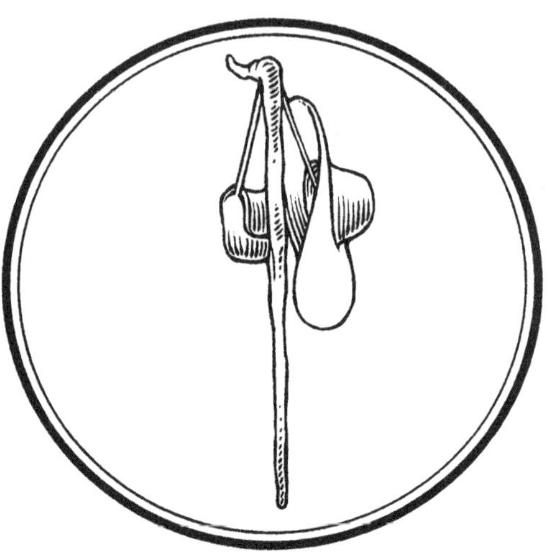

St. Brigid of Kildare, or Brigid of Ireland

FIGURES 209, 210

A patron saint of Ireland, Brigid was a fifth-century nun and, it is said, a friend of St. Patrick. One of her symbols includes an eternal flame and the oak wreath of Kildare. Possibly because she shared a name with a local pagan priestess, the saint also has an alternate symbol of a cross—of dubious pagan origin. Because little is known about her, some believe she is more myth than real, but since 2023, Ireland will observe a public holiday for her. St. Brigid is commemorated on February 1.

St. Capraisius of Agen, or St. Caprais

FIGURE 211

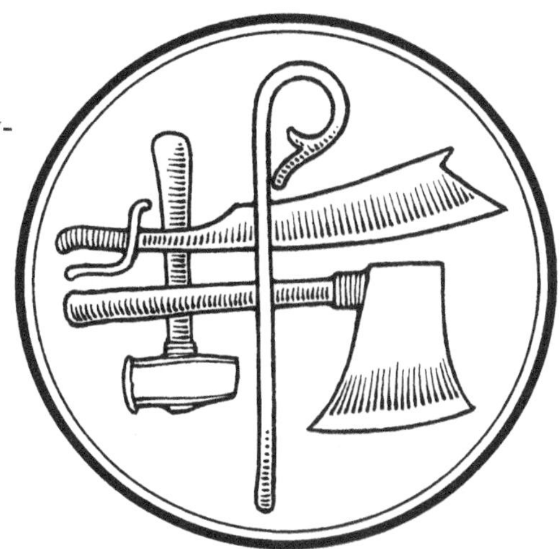

A lack of firsthand knowledge often allows several variations of symbols to represent a given saint. This one, a fourth-century French martyr, was the first bishop of Agen, France, according to legend. He was apparently beheaded, but a hammer also joins a sword and axe in one composite symbol. His death is commemorated on October 20.

St. Casilda of Toledo

FIGURE 212

Legends sometimes get the best of saints and their symbols. Among her acts of charity, Casilda, a Muslim princess, was known to smuggle bread to Christian prisoners. Once, when she was confronted, the bread allegedly turned into roses. Born around 950, she is remembered on April 9.

St. Catherine of Alexandria

FIGURE 213

Although eventually beheaded, this fourth-century martyr is represented by a symbol that reflects an implement of her torture—the spiked wheel, which, according to legend, shattered when she touched it. She is known for her intellect, piety, and virginity, but it is not known if she actually existed. November 25 is the commemoration of her death.

St. Catherine of Siena

FIGURE 214

This fourteenth-century Dominican nun had such influence on the Roman Catholic Church that she was occasionally entrusted with papal missions—something unheard of for a woman in medieval Italy. Declared a doctor of the church for her contribution to theology, she is known for her letter-writing and influence on the papal office and Italian government. Known for her holiness and spiritual discipline, Catherine is said to have had a mystical "marriage" to Christ and experienced visions of Him. She is commemorated on April 29.

St. Cecilia

FIGURE 215

A Roman martyr of the third century, Cecilia is said to have been skilled in singing and to have had angelic protection. Because she was often accompanied by musical instruments, the harp has become her symbol. Known for piety and purity, her martyrdom is commemorated on November 22.

St. Chad of Mercia, or St. Ceadda

FIGURES 216, 217, 218

A seventh-century English bishop, Chad went to Ireland as a monk, then to Yorkshire, where he became an abbot of several monasteries and eventually bishop over all of what is now northern England and parts of Scotland. Two variations of the cross potent quadrate are used as Chad's symbol, as well as depictions of Lichfield Cathedral, where he is buried. He is remembered on March 2.

St. Charles Borromeo

FIGURE 219

Although he studied law, Charles chose the priesthood and was made a cardinal as a young man. He promoted education among the clergy, founding both a university and several seminaries. But not all so-called saints led stellar lives. This well-known archbishop of Milan, a member of the de Medici family and nephew of Pope Pius IV, helped organize the Council of Trent and pressured the formulation of a counter-Reformation organization bent on burning Protestants at the stake. He did not, however, live to see its fruition. He is remembered by the Roman Catholic Church on November 4.

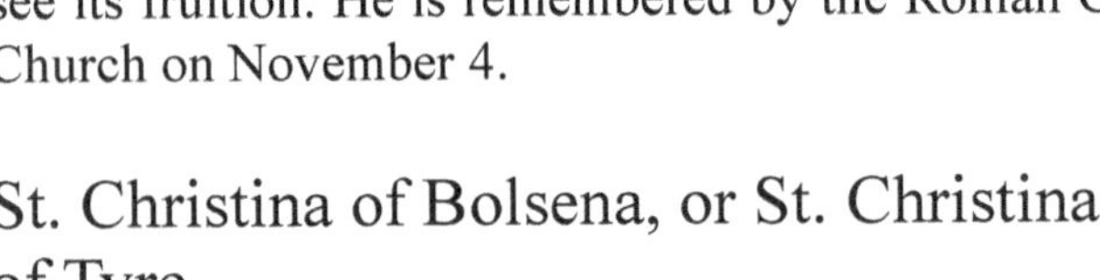

St. Christina of Bolsena, or St. Christina of Tyre

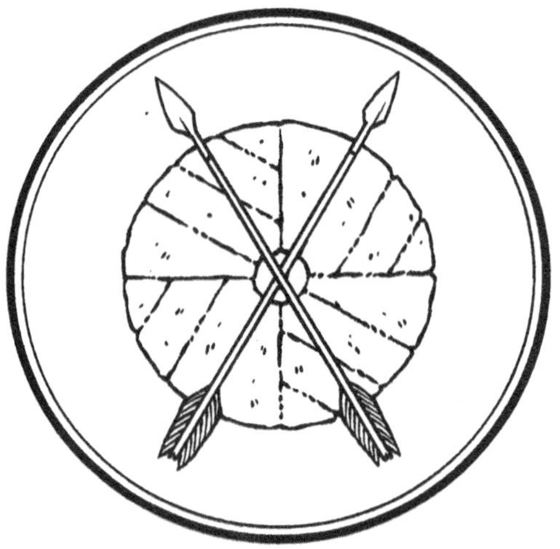

FIGURE 220

Much of this saint's story is based on legend, including where she was from (either Bolsena in central Italy or Tyre in Phoenicia) and that her father tried to have her executed by multiple gruesome means—but she survived. A third-century martyr, St. Christina is commemorated on July 24.

St. Christopher

FIGURES 221, 222

This beloved saint is well recognized on medallions showing him carrying the Christ Child. Many churches throughout Europe and even Asia bear his name, and in England there are more depictions of him than any other saint. His name literally means "Christ bearer," which relates to the legend that this third-century martyr carried the Christ Child across a river. Among his symbols are a dog-headed man and a lantern. He is remembered on July 25 and is called the patron saint of travelers.

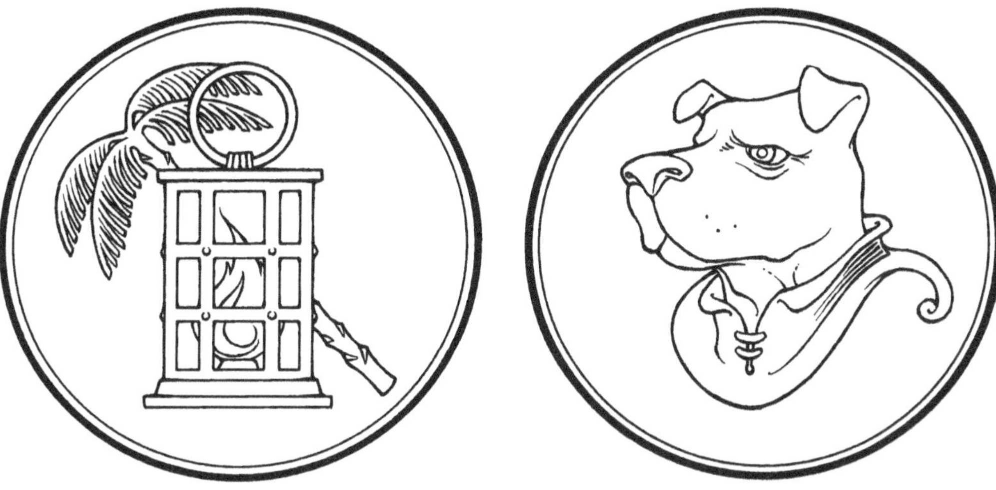

St. Chrysogonus of Aquileia

FIGURE 223

Martyred in the early years of the fourth century, St. Chrysogonus was a Christian soldier who became a victim of the Great Persecution. Beginning in 303 and continuing for the next ten years, Roman emperors gleefully and thoroughly persecuted those who did not comply with their religious practices and purged the Roman army of Christians. The death of Chrysogonus is commemorated on November 24.

St. Clare of Assisi

FIGURE 224

Inspired by hearing St. Francis of Assisi preach, this thirteenth-century woman joined a Benedictine convent and lead a life of prayer, seclusion, and poverty, having written the guidelines for her order. Clare supposedly fended off a Muslim attack on her convent with either a monstrance or host-filled ciborium. Either item can be used for her symbol. St. Clare is remembered on August 11.

St. Clement of Rome, or Pope Clement I

FIGURES 225, 226

This first-century Christian is considered to be the first apostolic father of the church and bishop of the church in Rome after Peter. Clement is mentioned in Paul's letter to the Philippians: "I ask you also, true companion, help these women, who have labored side by side with me in the gospel together with Clement and the rest of my fellow workers, whose names are in the book of life" (Philippians 4:3). According to tradition, he was martyred during the reign of Trajan by being tied to an anchor and drowned. Hence, his symbol is usually an anchor, but a miter with a pickax may also be used, as well as a papal cross. His commemoration is on November 23.

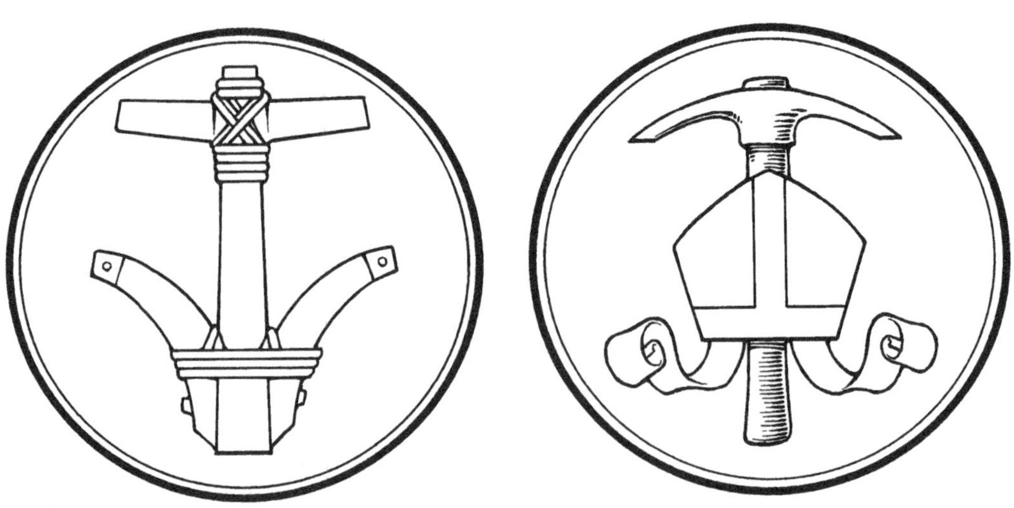

St. Columba

FIGURE 227

Columba influenced the spread of Christianity in Scotland and is the founder of the abbey on Iona, a center of monastic life. He is sometimes referred to as the apostle to the Picts. Some believe that in later years the monks at Iona would scribe the famous Book of Kells (also known as the Book of Columba). His symbol is the ionic cross—more informally known as St. Columba's cross. Columba died in 597 and is remembered on June 9.

St. Constantine, Emperor Constantine I, or Constantine the Great

FIGURE 228

Commemorated on May 21 along with his mother, Helena, Constantine was a successful figure in the powerful Roman army and was the first emperor to convert to Christianity (around 312, after the Great Persecution). Constantine convened the first Council at Nicaea, which was responsible for the Nicene Creed, and is credited with building a church at the site of Jesus' birth. His labarum, or royal standard, is Constantine's symbol. It is notably topped by a Chi-Rho.

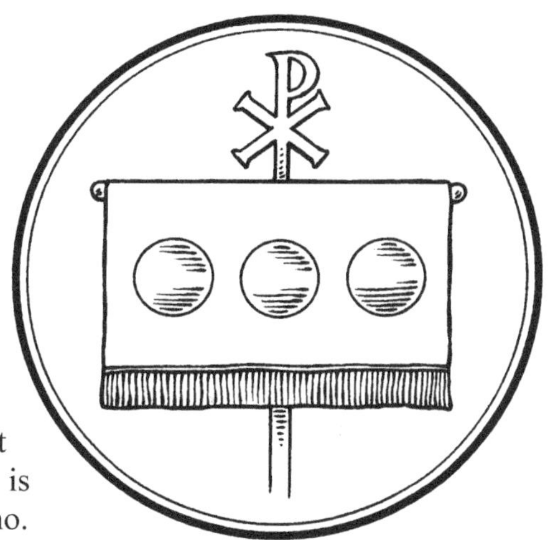

The Coptic Martyrs of Egypt

FIGURE 229

These twenty-one martyrs are a sobering reminder that Christians will be persecuted until the Lord's return. A militant extremist faction of the Islamic State kidnapped these men from their workplace. On February 15, 2015, the date on which they are now commemorated, a video was released of their beheading. A caption in the video calls them "people of the cross."

St. Cornelius, or Pope Cornelius

FIGURE 230

Because the name Cornelius is derived from the word *horn*, a horn and papal cross are used to symbolize this third-century saint. He was pope from 251 to 253, and his letters provided important documentation regarding the size and organization of the Church of Rome. While his martyrdom is disputed, he is commemorated on September 16.

SS Cosmas and Damian

FIGURES 231, 232

Faithful Christians and gifted physicians in ancient Syria, Cosmas and Damian refused payment from their patients. Their generosity attracted many to the Christian faith but also caught the attention of Emperor Diocletian, a pagan. Arabic twin brothers, their symbols may be twin pharmaceutical vials or a rod of Asclepius. Their martyrdom in 303 during the Great Persecution is commemorated on September 26.

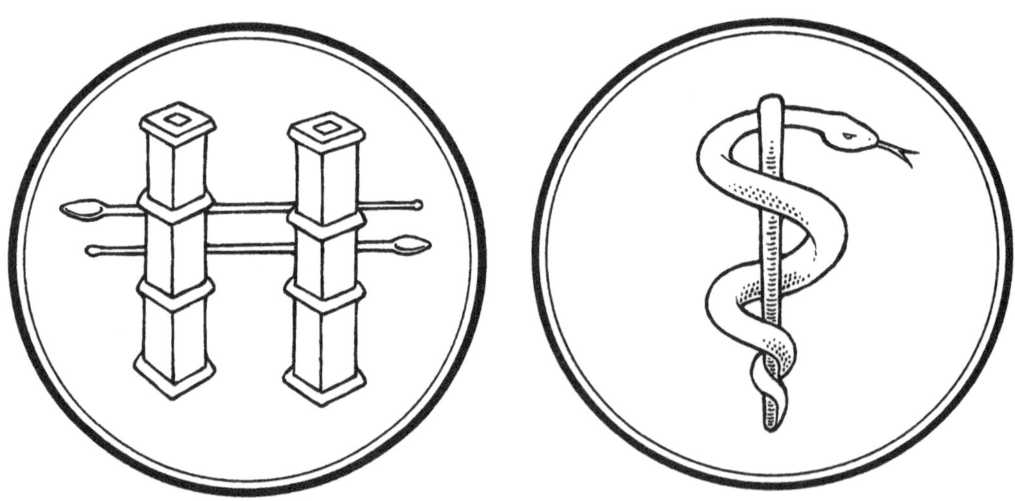

SS Crispin and Crispinian

FIGURE 233

Not to be outdone by Cosmos and Damian, these saints were also twins who suffered under Diocletian in the third century. To escape persecution because of their faith, they went to Gaul (modern day France), where they were cobblers by vocation, which their symbol reflects. October 25 commemorates their martyrdom.

St. Cuthbert of Lindisfarne

FIGURE 234

A shepherd as a boy, a soldier as a young man, St. Cuthbert became a monk, retired as a hermit, and was then called to serve as bishop of Northumbria. He was born in 634 or 635 and died in 687. Cuthbert's symbol is one of a few that use a unique cross shape. In this case, it follows the design of a pectoral cross found in his coffin, now interred at Durham Cathedral. St. Cuthbert's commemoration falls on March 20.

St. Cyprian of Carthage

FIGURE 235

This third-century bishop was of North African descent. As a gifted Latin linguist, he contributed so much to the church that he is among a few of the lesser-known saints to be included in the Lutheran sanctoral calendar. Many of his writings exist to this day. Cyprian was baptized at the age of 35 and two years later was named bishop of Carthage. His martyrdom is commemorated on September 16.

SS Cyril and Methodius

FIGURE 236

These Thessalonian brothers were missionaries to the Slavic peoples, used Slavonic in their worship services (over the traditional Latin), and even translated the Bible into the Slavonic language. Highly educated, Cyril was a university professor and Methodius was governor in Macedonia before they became priests. They created both the Glagolitic and Cyrillic alphabets, which appear on their symbol. They are commemorated on February 14.

St. Cyril of Alexandria

FIGURE 237

Remembered on June 27, this fifth-century pastor and confessor did much to defend the church. As archbishop of Alexandria, Cyril did not hesitate to use violence to strengthen the church (and eliminate its enemies). Nevertheless, his scholarship and extensive writings heavily influenced biblical theology, and he believed firmly in the two natures of Christ. His symbol bears two pens and the Greek inscription "God-bearer" for his defense of the mother of our Lord.

St. Cyril of Jerusalem

FIGURE 238

Although little is known of his life, Cyril of Jerusalem is recognized for his strong defense of Christian faith and doctrine in a series of lectures delivered in a clear and logical manner so as to be readily understood. His efforts at promoting Jerusalem were instrumental in that city becoming a pilgrimage destination. This fourth-century bishop once sold ornaments of his church to feed the poor. Hence, his symbol is a moneybag. He is remembered on March 18.

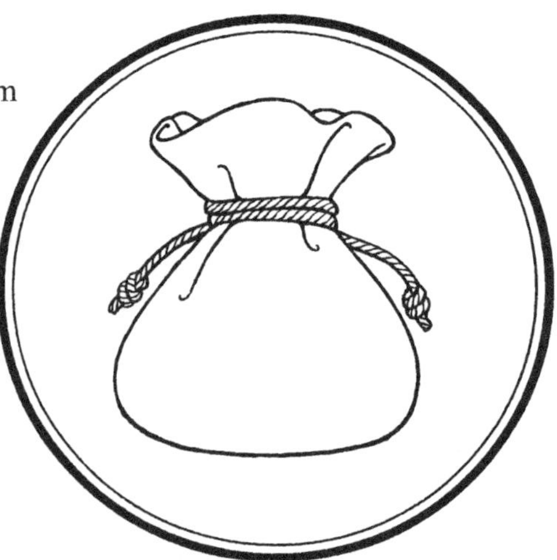

St. David of Thessalonica, or David the Dendrite

FIGURES 239, 240

This hermit was extremely popular in his own day for his wisdom and is usually symbolized by either a lion sejant-guardant or, owing to his alternate title, by a hermit sitting in a tree. David is said to have lived in the branches of an almond tree for three years, praying and fasting. He is believed to have lived between 450 and 540. David's commemoration day is June 26.

St. David of Wales

FIGURE 241

The patron saint of Wales, David is the subject of legend, though little of it can be substantiated. Among those legends, a white dove was said to have perched on his shoulder and the ground under his feet rose to create a new hill as he preached to a crowd outdoors. That legend is reflected in his symbol. It is known with some certainty that this sixth-century monk helped spread Christianity throughout Wales, established monasteries, and promoted the practice of fasting. He is remembered on March 1.

St. Denis of Paris

FIGURE 242

One of several missionaries sent to Gaul to convert the pagans, this third-century bishop has arguably one of the most bizarre legends attributed to him: after being beheaded, the bishop reportedly picked up his own head and then preached a sermon on repentance. His symbol, therefore, should come as no surprise. His martyrdom is commemorated on October 9.

St. Didacus of Alcalá, or San Diego

FIGURE 243

Besides being the namesake of a US city, this fifteenth-century Franciscan from Spain is also the subject of one of the more bizarre oddities in Christendom: a mechanized model of the saint who purportedly reenacts his dubious healing powers and beats his breast as a model of the mea culpa prayer. He is remembered on November 7.

St. Dominic

FIGURE 244

Born in Spain, this early-thirteenth-century saint was the founder of the Dominican Order, who are devoted to preaching. Because members of the order became known as watchdogs of the Lord, his symbol is a torch-bearing dog. St. Dominic is remembered on August 8.

SS Dorcas (Tabitha), Lydia, and Phoebe

FIGURE 245

These faithful women are recorded in the book of Acts and Paul's letter to the Romans. Their collective symbol reflects attributes of each—Dorcas (Acts 9:36) was known as a seamstress who made garments for the poor, Lydia (Acts 16:14) was a dealer in purple cloth (the dye of which came from a seashell), and Phoebe (Romans 16:1–2) was entrusted by St. Paul to deliver his letter to the church in Rome. They are commemorated on October 25.

St. Dorothy, or St. Dorothea of Caesarea

FIGURES 246, 247, 248

Little is known about this fourth-century martyr. Legends abound, however, and she is alternately symbolized by flowers, a burning lantern, or a crown-encircled flame. Her commemoration date is February 6.

St. Dunstan

FIGURES 249, 250, 251

Gifted in all manner of crafts, including metalworking, music, and illuminating manuscripts, this tenth-century Benedictine monk eventually rose to become archbishop of Canterbury. His symbols surround metalworking with a heavy dose of legend, such as a horseshoe with which he allegedly caused pain when shoeing Satan himself. May 19 is his commemoration day.

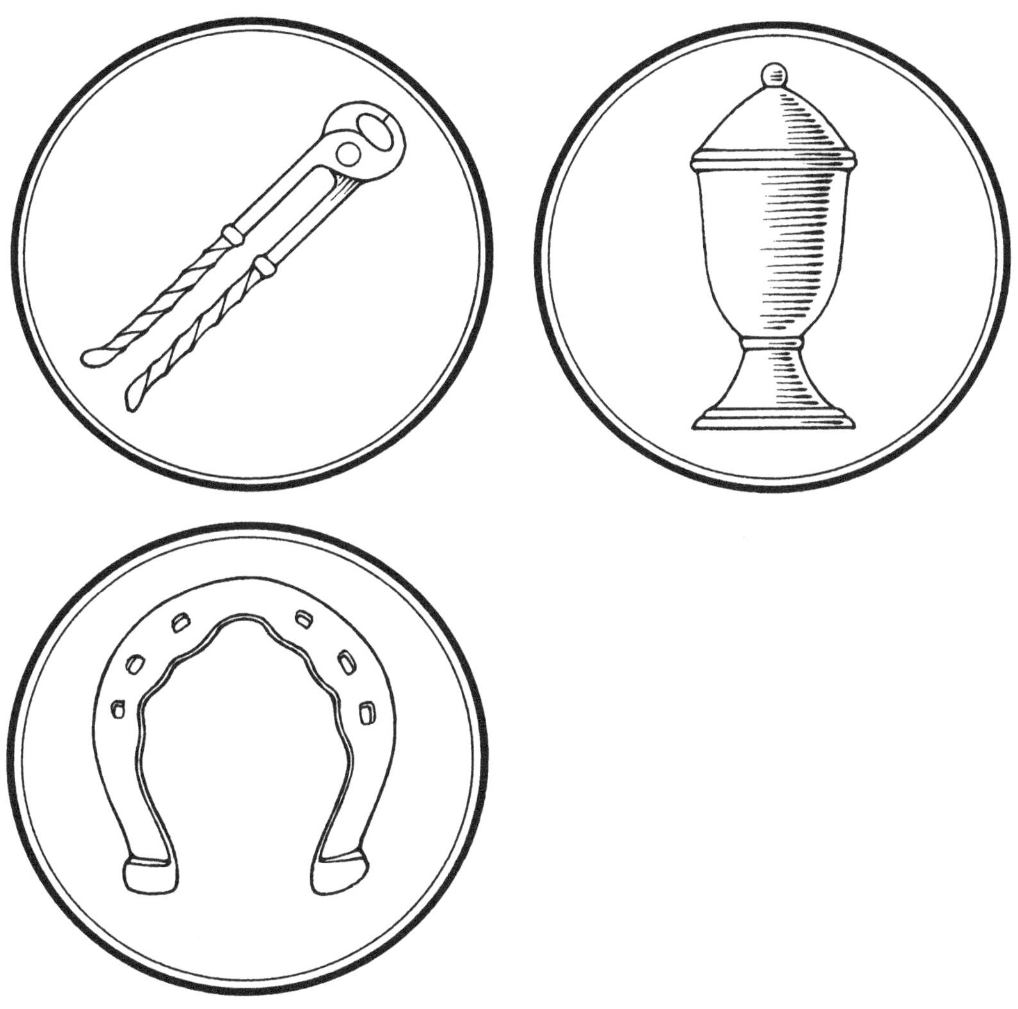

St. Edmund of East Anglia, or Edmund the Martyr

FIGURE 252

The ninth-century king was killed in battle by pagan Vikings, who felled him with arrows. Not much else is known about Edmund, who is said to have succeeded to the throne when he was fourteen. Some consider him to be the original patron saint of England. His death is commemorated on November 20.

St. Edward the Confessor

FIGURE 253

This tenth-century king founded Westminster Abbey, though the original church was demolished by Henry III. While his life was a checkered one, he gained fame—and his symbol—long after his demise. A replica of his crown is still on public display in the Tower of London and is used in coronations. He is remembered on October 13.

St. Edward the Martyr

FIGURE 254

A royal's life is not always easy—or long. This tenth-century English teenager gained the throne only to lose his life at the hands of his stepmother's family. His brutal death was memorialized in medieval English writings, and he became one of England's most popular saints. A dagger is added to symbols of a crown and scepter. His martyrdom is commemorated on March 18.

St. Eligius, or Eloi

FIGURE 255

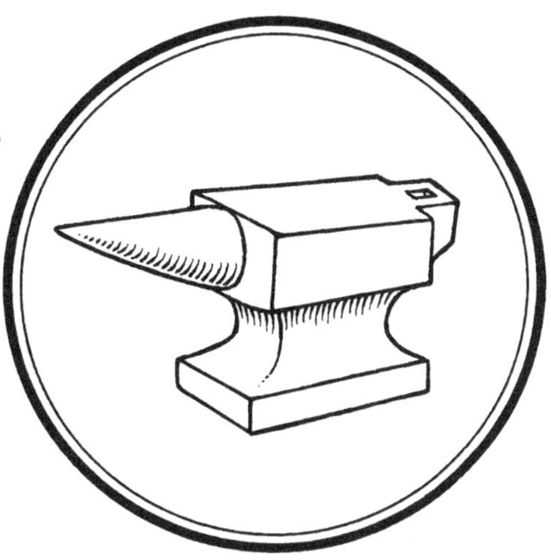

The patron saint of goldsmiths and other craftsmen, Eligius was a seventh-century Gallo-Roman whose craft was sought after by the Frankish king Clotaire II. Known for his honesty and generosity, he would later become a bishop. An anvil is his symbol, as are other implements of his trade. He is remembered on December 1.

St. Elizabeth

FIGURE 256

There are many saints bearing the name, but this Elizabeth is the mother of St. John the Baptist. Her extraordinary story is revealed in Luke 1. The two withered leaves at the base of her symbol refer to her barren years. She shares a feast day with her husband, Zechariah, on September 5.

St. Elizabeth of Hungary

FIGURES 257, 258, 259

Being arguably the most famous of the Elizabeths, this thirteenth-century royal has many symbols associated with her, including three crowns and a pitcher of wine. One symbol associated with her legend depicts contraband bread miraculously turning into roses. Also called Elizabeth of Thuringia, she is known for her charity and piety. She is remembered on November 17.

St. Erasmus of Formia, or St. Elmo

FIGURES 260, 261

According to legend, this early Christian bishop kept preaching even after a lightning bolt struck the ground next to him. In the centuries following, sailors began referring to the glow of a ship's mast before a lightning strike as "St. Elmo's fire" as an expression of their belief that the saint was protecting them. Thus, a lightning bolt is one of Erasmus's symbols, along with a windlass, with which he was tortured. His martyrdom is commemorated on June 2.

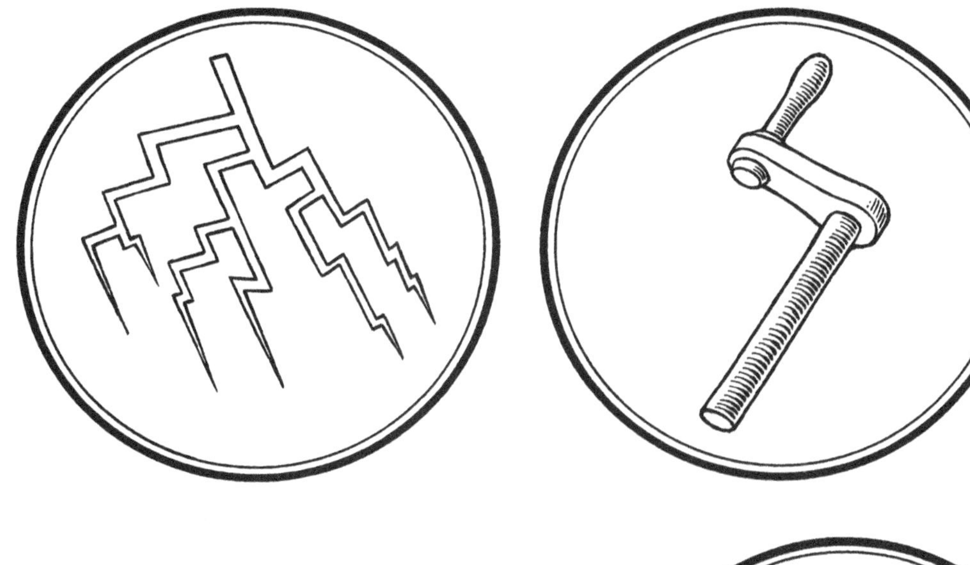

St. Eric IX of Sweden

FIGURE 262

Portrayed as a just ruler and defender of the Christian faith, this twelfth-century king helped to consolidate the church in Sweden, established a rule of law, and initiated aims at converting Finland to Christianity. Legend has it that he was killed while celebrating the mass. The commemoration of his martyrdom is May 18.

St. Etheldreda, or Æthelthryth, or St. Audrey

FIGURE 263

Born into Anglo-Saxon royalty, this queen and abbess of the seventh century is symbolized by three crowns. More medieval writings exist about her than about any other female saint from England. She is remembered on June 23.

St. Eustace, or Placidus

FIGURE 264

Some saints share similar symbols—in this case a white stag with a cross on its head. Although the accuracy of legends about Eustace cannot be verified, and some believe he is a work of fiction, his story is one of faith in the face of great tribulation. A second-century centurion, he is said to have converted when he saw a stag with a cross in its antlers. Eustace was martyred under Hadrian around the year 119. His death is commemorated on September 20.

St. Faith of Conques

FIGURES 265, 266

This Christian lived in the third or fourth century under Roman rule in what is southwest France today. She was martyred at the age of 12 or 13 when she refused to deny the faith and is commemorated on October 6. As with all other martyrs, one of her symbols is the palm frond.

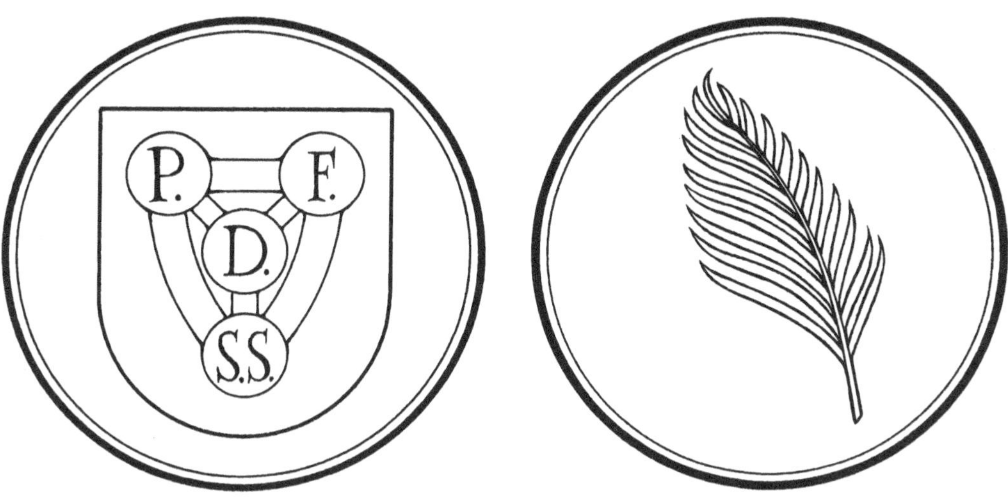

St. Felicitas, or St. Felicity

FIGURE 267

Not to be confused with the saint of the same name associated with St. Perpetua, this second-century saint has a symbol of seven swords, which alludes to the legend that she had seven sons who became martyrs along with her. Her martyrdom is commemorated on November 23.

St. Ferdinand III of Castile

FIGURE 268

This thirteenth-century Spanish king of Castile greatly expanded his kingdom and protected it against the Moors and Islamic invaders. As is the case with some regal figures declared saints by the Vatican, little of his life indicates any significant contribution to Christendom other than being steadfast in his vocation, though he is said to have founded monasteries, hospitals, and churches. He is commemorated on May 30.

St. Francis de Sales

FIGURE 269

Born in 1567 into nobility in Savoy, Francis studied law in Padua before he entered the priesthood. Although known for his gentleness in dealing with fallout from the Protestant Reformation and for his writings for laypeople about spiritual formation and devotion to God, St. Francis was nonetheless labeled a sorcerer by the Calvinistic ministers of Geneva. He is remembered on January 24.

St. Francis di Paola, or Francis the Fire Handler

FIGURE 270

Hallmarks of this saint include the fact that he was never ordained as a priest, his introduction of "the fourth vow" (a strict diet that has firmly placed him as one of the first vegans in history), and his alleged miracles of reviving dead animals, including a fully cooked lamb from a furnace. Although a hermit, he nevertheless built a large monastery and church because his order was so popular. He is remembered on April 2.

St. Francis of Assisi

FIGURES 271, 272

This Italian friar and mystic was born in 1181 and lived a raucous life before he was on the receiving end of a series of divine visions. He established the Franciscan Order, among others, and is said to have arranged for the first live nativity scene. This Francis is symbolized by a tau cross or a cross bearing the stigmata of Christ, which the saint also bore on his hands and feet. He is also known for preaching to the birds, although Scripture makes it quite clear that we are to instead preach to mankind. He is remembered on October 4.

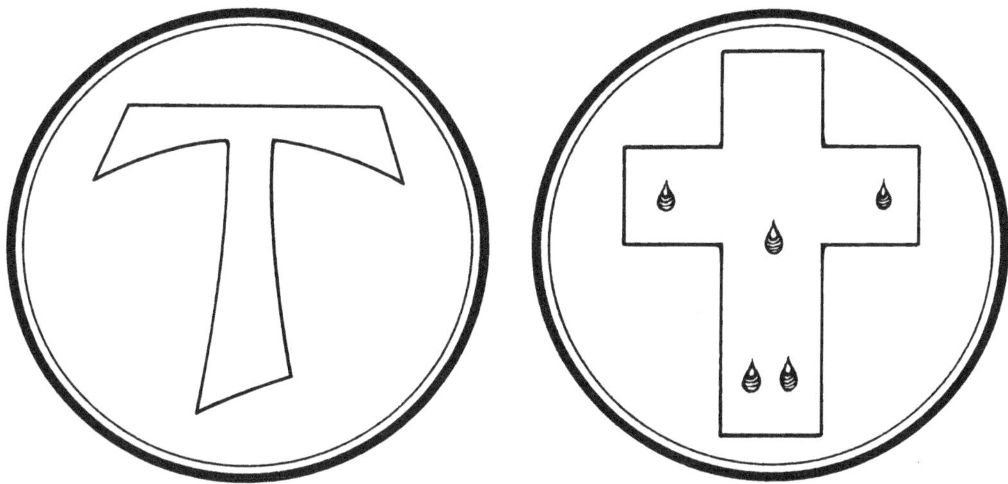

St. Francis Xavier

FIGURE 273

A sixteenth-century Spanish missionary to India, Japan, China, and other lands along the way, St. Francis Xavier was also a cofounder of the Jesuits. Because of the many conversions that happened along his travels to Asia, he is considered a great missionary. His symbol is a baptismal font, indicative of the tens of thousands of Baptisms he reportedly performed. He is remembered on December 3.

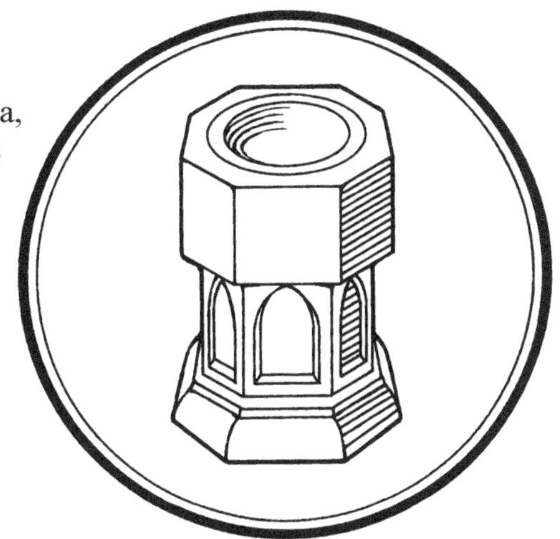

St. Gabriel, Archangel

FIGURES 274, 275

One of two archangels mentioned in the Protestant Bible (the other is Michael), we read of Gabriel specifically when he appeared to Daniel (Daniel 9:20–23), to Zechariah (Luke 1:5–19), and to Mary (Luke 1:28–33). Although his name derives from "God is my strength," Gabriel has come to be associated with his role as a messenger. In art he is shown in blue or white and carrying a lily, trumpet, lantern, or scroll. Gabriel is remembered, along with all angels, on September 29.

St. Geneviève

FIGURE 276

St. Geneviève was a fifth-century Parisian nun who led a life of prayer and fasting. She purportedly held off attacks on her city from not only the Merovingian king Childeric but also Attila the Hun. Her symbol reflects images gleaned from legends surrounding her life but may also include a lit candle, bread, keys, or cattle. She is commemorated on January 3.

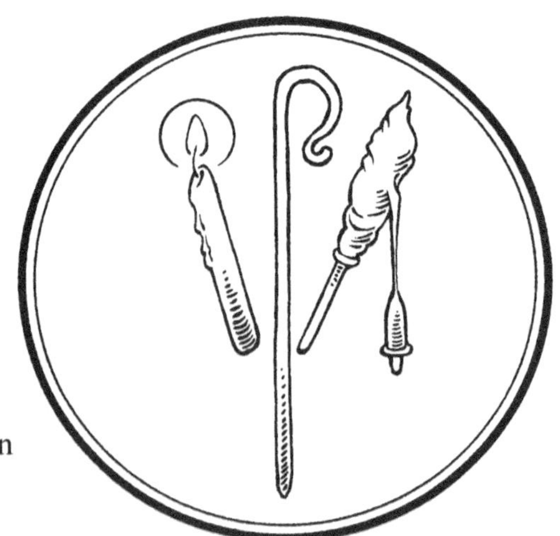

St. George, or George of Lydda

FIGURES 277, 278

A member of the Praetorian Guard under the Roman Emperor Diocletian, the life of St. George can hardly be separated from the legend of his battle with the dragon. Tradition holds that George was beheaded in 303 because he would not renounce his faith in Christ. By the time of the Crusades, around 1090 to about 1290, he was regarded as a military saint. And the countries of England, Ethiopia, Ukraine, and Georgia, along with regions in Spain, France, and Russia consider him as their patron saint. The red cross of St. George and the slain dragon are his symbols. His martyrdom under Diocletian for refusing to recant the faith is commemorated on April 23.

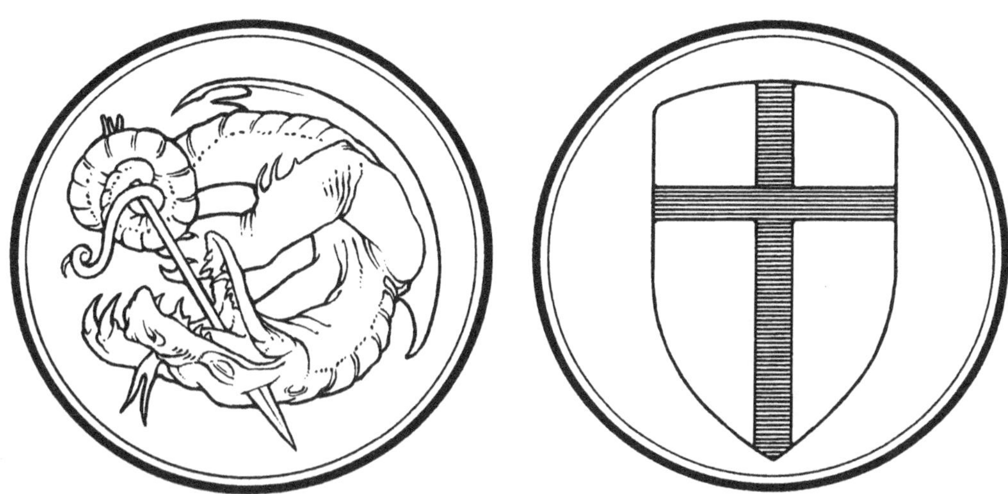

St. Gertrude of Helfta, or Gertrude the Great

FIGURE 279

A German mystic who allegedly received visions from the Christ Child, this fourteenth-century nun gained the rare title of "great" because of her spiritual and theological insight. The new invention of the printing press was key to spreading her writings. Although a prolific author, only five of her books are still in existence. She is remembered on November 16.

St. Giles, or Giles the Hermit

FIGURE 280

The product of legend, this seventh-century monk is purported to have sheltered a wounded doe from hunters, from which his symbol derives. His origins (Greece or France) are uncertain, but he is said to have lived in solitude in France and to have built a monastery that became a popular place of respite for pilgrims. He is remembered on September 1.

St. Gregory the Great, or Pope Gregory I

FIGURE 281

Known for his writings and for initiating the first mission to the Anglo-Saxons, Gregory is credited with establishing the medieval papacy. Throughout the Middle Ages, this bishop of Rome was considered the father of Christian worship and was known for his generosity to the poor and influence on music and liturgy. He is one of the Latin fathers and a doctor of the church. Founder of seven monasteries, he is remembered on September 3.

St. Gregory of Nazianzus

FIGURE 282

A fourth-century bishop of Constantinople, St. Gregory of Nazianzus was a defender of the Nicene Creed and is regarded as the "Trinitarian Theologian." An accomplished speaker and poet, Gregory helped to further the understanding of God as three Persons. He is commemorated in the Lutheran Church on January 10 along with his fellow confessors, Basil the Great of Caesarea and Gregory of Nyssa.

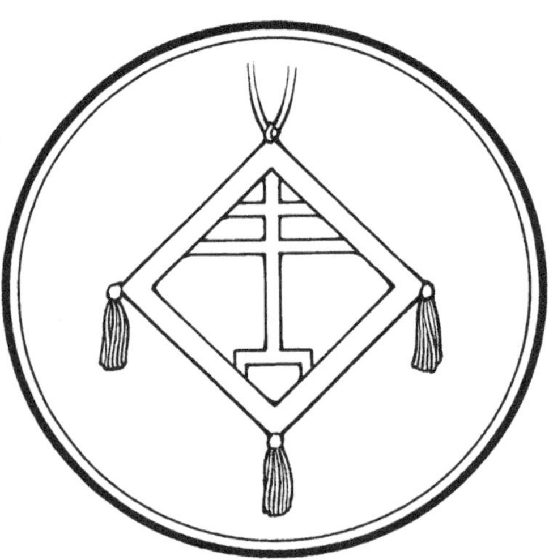

St. Gregory of Nyssa

FIGURE 283

Following somewhat in the shadow of his fellow confessors, St. Gregory of Nyssa still made important written contributions to the doctrine of the Holy Trinity and the Nicene Creed. Brother of the better-known Basil, Gregory of Nyssa was among the first theologians to teach that God is infinite. He is believed to have died in 395. January 10 is his commemoration date.

St. Helena

FIGURE 284

The early-fourth-century empress of the Roman Empire is commemorated on May 21, along with her son, Emperor Constantine I. She is remembered for her pilgrimage to the Holy Land and overseeing excavations in search of the true cross.

St. Hilarion of Gaza, or Hilarion the Great

FIGURE 285

A student of Anthony the Great, this fourth-century Palestinian monk grew in popularity for being a miracle-worker. So much so, it became nearly impossible for him to live in the hermit-like seclusion of his anchorite calling. He is remembered on October 21.

St. Hilary of Poitiers

FIGURE 286

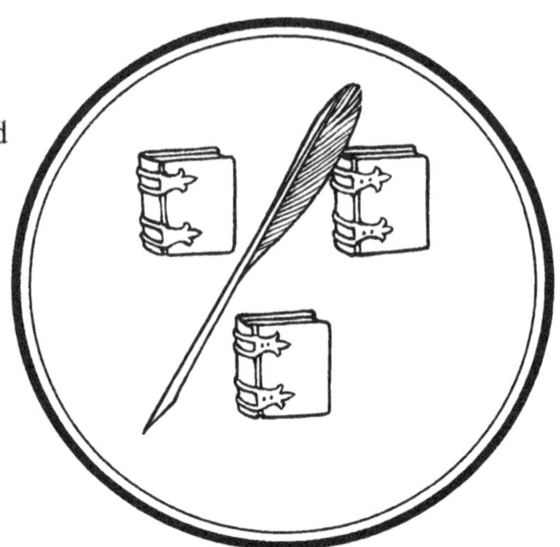

Born and educated a pagan, Hilary studied the Old and New Testaments, which caused him to abandon his old ways and be baptized into the Christian faith. Sometimes referred to as the "Athanasius of the West," this fourth-century French bishop and doctor of the church did much to defend the doctrine of the Holy Trinity. Hence, his symbol is a pen and three books. He is commemorated on January 13.

St. Hilda of Whitby, or Hild of Whitby

FIGURE 287

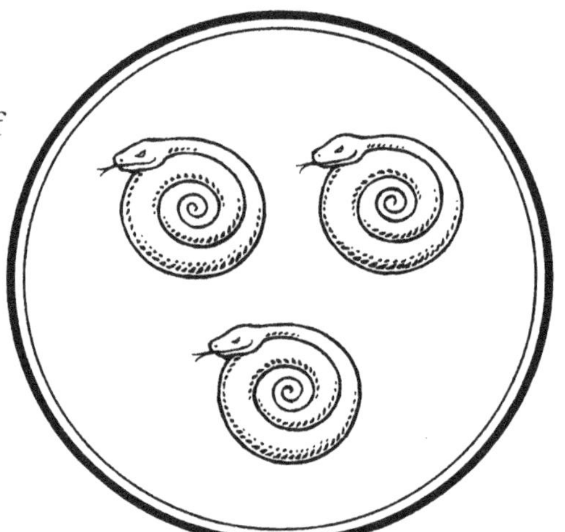

This seventh-century English nun became abbess of several monasteries, including Whitby Abbey, which she founded. She was known for her energetic daily work as a landowner, her wisdom in business matters, and her skill as a teacher. According to legend, she once turned snakes into stones. That legend is the basis for her symbol. Her feast day is November 17.

St. Hippolytus of Rome

FIGURE 288

Legends do nothing to help Christendom, and St. Hippolytus is an example of this. His third-century life is a blur as bishop of Pontus, converted Roman soldier, and a near copy of his mythological namesake. He is considered an important theological scholar, especially regarding his view of the Trinity, but many of his writings are available via translations and not original manuscripts. Some credit him with establishing the apostolic tradition. Hippolytus is remembered on August 13.

Holy Innocents

FIGURE 289

This is one such case when the title "saints" is not given, although it is assumed. The Holy Innocents are the young boys destroyed by Herod when he searched for the new King of the Jews, according to Matthew 2:16–18 (and prophesied in Jeremiah 31:15). Considered to be the first Christian martyrs, they are often depicted as naked babies playing around the virgin Mary. Their symbol is Mary's lily with two crowns. Their martyrdom is commemorated on December 28.

St. Hubert of Liége

FIGURE 290

Born into French royalty and a member of the royal court, Hubert primarily pursued hunting. Until, that is, he was converted when a stag appeared with a cross between its antlers. Hubert then immersed himself in religious studies, renounced his worldly ways, gave his wealth to the poor, and was made bishop. St. Hubert is remembered on November 3.

St. Hugh of Lincoln

FIGURE 291

French-born, Hugh was educated at a convent, ordained as a deacon at the age of 19, and named a bishop by Henry II. Among his accomplishments, St. Hugh initiated the restoration of the Lincoln Cathedral in England. Legend has it that a white swan adopted the bishop, following him around and even guarding him as he slept. The swan became his symbol. St. Hugh is remembered on November 16.

St. Ignatius of Antioch, or Ignatius Theophorus

FIGURE 292

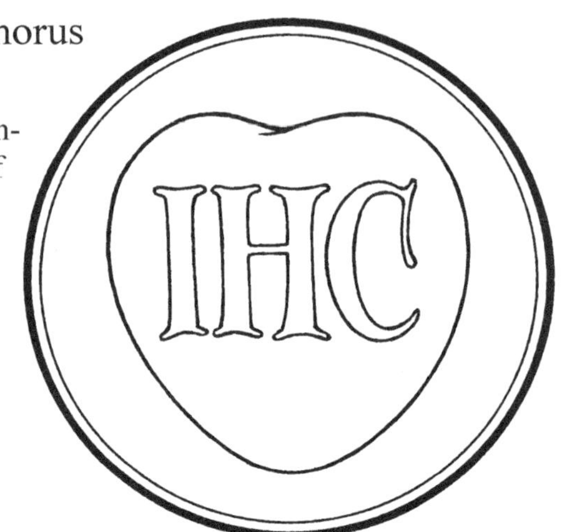

This second-century Syrian became bishop of Antioch and was, according to tradition, a disciple of the apostle John. The author of seven letters covering topics such as ecclesiology, the sacraments, and the Sabbath, Ignatius met his martyrdom with lions in the arena in Rome. He is commemorated on October 17.

St. Ignatius of Loyola

FIGURE 293

A contemporary of Martin Luther, Ignatius was a reformer in his own right. Born into Spanish nobility, he served as a knight. It is said that he became bored during his recovery from an injury received during battle and began reading about the lives of the saints and about the life of Christ. It changed his life. He eventually went to Paris to study, where he and like-minded priests founded the Society of the Jesuits. Where Luther's efforts to reform the church resulted in his excommunication, Ignatius's own efforts were kept within the church. Attempts to excommunicate him were not successful, but he was kept under watch in the Vatican, near the pope's own office. The AMDG letters on his symbol stand for "To the greater glory of God," the motto of the Jesuits. He is remembered on July 31.

St. Irenaeus of Lyons

FIGURE 294

This second-century Greek became bishop of Lugdumum, in what is now Lyons, France. A student of Polycarp (who was a disciple of John), Irenaeus did much to refute the Gnostics and helped to spread the Gospel in modern-day southern France. St. Irenaeus is commemorated on June 28.

St. Isadore the Laborer, or Isadore the Farmer

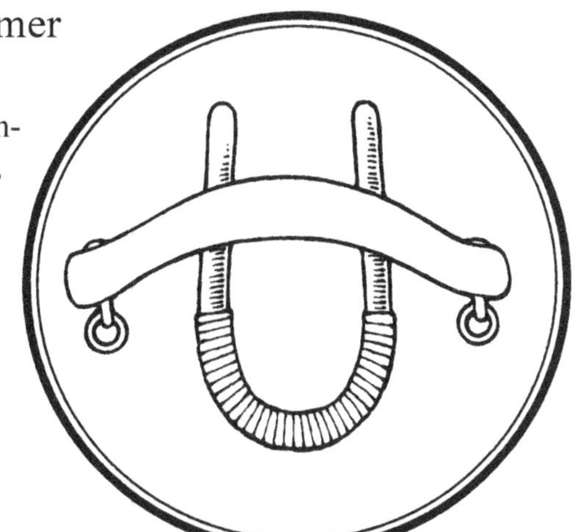

FIGURE 295

Many legends surround the life of this twelfth-century Spanish farm worker, an otherwise faceless saint, who has gained notoriety among laborers around the globe as a model of the dignity of work. His symbol can be a yoke or other farming equipment. He is remembered on May 15.

St. James the Greater, St. James the Elder, or James, the son of Zebedee

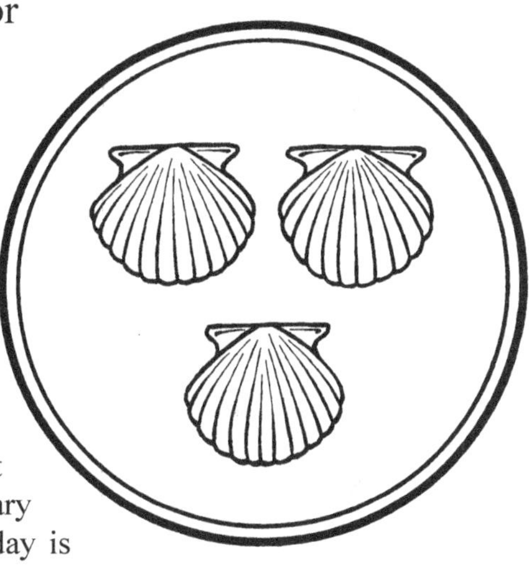

FIGURE 296

One of the twelve apostles, this saint has the label "greater" because he was either older or taller, not because he was of more importance. A son of Zebedee and Salome and brother of John, he was among the first disciples called to follow Jesus, was an eyewitness at the transfiguration—among other important events—and was the first to be martyred. Before scallop shells became symbolically connected to Holy Baptism, they denoted pilgrimage. Because this saint was one of the first to be mentioned going on a missionary journey, his symbol is three scallop shells. His feast day is July 25.

St. James the Lesser, or St. James the Younger

FIGURES 297, 298, 299

Another of the twelve apostles, this James is considered to be a brother or cousin of Jesus (Matthew 27:56 and Mark 15:40 or Mark 16:1 and Luke 24:10). Tradition is less clear on his death, so symbols of saws, fuller's clubs, and halberds are among those pointing to his martyrdom, which is commemorated on October 23.

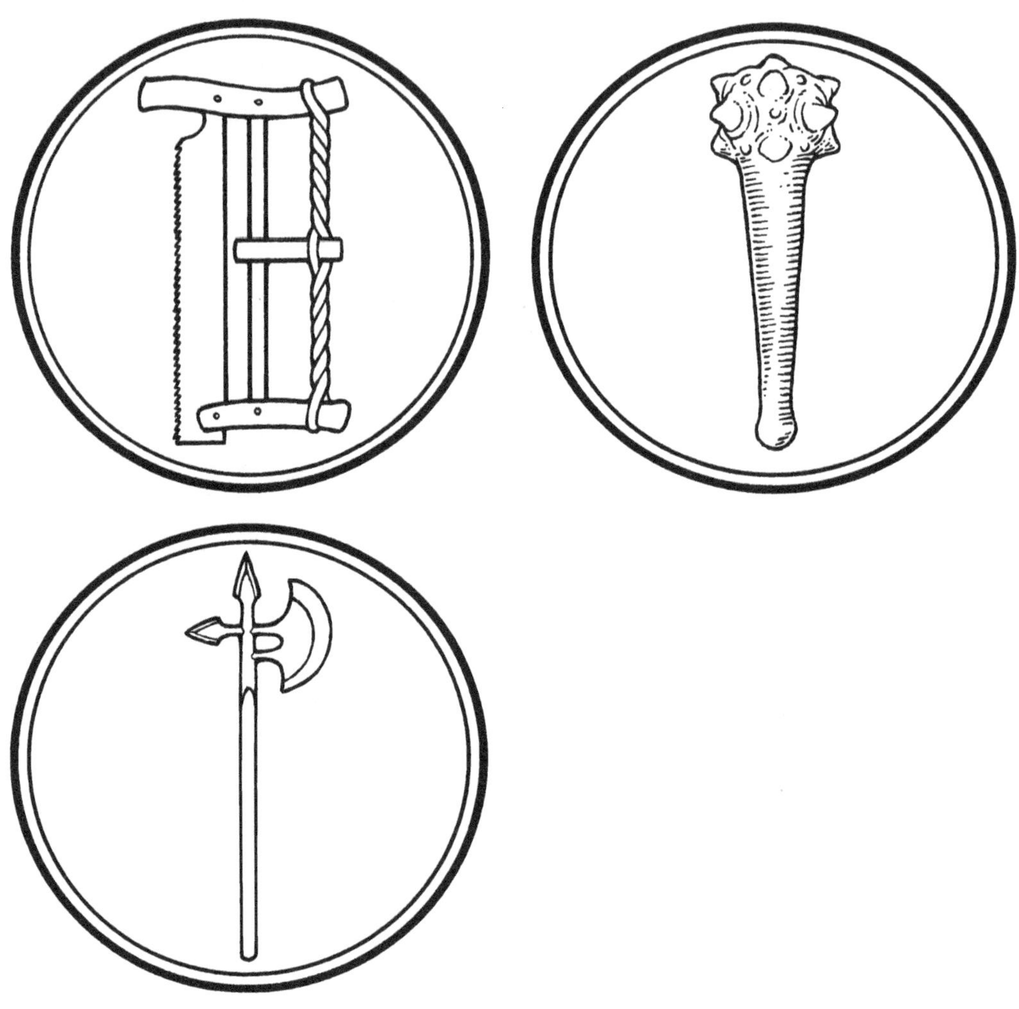

St. Jerome

FIGURES 300, 301

Born in present-day Croatia, Jerome undertook a Latin translation of the Greek New Testament, known as the Vulgate. Because he is often portrayed as a hermit, one symbol for the saint is a skull and cross. A fitched potent cross may also be used. He is commemorated on September 30.

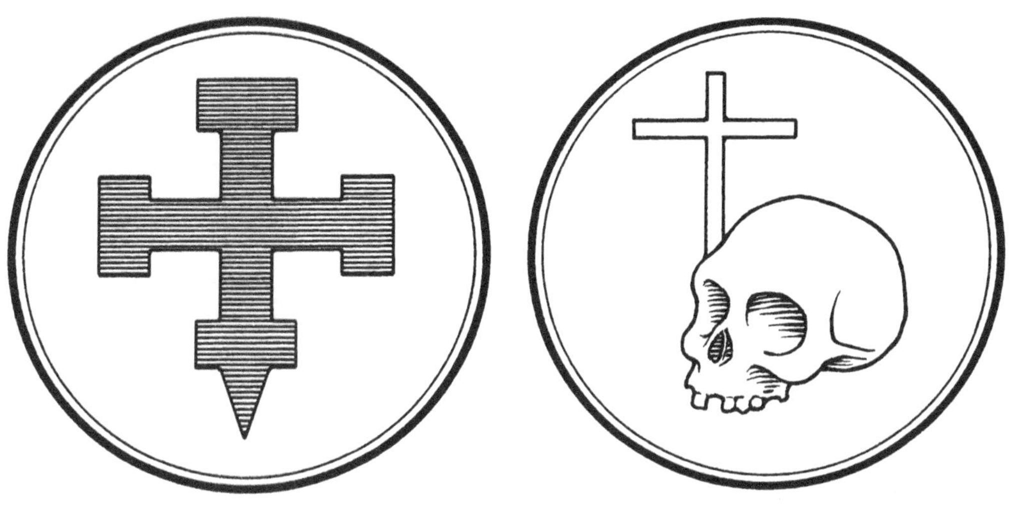

St. Joan of Arc, or The Maid of Lorraine

FIGURE 302

This beloved, larger-than-life military leader has become even more popular in the centuries following her death at age 19. After having a vision at the age of 13, this Joan convinced the local French officials that God had chosen her to help lead France during the Hundred Years' War. Despite some military success, she was captured, tried for heresy, and found guilty. Her symbol is the coat of arms granted to her brothers and their descendants. Her martyrdom of burning at the stake is commemorated on May 30.

SS Joanna, Mary, and Salome

FIGURE 303

According to the Gospels of Matthew (28:1), Mark (16:1), and Luke (8:3), Joanna was the wife of Chuza, a steward in Herod's household; Mary was the wife of Alphaeus and mother of James the Younger; and Salome was the wife of Zebedee and mother of James the Greater and John. August 3 is the commemoration of these three myrrh-bearers who went to the tomb on Easter morning to anoint the body of Jesus after His death. Their collective symbol is comprised of three small jars of the costly ointment.

St. John the Apostle

FIGURE 304

This son of Salome and Zebedee was one of the first disciples called by Christ and the only one of the Twelve who did not forsake Jesus and who witnessed His crucifixion. While given the symbolic eagle in his role as an evangelist, St. John's symbol as an apostle is that of a serpent in a chalice. This stems from a legend in which he was challenged to drink a cup of poison to demonstrate the power of his faith. John is believed to be the longest-living apostle and the only one to die a natural death. His feast day is December 27.

St. John the Baptist, or St. John the Forerunner

FIGURES 305, 306, 307

The forerunner of Christ, this "voice in the wilderness" was the first prophet after Malachi. Whether it was his miraculous birth or his distinct life, it is hard to avoid depictions of this saint, both in life and in death. He is alternately shown as a fiery, wild-haired preacher in animated exhortation or as a lifeless head on a platter. He is also frequently shown with a scallop shell. This is one saint who has the distinction of having two entries in the sanctoral calendar—his birth is celebrated on June 24, and his martyrdom is commemorated on August 29.

St. John Chrysostom, or St. Chrysostom

FIGURES 308, 309, 310

Many significant saints have numerous symbols, and this early church father of the fifth century who became archbishop of Constantinople is one. A chalice on a Bible, a dove, or a bee skep may be used as his symbol. Highly educated, he was a prolific author, a lawyer, a priest, and a hermit. He memorized the Bible and adopted a literal interpretation of it. He is remembered on January 27.

St. John of the Cross

FIGURE 311

It should come as no surprise that a cross is the symbol of this sixteenth-century priest who was active in the Spanish Reformation. His writings are counted among the great works of Spanish literature and theology. The symbol's split design reflects his monastic background as both a Jesuit and a Carmelite. He is remembered on December 14.

St. John of Damascus

FIGURE 312

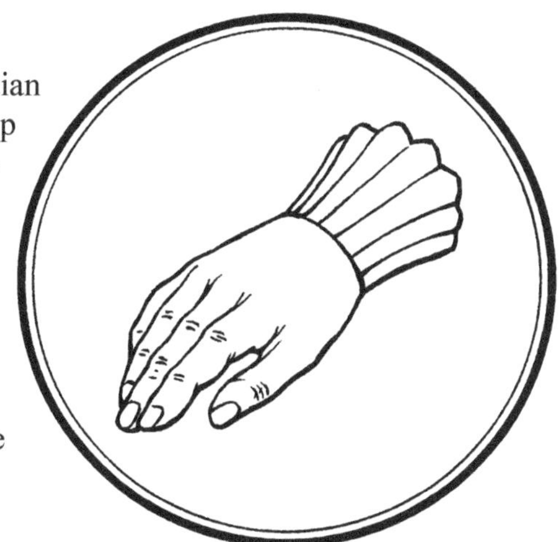

This saint was born into a wealthy Arab-Christian family and held a position in court. He gave that up for the priesthood and lived at a monastery near Jerusalem. John became involved in a controversy over whether icons should be worshiped. He is credited with writing theological works that are important to Eastern Orthodoxy. His symbol, like others, begs for explanation. According to legend, the ruling caliph had John's hand unjustly cut off for an offense. After much prayer, his hand was miraculously reattached. He is remembered on April 30.

St. John Eudes

FIGURE 313

Known as a missionary and eloquent preacher and writer, this seventeenth-century French priest had a reputation for compassionate evangelism and for working to improve the spiritual lives of priests and prostitutes. He authored the Roman Catholic propers for the Sacred Heart of Jesus and the Blessed Virgin, which is reflected in his symbol of the flaming heart. He is remembered on August 19.

St. John the Evangelist

FIGURE 314

Brother of James, son of Zebedee and Salome, John was one of the first disciples whom Jesus called and was part of His inner circle. He is always listed after James, the older of the two sons. John was present at the transfiguration, helped Peter prepare for the Last Supper, sat next to Jesus at that meal, was present at the foot of the cross, and raced to the Lord's tomb on the day of the resurrection. Here the saint is symbolized as one of the four living creatures—the eagle—because of the lofty, soaring words his Gospel contains in the opening chapter. For both his role as evangelist and apostle, St. John has December 27 as his feast day.

St. John Nepomuk

FIGURE 315

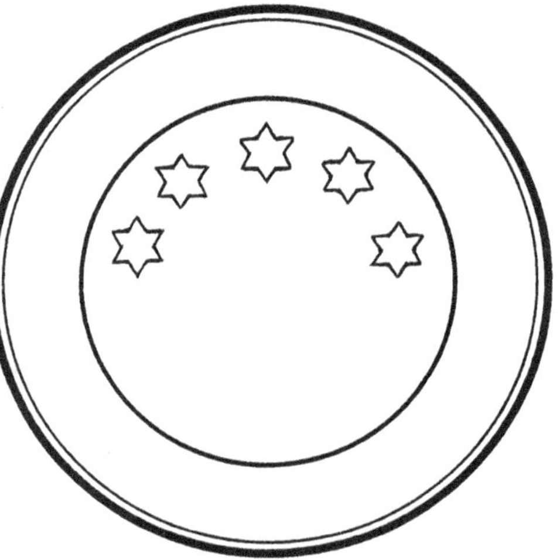

A doctor of canon law and vicar general in Prague, this fourteenth-century Czech saint is said to have been the confessor of the queen of Bohemia. Because he did not divulge the secrets of her confession, King Wenceslaus IV had the priest tortured with fire and drowned in the Vltava River. He is designated by a halo of five stars, and his martyrdom is commemorated on May 16.

St. Joseph of Arimathaea

FIGURE 316

All four Gospel books tell us that Joseph of Arimathaea was responsible for Jesus' burial. With Pilate's permission, Joseph took Jesus down from the cross, wrapped Him in a linen shroud, and buried Him in his own tomb. He is the fulfillment of Isaiah 53:9— that the Messiah would lie in a rich man's grave. This saint's symbol chiefly derives from legends surrounding him. The Holy Grail, for example, was supposedly given into his care, and one legend records his walking staff turning into a Glastonbury thorn. St. Joseph of Arimathaea is remembered on July 31.

St. Joseph of Nazareth

FIGURE 317

A descendant of King David, the earthly guardian of Jesus has many symbols. The one pictured here shows a carpenter's square superimposed over a lily with a conspicuous *M*, a symbol for Mary. Joseph may also be depicted either holding a lit candle or sleeping or both. These point to the fact that he literally carried the Light of the world and that he was given direction through dreams. His profession as a carpenter (or skilled tradesman) is mentioned only once, in Matthew 13:55. Outside of Scripture, legends surrounding Joseph abound. For example, according to tradition, he died in the arms of Mary and Jesus. His feast day is March 19.

Judas Iscariot

FIGURE 318

An example of avarice, the story of Judas shows that we cannot know what is in another's heart or thoughts. The other disciples did not know Judas as anyone other than another follower, called by Jesus to walk with Him. Our Lord did know, however, and knew that Judas was unrepentant. He is often symbolically included with the apostles, but only as a warning to the viewer. His symbol is the thirty pieces of silver and the rope, in the shape of a *J*, with which he hanged himself.

St. Jude the Apostle

FIGURES 319, 320, 321

One of the Twelve, Jude was believed to have been a relative of Jesus through both His earthly father and mother. Luther believed that he was not the author of the book of Jude. Some ancient writers claimed Jude was the groom in the wedding at Cana. From John 14, we know that he was present at the Last Supper. According to tradition, he was martyred in what is present-day Lebanon. Because accounts vary, he can by symbolized by a club, sword, or axe. Alternately, a ship may be used to represent his missionary journeys. His death is commemorated, along with St. Simon's, on October 28.

St. Julia of Corsica

FIGURE 322

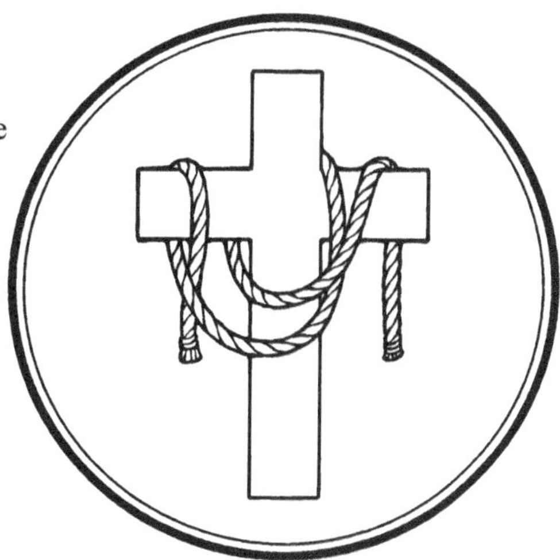

As with most people who lived in the 400s, little is known of this Carthaginian saint's life, but legend about her abounds. It is said that she was captured during a barbaric Roman attack, sold as a slave to Eusebius, and remained faithful to God even while being tortured. She often appears crucified on a cross. An alternate symbol is an empty cross entangled with a rope. Her martyrdom is commemorated on May 22.

St. Julian of Le Mans

FIGURE 323

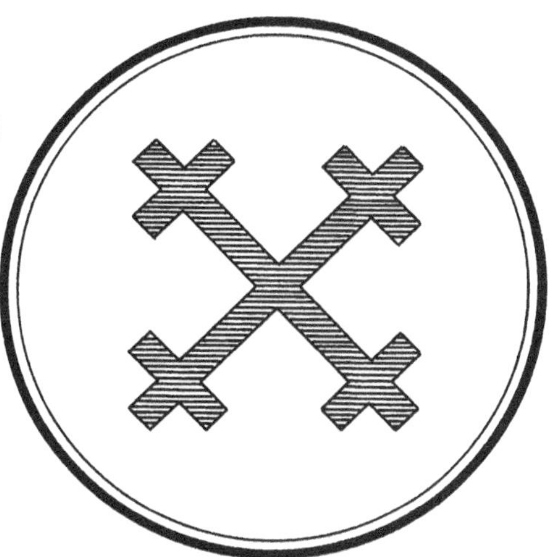

Julian was sent from Rome to Gaul during the third century to the city that is now Le Mans, France, where he became the first bishop. According to legend, the city had a water shortage. Julian is said to have jabbed his staff into the ground and water gushed out. This inspired the residents to convert to Christianity. Julian is credited with ministry to the poor and to orphans. He is remembered on January 27.

St. Justin of Rome, or Justin Martyr

FIGURES 324, 325

A Greek philosopher who was not satisfied with philosophies he encountered, Justin eventually converted to Christianity and held to the examples of the martyrs. After moving to Rome, he founded a Christian school. One of his few surviving works is a piece that defends the Christian faith to the Romans and describes what worship was like in the early church. He paid the ultimate price for his newfound faith, becoming a martyr himself in the second century. His death is commemorated on June 1. His symbol may be a flaming Roman helmet or a Roman gladius with a pen.

St. Justina of Padua

FIGURES 326, 327

A childless Italian nobleman and his wife converted to Christianity, and Justina was born after they prayed for a child. This daughter was devoted to the faith and took a vow of virginity. She was captured by the brutal Maximian and put to death because she would not renounce her faith. Symbols for this fourth-century martyr may either be a sword or a unicorn. The mythical unicorn was alternately used in the Middle Ages to symbolize chastity, as in this case, or Christ Jesus. St. Justina's martyrdom is commemorated on October 7.

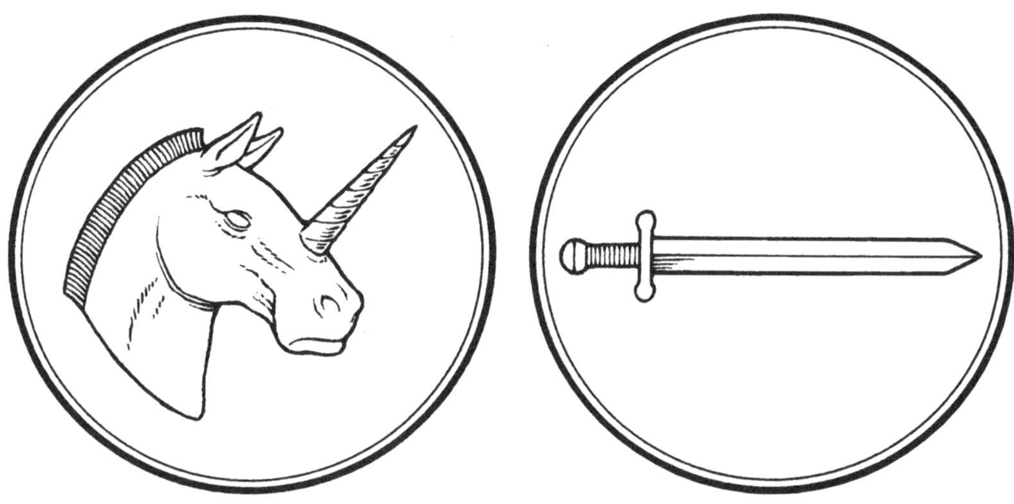

St. Justinian, Justinian I, or Justinian the Great

FIGURE 328

This sixth-century Byzantine ruler was not only an ambitious leader—"the emperor who never sleeps"—but also a confessor of the church. Under his leadership, the Roman Empire underwent a partial restoration in the western Mediterranean. He rewrote Roman law, which underpins civil law in many areas to this day. He led a building plan that resulted in magnificent buildings and civil works like bridges, dams, and cisterns. His odd symbol is taken from a condensed monogram found inscribed on architectural columns. He is remembered on November 14.

St. Kentigern, or St. Mungo

FIGURE 329

Born in what is now Scotland, this sixth-century saint is beloved for his missionary work throughout the British Isles. Kentigern was the son of a princess and raised in a monastery. He built a church that eventually became part of the cathedral in Glasgow and is credited with founding that city. His symbol refers to a legend in which he restored the honor to an indiscreet queen. St. Kentigern is commemorated on January 13.

St. Kilian

FIGURE 330

This seventh-century Irish missionary to Germany was beheaded after unveiling a ruler's infidelity. His martyrdom is commemorated on July 8.

St. Lawrence

FIGURE 331

A third-century archdeacon of Rome, St. Lawrence was one of seven Christians martyred on a gridiron during the Valerian persecution. It is said that when pagan rulers ordered Lawrence to produce the treasures of the church, he presented to them the poor and the widows instead of turning over his riches to the emperor. His death is commemorated on August 10.

St. Lazarus of Bethany

FIGURE 332

A follower of Jesus, Lazarus lived near Jerusalem with his sisters Mary and Martha. The occasion of Jesus teaching in the home of Lazarus and his sisters appears only in Luke 10. The account of Jesus restoring Lazarus from death back to life appears only in John 11 and was a miracle that caused much anxiety among the Pharisees and chief priests because it inspired many people to believe in Jesus as the promised Messiah. Nothing else is said about Lazarus in the Bible, though much has been speculated about his life afterward. Together with his sisters, Lazarus is celebrated on July 29. His symbol is often a living man swaddled in funeral cloths.

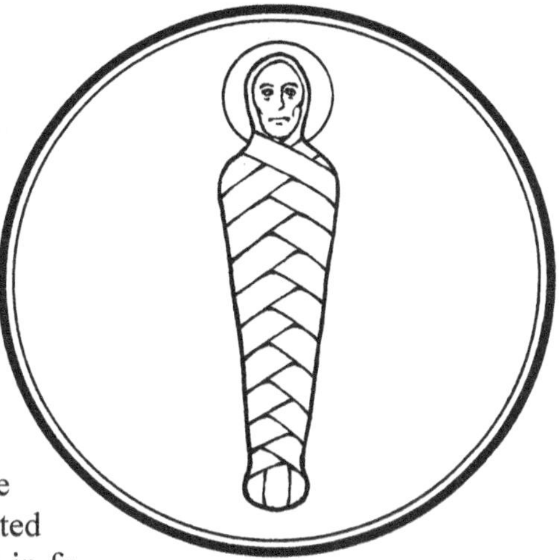

St. Leonard of Noblac

FIGURE 333

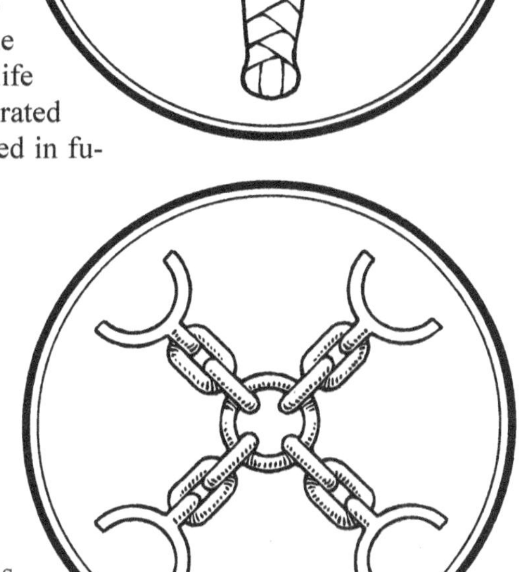

All that is known of this sixth-century French saint comes from a biography written five hundred years after his death. According to that publication, Leonard was a noble during the reign of Clovis I. He supposedly asked the king's favor to release prisoners of his choosing. He is the patron saint of prisoners, and his symbol is comprised of broken shackles. His commemoration day is November 6.

St. Louis IX of France

FIGURE 334

This thirteenth-century king was known for his just rule and is the only canonized ruler of France. Louis became king at the age of 12, and he is credited with civic and religious building projects in France and Palestine. He led the seventh crusade to the Holy Land and helped to end conflicts with England and elsewhere in France. Diplomatic and pious, Louis was known for his charitable acts, fairness, and life of faith. His symbol is the ancient arms of France. Louis IX is remembered on August 25.

St. Lucian of Antioch, or Lucian the Martyr

FIGURE 335

Lucian was a fourth-century Syrian who was tortured and killed under Maximinus Daia. One legend describes his death by drowning, after which a porpoise—his symbol—brought his body to shore. He is credited as a theologian and for biblical linguistic scholarship that influenced how we view the Bible. His martyrdom is commemorated on January 7.

St. Lucia of Syracuse, or St. Lucy

FIGURES 336, 337, 338

How a fourth-century Sicilian woman became so beloved in Scandinavia is a wonder; perhaps it is her association with light that helps fight off the darkness shortly before the winter solstice. Her symbols may be a lantern, a headdress of candles, or a set of eyes. The latter symbol points to a legend that her eyes were gouged under torture before her death by sword. The account of her martyrdom in 304 was included in *Acts of the Martyrs,* compiled by various scholars beginning in the 300s, and her story is recorded in the catacombs of St. John in Syracuse, which were built between 300 and 500. Her martyrdom is commemorated on December 13.

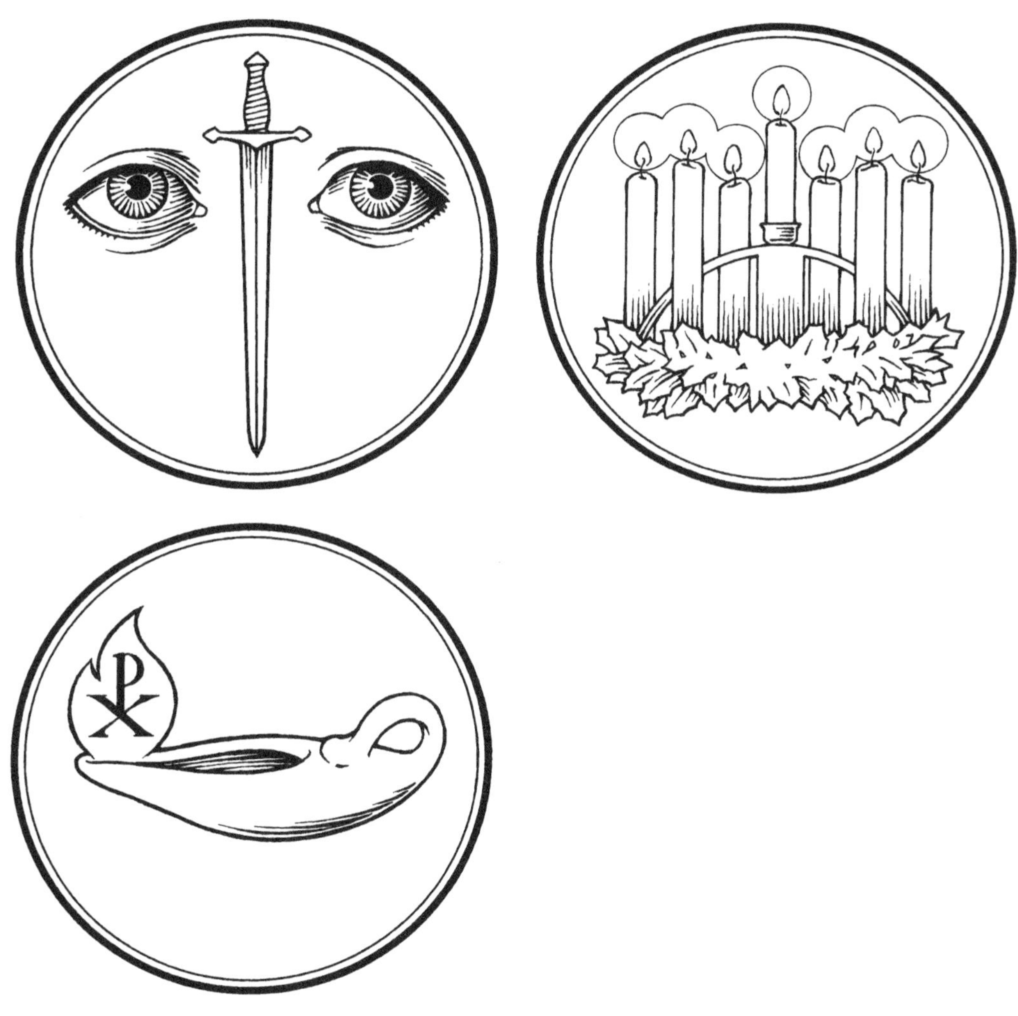

St. Luke the Evangelist

FIGURES 339, 340

A highly educated Gentile physician from Antioch, though perhaps a slave, Luke was a disciple of Paul and is credited with writing the book of Luke and the Acts of the Apostles, recording several accounts that are not included elsewhere. Much of what we know about him is inferred from the New Testament, but it is commonly believed that he met Paul around the year AD 51 and traveled with him on several missionary journeys. Luke's writings emphasize Christ's compassionate forgiveness and mercy for sinners. Because the great sacrifice of the Old Testament was the ox, and because the Gospel of St. Luke revolves around the theme of sacrifice, the winged ox—one of the four living creatures mentioned in the Revelation of St. John—has become the symbol of St. Luke. Apart from his role as an evangelist, St. Luke is often shown painting, especially images of Christ. As such, he has become the patron saint of artists. He is celebrated on October 18.

St. Margaret of Antioch, or St. Margaret the Virgin

FIGURE 341

Little is known of this martyr, but according to one of many legends, this fourth-century Christian convert was swallowed by Satan, but the cross she carried grew so large that it pried open his mouth and she escaped. Other legends have her sentenced to death by fire, drowning, and beheading and hold that hers was among the voices Joan of Arc heard (along with St. Michael's and St. Catherine's). She is remembered on July 20.

St. Mark the Evangelist

FIGURE 342

A son of Mary (Acts 12:12) and cousin of the apostle Barnabas, Mark was closely associated with Paul and Peter, is thought to have been present when Paul was martyred, and is considered the founder of the church of Alexandria. Mark is held as one of Jesus' seventy-two disciples and to be the young man who fled at Jesus' arrest (Mark 14:51–52). St. Ireneaus, who assigned the four living creatures described in the Revelation of St. John to the four evangelists, assigned the winged lion to Mark because he begins his Gospel with John the Baptist crying in the wilderness. That cry was likened to the roar of a lion. St. Mark is celebrated on April 25.

St. Martha

FIGURES 343, 344

A model of diligent Christian service and faith, Martha is sometimes depicted holding a torch, which in earlier days symbolized enlightenment or zeal. However, because of her domestic role when Christ Jesus visited, she is more often associated with household tools, such as buckets, brooms, and cooking utensils. She is remembered, along with her sister, Mary, and brother, Lazarus, on July 29.

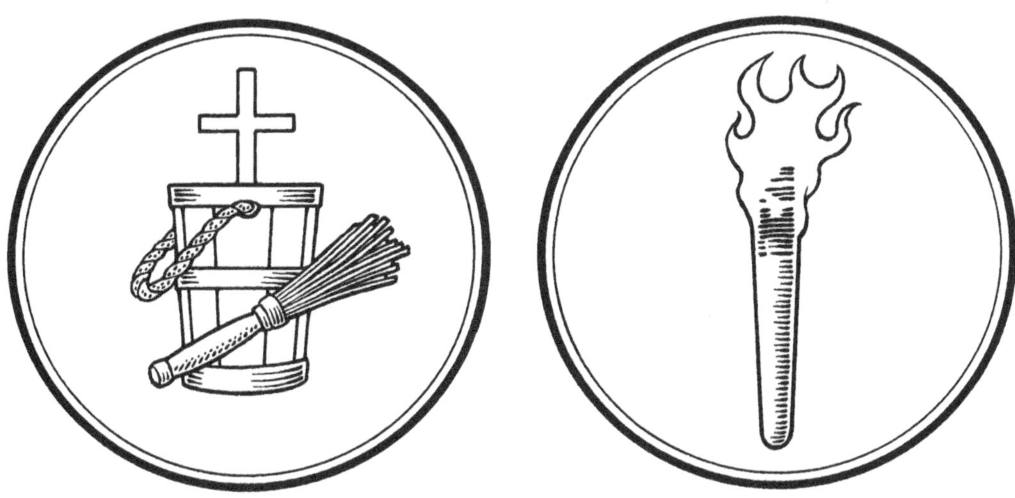

SS Martha, Mary, and Lazarus of Bethany

FIGURE 345

Because Mary is often associated with the sinful woman who anointed Jesus' feet, her symbol is a jar of myrrh. Besides his fame of being raised from the dead, legend holds that Lazarus became bishop alternately of Cyprus and Marseilles. Hence, a stole is here used for his symbol. Martha's symbol of a bucket and asperge is also used in a reprise. Together, their day of commemoration is July 29.

St. Martin of Tours

FIGURE 346

This Martin was born in the fourth century in what is now Hungary and grew up in Italy shortly before Christianity was accepted and the brutalities against Christians ended. Martin Luther was named for him because he was baptized on the saint's commemoration date of November 11. As a young man, Martin of Tours was a Roman soldier who, according to legend, once cut his cloak in two with a sword in order to share it with a poor beggar. Among the many stories about him is that he was the first conscientious objector.

St. Mary of Egypt

FIGURE 347

This fifth-century hermit did not always live a chaste life and is sometimes visually confused with Mary Magdalene. Her biography, written three hundred years after she lived, claims that she lived as a prostitute but had a conversion experience in Jerusalem, after which she wandered alone in the desert and lived on bread and herbs. Legend has it that her grave was dug by a lion and is therefore symbolically associated with the same. She is remembered on April 1.

St. Mary of Magdala, or Mary Magdalene

FIGURE 348

Confusion, speculation, and fiction have colored our view of Mary of Magdala. What is known for certain from Scripture is that she was one of the early followers of Jesus, helped support His ministry financially, and witnessed His crucifixion. In addition, Luke tells us that Jesus healed her of demonic possession, and John tells us that the resurrected Jesus gave her instructions to tell the disciples that He had returned. Images of her hair, tears, and myrrh flask are used to symbolize this saint, who became associated with the unnamed sinful woman who anointed Jesus' feet. She is commemorated on July 22.

St. Mary, Mother of our Lord, or the Virgin Mary

FIGURES 349, 350, 351, 352

It makes sense that the mother of our Lord is the subject of innumerable pieces of artwork and written tributes. Although mention of her in Scripture is scant, it is enough to give us a picture of her character: she was faithful to God, pious, humble, obedient, and devoted. A plethora of symbols are used to identify this Mary from the single lily and its stylized cousin, the fleur-de-lys; to a winged, sword-pierced heart; and beyond that to lesser-known symbols such as a crescent moon. She is remembered on August 15, but is associated with other days on the sanctoral calendar, such as the Annunciation, the Purification of Mary, and the Visitation.

St. Matthew the Apostle

FIGURES 353, 354

In his role as despised-tax-collector-turned-beloved-apostle, Matthew is often symbolized by three money bags. Alternately, the manner of Matthew's death is often alluded to with spear, battle axe, sword, and other implements, although such symbols are based on tradition and legend.

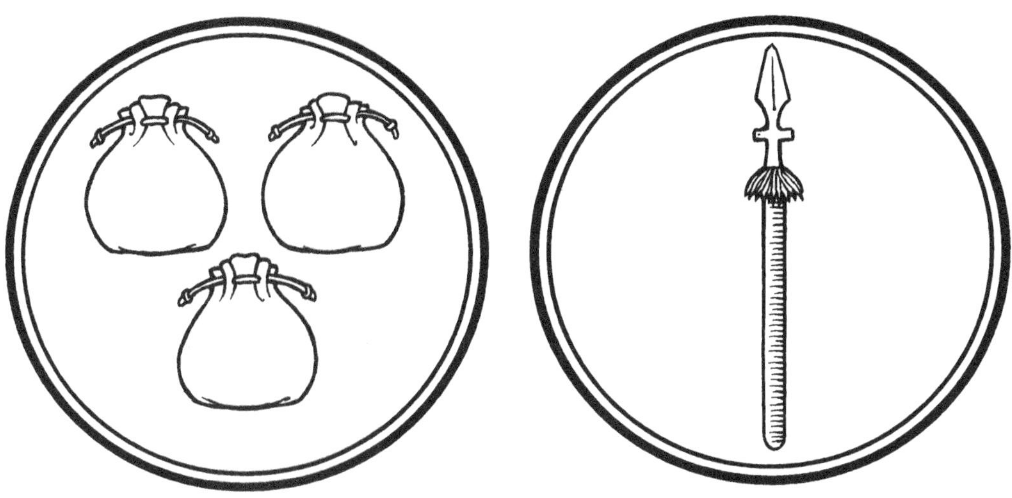

St. Matthew the Evangelist

FIGURE 355

It may seem that hairs are being split regarding this evangelist's symbol, but a winged man—not an angel—points to Jesus' incarnation, which is the thematic point of the opening chapters of the Gospel. Matthew emphasized for his Jewish readership that Jesus was the promised Messiah. Therefore, this symbol is an attempt to point to the two natures of Christ. St. Matthew, apostle and evangelist, is celebrated on September 21.

St. Matthias

FIGURE 356

A follower of Jesus from the beginning of His earthly ministry, Matthias was chosen to replace Judas. He is mentioned only in Acts 1:23–25. By tradition, St. Matthias was beheaded, so this saint is represented by an axe, which is ironically placed with an open book with the Latin inscription *super Mathiam*, meaning "on Matthias." This is a scriptural phrase used when describing how Matthias became an apostle: "and the lot fell on Matthias." He is commemorated on May 14.

St. Maurice

FIGURE 357

This third-century Egyptian became a soldier in the Roman army and eventually commanded the Theban Legion, which was composed entirely of Christians. Although he dedicated his military service to Rome, he was a Christian above all else. He and his legion refused to torture Christians, for example, and refused to worship Roman gods. For this confession of faith in Christ Jesus, Maurice was executed. His martyrdom is commemorated on September 22.

St. Michael, Archangel

FIGURES 358, 359

The chief of all angels, Michael is given specific responsibilities in Scripture, including leadership of God's army of angels and guiding the faithful to heaven upon their death. He is one of four archangels mentioned in the Bible, along with Raphael, Gabriel, and Uriel. Because Michael is described in the book of Revelation as battling the dragon, his symbolic attributes differ from those of Gabriel, who delivered God's message of the coming Messiah to Mary and to the shepherds. Michael is often shown with armor and a sword, with or without the scales of justice. He is sometimes referred to as "the warring angel." St. Michael and all angels are celebrated on September 29.

St. Monica

FIGURE 360

Born sometime around 330 AD in North Africa, Monica was a pious woman who not only prayed continuously for the conversion of her pagan son, Augustine, but also suffered the abuses of her husband's infidelity and capricious nature. She is remembered on August 27, and is often symbolized by her weeping eyes.

St. Neot

FIGURE 361

This ninth-century British monk became famous enough in life to gain an audience with King Alfred the Great and Pope Nicholas I in Rome, although St. Neot preferred seclusion and the life of a hermit. He was known for his life of prayer, evangelism, wisdom, and short stature. A spring-fed well where he had his midday meal still exists in Hamstoke (Cornwall) and is a popular tourist stop. He is commemorated on July 31.

St. Nicholas of Myra

FIGURE 362

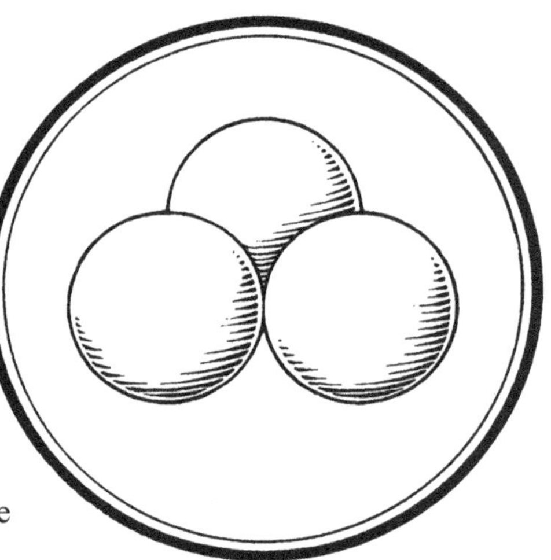

The fact is that not much is known about this figure. The first documented mention of him comes from about two hundred years after his death, when a church was built to honor him. His legend was well established by that time, however. It is believed that Nicholas lived during the late 200s and early 300s in what is now Turkey. Some historians believe he was present at the First Council of Nicaea in 325. Among the legends of this Greek bishop is one that he provided dowries for three sisters who would have otherwise been destined for prostitution. Hence, three golden spheres are his symbol. He is commemorated on December 6.

St. Nilus of Rossano, or Nilus the Younger

FIGURES 363, 364

This saint was a tenth-century abbot who established Eastern Orthodoxy in southern Italy. Known for his virtuous life as a hermit and for his theological understanding, Nilus built the Greek monastery of Grottaferrata after a vision of the virgin Mary directed him to do so. The monastery has been in continuous operation since 1004. He is remembered on September 26.

St. Norbert of Xanten

FIGURE 365

A twelfth-century German bishop, St. Norbert gained influence throughout Europe as an itinerant preacher. For his role in attempting to tighten discipline within his jurisdiction, several attempts were made on his life. Norbert was said to have been inspired during a severe thunderstorm to abandon his worldly ways and dedicate his life to prayer and penance. St. Norbert may be symbolized by a ciborium or a monstrance. His death is commemorated on June 6.

St. Osmund

FIGURE 366

A Norman of noble heritage, St. Osmund not only served as lord chancellor of England under William the Conqueror but also became the second bishop of Salisbury after England fell to the Normans in 1066. Osmund's dioceses included Old Sarum, near Stonehenge. And he is known as one of the contributors of the Domesday (Doomsday) Book. He is remembered on December 4.

St. Oswald of Northumbria

FIGURE 367

The seventh-century Anglo-Saxon king of Northumbria helped spread Christianity throughout what is now central and northern England throughout the mid-600s. Bede credited him with uniting provinces of Britain. Due to a legend surrounding his death, a crowned raven clutching a ring is his symbol. His martyrdom is commemorated on August 5.

St. Pantaleon

FIGURE 368

This fourth-century martyr was in life a gifted and generous physician, often treating the poor without charge and giving his wealth to charity. That said, so many legends became associated with him that even the most basic events of his life are somewhat suspect. His death under the rule of Maximian is commemorated on July 27, and his symbol is an apothecary chest.

St. Patrick

FIGURES 369, 370

Patrick's autobiography tells us that he was born in 387 in Britain to wealthy Roman parents, kidnapped at age 14, enslaved in Ireland, and turned to God as he tended sheep. After escaping and returning to Britain, Patrick studied, became a priest, and returned to Ireland, this time as a missionary. The paramount saint of Ireland, Patrick has several symbols related to him—none of which is the leprechaun. Legends surrounding the saint account for the expulsion of snakes—which is entirely fictious. His preaching on the Holy Trinity can be symbolized through depictions of the three-leafed shamrock. A red saltire cross, similar to St. Andrew's cross, may also be used. He is, of course, commemorated on March 17.

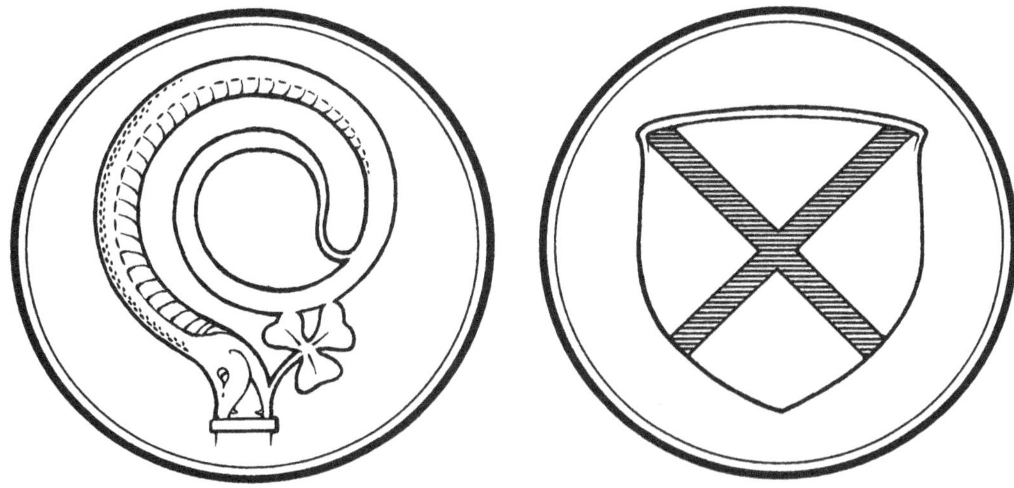

St. Paul

FIGURE 371

The well-educated, zealous tormenter of Christians, Paul knew the Old Testament very well but didn't grasp the Gospel until Christ Jesus Himself confronted him. He then became one of history's most influential figures, giving us most of the New Testament and setting for us an example of humility, repentance, and Christian living. The sixth chapter of St. Paul's letter to the Ephesians is the basis for this apostle's symbol. An open Bible bears the Latin words *Spiritus Gladius,* or "Sword of the Spirit," while a Roman gladius visually underscores the theme.

St. Paul the Hermit, St. Paul of Thebes, or St. Paul the Anchorite

FIGURE 372

This fourth-century Egyptian lost his inheritance and sought refuge in the desert while under persecution, becoming one of the first Christian hermits. According to legend, a raven brought daily bread to the hermit. He is also said to have derived his food from a date palm and to have been buried—at age 113—in a grave dug by lions. He is remembered on January 15.

SS Perpetua and Felicity

FIGURES 373, 374

These third-century African martyrs point to the obvious fact that the church is not bound by race or status or age. Vibia Perpetua was a well-educated young noblewoman with a nursing child. Her maid, Felicity, was with child. They were among a group of Christian catechumens who were put in the arena as entertainment during Emperor Septimius Severus's birthday. The pair may be symbolized by a mad cow—the manner in which they met their death—or by a dragon and ladder. Their martyrdom is commemorated on March 7.

St. Peter

FIGURES 375, 376, 377, 378

His confession of Jesus as Messiah and devotion to the Lord, despite his human weaknesses, helped Peter emerge as the leader of the early church after Jesus' ascension. Peter embarked on wide-ranging missionary journeys and is identified as the first pope. St. Peter has several symbols to his name. A crowing rooster may be used. An inverted Latin cross may also be used, which refers to his traditional—though not scriptural—manner of death. Add to these the crossed keys, which are also used for the Office of the Keys, and various combinations of these symbols. St. Peter is remembered, together with St. Paul, on June 29, but his confession is commemorated on January 18.

SS Peter and Paul

FIGURE 379

It is common to speak of these two saints in the same breath because of their personal experiences with Jesus and their contribution to the early church and to the New Testament. Together they show us the transformative work of the Holy Spirit in the life of the sinner. They are commemorated on the same day. To symbolize them together, a gladius may be superimposed by crossed keys. In our example, the conspicuous cut of the keys is formed into patriarchal crosses.

St. Peter Nolasco

FIGURE 380

Never ordained as a priest, this thirteenth-century French-Spaniard was originally a soldier in the war against the Moors. He eventually helped to found the Mercedarians and used his personal wealth as an official ransomer of Christian captives in Moorish regions in Spain and Algiers. Nearly three thousand captives were released during Nolasco's lifetime. The order he founded worked throughout Europe and even in the New World. His symbol bears the banner of his order and broken chains. St. Peter Nolasco is remembered on May 6.

St. Peter of Verona

FIGURES 381, 382

This thirteenth-century Dominican priest was celebrated for his oratory skills and zealous work against heresy. St. Peter of Verona always makes an impression when he shows up in artwork. He may have a large knife or axe lodged in his head, pointing to his manner of death. The word *credo* may also accompany the weapons with which he was killed, for he supposedly began reciting the Apostles' Creed as he was attacked by assassins. His martyrdom is commemorated on April 6.

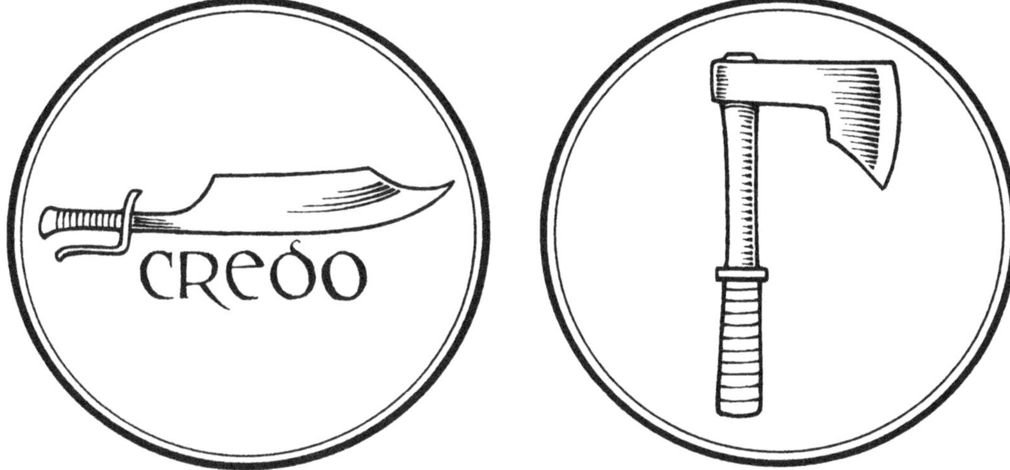

SS Philemon and Onesimus

FIGURE 383

Onesimus, once accused of thievery and being a runaway slave, later became extremely useful to his wealthy master, Philemon. It was Paul, who knew them both, who encouraged the master to extend brotherly love to the slave. These two biblical figures are commemorated together on February 15. An open chest of coins and broken shackles represent them both.

St. Philip

FIGURES 384, 385

By tradition, Philip is said to have been the disciple who figured how much money it would take to feed the five thousand (John 6:7), and he preached in areas of Greece. This may not be such a stretch since Philip himself had a Greek name. One of St. Philip's many symbols, therefore, is a tall column. He may also be represented by a cross with two roundels, which represent the two hundred denarii worth of bread he suggested at the feeding of the five thousand. St. Philip is commemorated, together with St. James, on May 1.

St. Polycarp of Smyrna

FIGURES 386, 387

One of the three apostolic fathers, Polycarp is said to have had conversations with John the evangelist and others who had firsthand interaction with Jesus. What we know of Polycarp comes from his own writings and those of others, some of which verified first-century Christian material. "Fourscore and six years have I served Him, and He has done me no harm. How then can I curse my King that saved me?" Thus the elderly Polycarp responded when told to denounce his Christian faith. This early church father met his martyrdom by being burned to death, which is depicted in one of his symbols. According to legend, a dove flew out of the flames, which is the basis for an alternate symbol. St. Polycarp's martyrdom is commemorated on February 23.

SS Praxedes and Pudentiana

FIGURE 388

Apart from legend, not much is known about these second-century Roman sisters who, despite Roman persecution, distributed food to fellow saints and cared for their dead. According to legend, they were daughters of one of Paul's disciples and lived in Rome. Each has a church named for her. The sisters' supposed martyrdom is commemorated on May 19.

St. Prisca

FIGURE 389

In spite of legends suggesting otherwise, it is likely that this saint is not the Priscilla mentioned in Scripture. She was, however, a first-century martyr, put to death by Claudius for refusing to denounce Christ. At one point during her ordeal, she was thrown into the arena with a lion, which allegedly lay down quietly at her feet. St. Prisca's death is commemorated on January 18.

St. Quentin

FIGURE 390

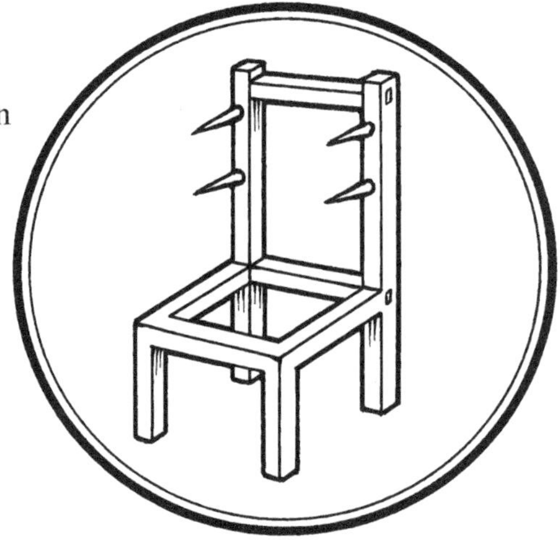

Although there is no connection to the infamous San Quentin State Prison, this saint's symbol shares a dark similarity with the penal institution. The third-century Roman, also known as Quintinus, traveled with eleven other missionaries and eventually arrived in Gaul, where he proclaimed the Gospel. However, he was captured, endured brutal torture, and was ultimately martyred by Roman soldiers. He is remembered on October 31.

St. Radegund

FIGURE 391

Born into royalty, this sixth-century Germanic woman was one of several wives of Theuderic and the last surviving member of the Thuringian family. Radegund eventually sought refuge in the church and thereafter led an ascetic life. She is credited with establishing the monastery of Sainte-Croix. Legend has it that wild animals became tame in her presence. Hence, two wolves couchant are her symbol. St. Radegund is remembered on August 13.

St. Raphael, Archangel

FIGURE 392

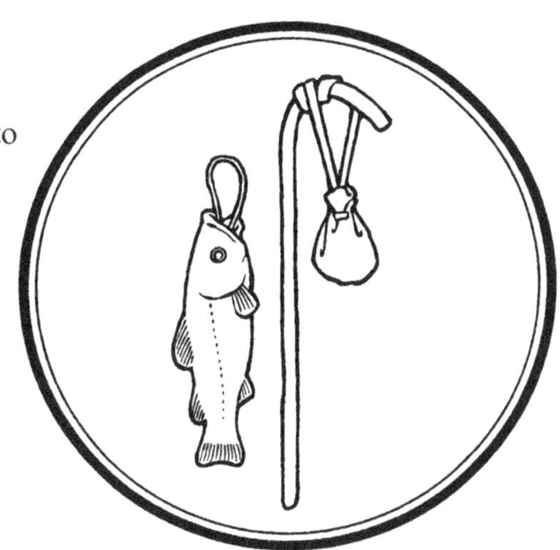

Named only in the Apocrypha, Raphael is said to be one of three angelic visitors to Abraham. This archangel is sometimes shown carrying a fish. He is also known as a healer. For his symbol, a fish and a healer's staff are combined. Along with all other angels, he is celebrated on September 29.

St. Remigius of Reims

FIGURE 393

This well-educated son of nobility lived in the late 400s and early 500s. Remembered for baptizing Clovis I, king of the Franks, and thereby converting an entire people to Christianity, this bishop of Reims established many churches on land that Clovis granted to him. He lived nearly 96 years. A vial of holy oil and miter are his symbols. St. Remigius is remembered on October 1.

St. Roch, or St. Rocco

FIGURE 394

This fourteenth-century Majorcan was said to have been born with a mark in the shape of a cross on his chest. He renounced the wealth of his youth, traveled to Rome, and set about caring for the sick during the plague until he became ill himself. According to legend, he then retreated to a forest and was fed by a hunting dog. Hence, a dog holding a loaf of bread became one of his symbols. His death is commemorated on August 17.

St. Romuald

FIGURE 395

This eleventh-century abbot was an ascetic hermit who spent thirty years traveling throughout Italy, founding monasteries and hermitages. His symbol points to the rather unfortunate idea of his spiritual ascent. He is remembered on June 19.

St. Rose of Lima

FIGURE 396

A crown of roses with thorns is the symbol for this seventeenth-century Peruvian nun who wore a heavy silver crown of thorns to emulate the Passion of Christ. Known for her piety from a young age, she performed frequent and extreme penance, spent most of her time in prayer and in fasting, and followed a strict diet. Her patronage includes the indigenous peoples of the Americas and the whole of Latin America. She is remembered on August 23.

St. Sabbas the Sanctified

FIGURE 397

This sixth-century Cappadocian monk is said to have feared God so much that he feared no man. Born near Caesarea, he entered a monastery in Jerusalem at the age of 18, then lived as a hermit for several years. He founded a monastery in a remote area between Jerusalem and the Dead Sea that is still inhabited by Eastern Orthodox monks and is thought to be one of the four oldest monasteries in the world. A lion statant, therefore, is his symbol. His death is commemorated on December 5.

St. Saturnin of Toulouse

FIGURE 398

A third-century Greek missionary to what is present day France, this saint was martyred for refusing to offer sacrifices to pagan deities. He was dragged to death by a harnessed bull, his symbol. His martyrdom is commemorated on November 29.

St. Scholastica

FIGURES 399, 400

The twin sister of Benedict of Nursia, this sixth-century nun is regarded as the founder of the Benedictine nuns. Legend states that a dove ascended when this saint died. Her symbol is therefore a dove—without a tri-radiant nimbus—either on an open book or with a crozier. She is remembered on February 10.

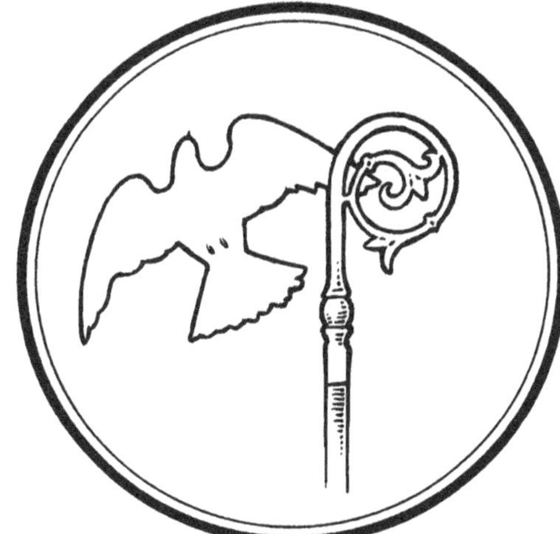

St. Sebastian

FIGURE 401

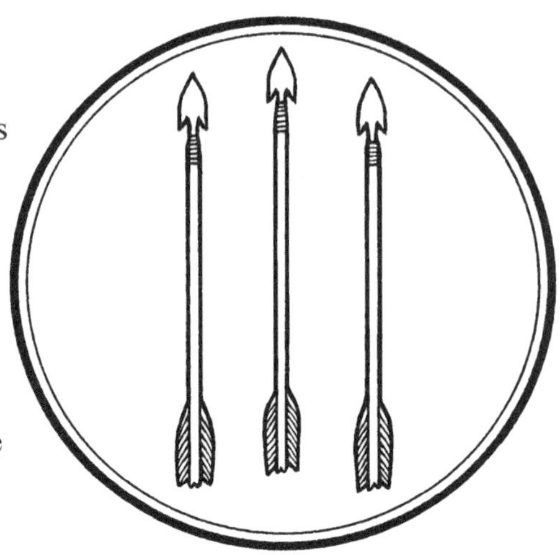

One of the oft-depicted martyrs in sacred art, this fourth-century commander of the Praetorian guard met his fate during the Diocletian persecution. Legend states that he was tied to a tree and shot with many arrows, then was nursed back to health only to publicly harangue Diocletian for his mistreatment of Christians. He was later beaten to death. He is first mentioned in a chronological work by Furius Dionysius Filocalus, a Roman scribe, produced in 354. The commemoration of his death is on January 20.

St. Silas, or St. Silvanus

FIGURE 402

A contemporary of Christ Jesus, Silas was a fellow worker of saints Peter, Paul, and Timothy. Silas traveled with Paul on his second missionary journey to Syria, Cilicia, and Macedonia. He was imprisoned with Paul when the chains were miraculously broken. Hence, his symbol is often broken shackles or a ship to represent his missionary travels. He is commemorated on February 10.

St. Simeon Stylites

FIGURE 403

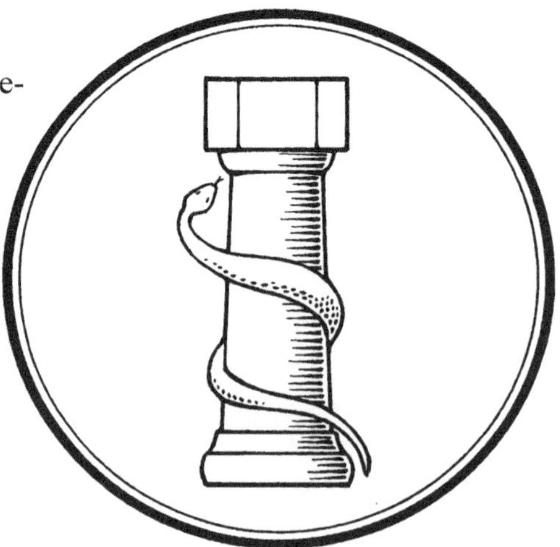

This saint's title refers to his rather odd—yet sometimes copied—ascetic existence atop a large architectural column. A biography of him written during his lifetime gives his extreme and strange life credibility. As a teenager, he entered a monastery and began the life of an ascetic. Simeon would pray and fast throughout Lent, standing on his pillar the whole time. By some accounts, he lived for 35 or 42 years on a little platform atop his pillar, fifty feet off the ground. His symbol is a serpent coiled around a column, and he is remembered on January 5.

St. Simon, or Simon the Zealot

FIGURES 404, 405, 406

One of the twelve disciples, this Simon is mentioned only in passing in the Bible and is one of nine men with that name in the New Testament. To distinguish him from Simon Peter, he often bears the title "zealot," although there is some speculation about whether he was part of the group known for their more aggressive behaviors. Because he was a "fisher of men," his symbol may be a fish on a Gospel book, or it may be combinations of oars and a saw, the traditional method of his martyrdom. He is commemorated together with St. Jude on October 28.

St. Stanislaus the Martyr, or Stanislaus of Sczcepanów

FIGURE 407

Known for his preaching and teaching, this eleventh-century bishop of Kraków, like some others in history, made the bold move to openly chastise the ruling king for cruelty and immorality and eventually got him excommunicated. It cost St. Stanislaus his life but elevated him to be one of the most beloved Polish saints. His martyrdom is commemorated on May 8.

St. Stephen

FIGURE 408

According to Acts 6, Stephen was the archdeacon, one of seven deacons chosen to extend pastoral care to widows. He was known for his preaching, miracles, and popularity among Jews. Remembered as the protomartyr of the Christian Church, St. Stephen was stoned to death for denouncing the religious leaders. His symbol is a dalmatic and three stones. His martyrdom is commemorated on December 26.

St. Swithun

FIGURE 409

Posthumous legends, wives tales, and superstition have superseded the actual life of this ninth-century English bishop. His symbol is an apple and raindrops, which is owed to the ridiculous notion that if it rains on St. Swithun's Bridge on his feast day, July 15, then it will certainly rain for the next forty days. Of course, it always rains there, so the miracle is oversold.

St. Sylvester, or Pope Sylvester I

FIGURE 410

According to legend, it was Sylvester who baptized Constantine, the first Christian Roman emperor. Pope Sylvester I was bishop of Rome during the fourth century and was invited to the Council of Nicaea, though he did not attend. His symbol is the papal cross on a shield, and he is remembered on December 31.

St. Thaïs

FIGURE 411

This fourth-century Egyptian woman was born into royalty but led a wayward life until her conversion to Christianity. She became a nun and led a life of solitude for three years before her death. Her penance during those years was to repeat the words that are her symbol, "Thou who hast made me and redeemed me by Thy Passion, have mercy on me." She is remembered on October 8.

St. Thecla

FIGURE 412

"The stuff of legends" may be an understatement for this saint. A first-century woman of Iconium in present day Turkey, St. Thecla was once supposedly protected by wild lionesses while being attacked by men. She is also said to have been a follower of St. Paul, to have preached the word of God in Myra, to have been a healer in Syria, and to have survived a burning at the stake by a sudden rainstorm. She is remembered on September 23.

St. Theresa of Ávila

FIGURES 413, 414

Born in 1515 in Spain, St. Theresa was already a celebrity when she became a nun. The author of several books on spirituality, she was known as one of the great women of the Roman Catholic tradition. Her influence continued to spread in her life and death. Her symbols include hearts—wounded, flaming, encircled with thorns, and otherwise. She is remembered on October 15.

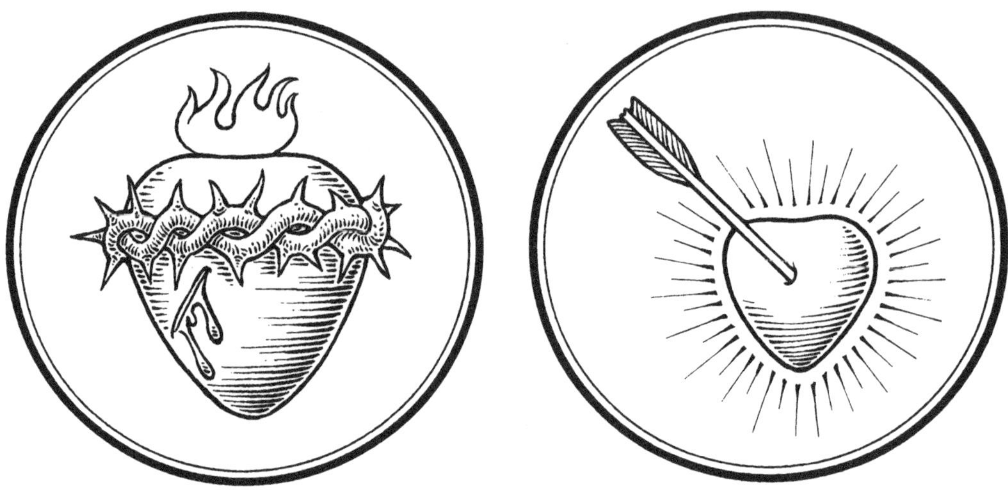

St. Thomas

FIGURES 415, 416

An apostle of Christ, St. Thomas was, according to tradition, a carpenter by trade. Perhaps best known as the one Jesus rebuked for his lack of belief in His resurrection, he was an evangelist to Persia and India. His symbols may include a carpenter's square and spear, or an axe. The two latter implements are variously attributed to his martyrdom. His death is commemorated on December 21.

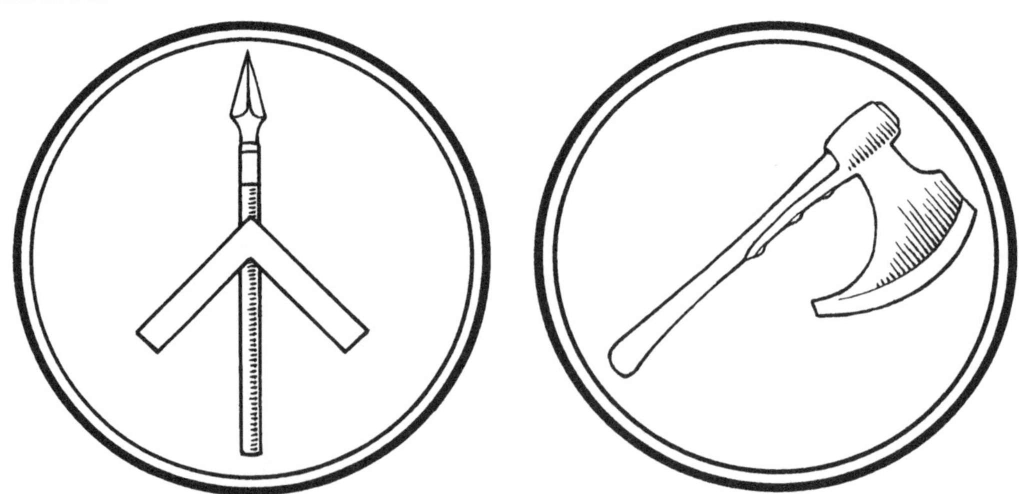

St. Thomas Aquinas

FIGURE 417

Born in Sicily, this saint was a thirteenth-century theologian, philosopher, and doctor of the church. The author of several important theological works, his far-reaching influence crossed denominational and secular lines. A blazing sun almost always shows up in his symbols. He is remembered on January 28.

St. Thomas of Canterbury, or Thomas Becket

FIGURE 418

A twelfth-century English archbishop, Thomas is famously known for being assassinated after pushing for the rights of the church. He was the archbishop of Canterbury and companion of Henry II, but he fell out of favor with the king and, despite a reconciliation with him, was killed by some of the king's knights. The coat of arms bearing three crows was assigned posthumously during the age of heraldry. His martyrdom is commemorated on December 29.

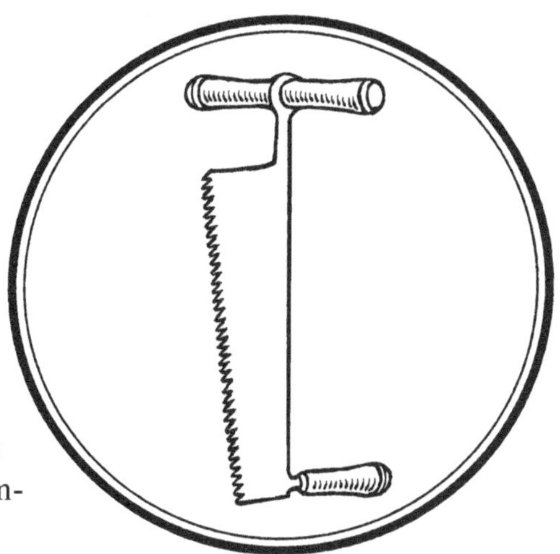

St. Thyrsus

FIGURE 419

Of this third-century Greek, little is known except that he was martyred during the Decian persecution. His symbol is a saw, indicating his ordeal. Legend states, however, that the saw was not sharp enough and was too heavy to wield, so he was hanged. That didn't work either, so he was beheaded. Such was the plight common to Christians. St. Thyrsus is remembered on January 28.

St. Timothy

FIGURE 420

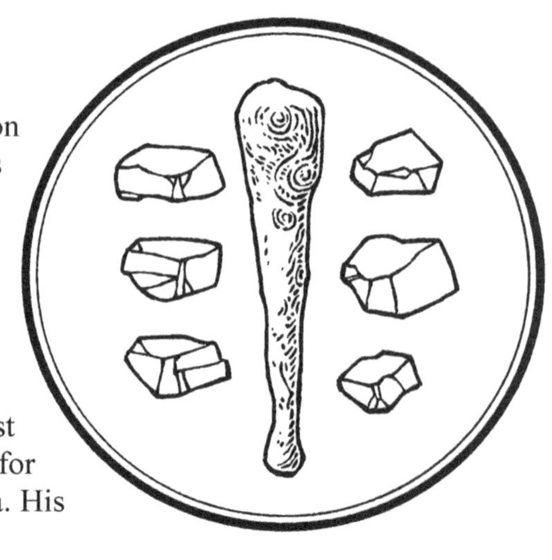

Born in Lystra, St. Timothy replaced Barnabas on St. Paul's second missionary journey and became his companion and friend. Timothy delivered Paul's first letter to Corinth and traveled with Paul to Macedonia and Galatia, among other places. He may have been with Paul during his imprisonment at Caesarea and Rome. Paul wrote two letters to Timothy, which established the guidelines used today for the pastoral office. According to tradition, St. Timothy was the first bishop of Ephesus but was beaten and stoned to death for trying to disrupt a celebration to the pagan god Diana. His martyrdom is commemorated on January 24.

St. Titus

FIGURE 421

Another associate of Paul, Titus was entrusted to deliver Paul's second letter to the Christians in Corinth and assisted Paul as his secretary and interpreter. Paul sent Titus to Jerusalem to collect alms there and appointed him to establish the church in Crete. Titus is mentioned in Galatians along with Barnabas. He also traveled to what is now Croatia and to Macedonia. His symbol is the ruins of a Greek temple, and he is remembered on January 26.

St. Ursula

FIGURE 422

What information there is about this saint has been cobbled together from questionable histories. According to legend, this fourth-century English princess sailed to Germanic lands. While there, she tried to fend off an attack of Huns as she was guiding a group of girls. Despite her efforts, all were massacred. Her name is used for the Order of Ursulines, a group dedicated to the education of young girls. Her martyrdom is commemorated on October 21.

St. Valentine

FIGURE 423

This is one of several saints whose real lives have been supplanted by ridiculous tradition. While little verifiable information is available, he was known for evangelistic efforts, officiating at Christian marriages, and assisting Christians who were persecuted by the Roman emperor Claudius II. Hearts are not appropriate, but roses, a bishop's crozier, or a martyr's palm branch may be used as his symbols. His death as martyr is commemorated on February 14.

St. Veronica

FIGURE 424

While not mentioned in Scripture, this saint shows up in a station of the cross as a woman who offered her veil so that Jesus might wipe His brow. The veil then supposedly became imprinted with the face of our Lord. Existence of the cloth itself was not known until the Middle Ages when it was put on display. Its authenticity cannot be proven, of course, but six copies are said to be held in churches throughout Europe. St. Veronica is remembered on July 12.

St. Victor of Marseilles

FIGURE 425

This fourth-century Roman commander converted to Christianity, openly confessed the Lord, and converted several of his fellow soldiers. He refused to make an offering to a Roman god, and for that, he met his martyrdom under a millstone at the command of Emperor Maximium. He is commemorated on July 21.

St. Vincent of Sargossa

FIGURES 426, 427, 428

Another fourth-century saint, Vincent is the protomartyr of Spain. Spokesman for the bishop of Saragossa, Valerius, he was bold to profess his faith to the Roman governor under Diocletian. He met his end, as one legend has it, with torture, with imprisonment, and with a millstone tied to his neck before he was thrown into the sea. Another legend states that ravens guarded his body against scavenging vultures until fellow Christians could care for his body. Yet another legend includes a cross and meat hooks from his lengthy ordeal. His martyrdom is commemorated on January 22.

St. Wenceslas, or Wenceslas I, Duke of Bohemia

FIGURE 429

A pious leader of Bohemia, Wenceslas was zealous in his efforts to spread the faith. He was unpopular with non-Christians, among whom were his own mother and brother. Legend has it that he was murdered by his brother on his way to church. Referred to in song as "Good King Wenceslas," this tenth-century figure was given the title of king after his assassination. He is the patron saint of the Czech Republic and his symbol includes an eagle of the land's ancient arms. He is remembered on September 28.

St. Wilfrid

FIGURE 430

The bishop of York, Wilfrid was educated in Rome and Lyons before returning to his homeland of Northumbria. He founded Benedictine monasteries and built churches in his efforts to convert undisciplined England to the Christian faith. The three stars representative of this seventh-century saint can be seen in many church windows of his native England. He is remembered on October 12.

St. William of York

FIGURE 431

Archbishop of York, William was known by some as kind and generous and by others as corrupt and guilty of bribing his way to leadership. As archbishop, he was popular with the people for his church reforms. Legend has it that his death was caused by poisoning. The symbol of this twelfth-century archbishop is a shield bearing seven lozenges. It still is used by parishes and schools bearing his name. He is remembered on June 8.

Prophets, Patriarchs, and Other Figures of the Old Testament

Old Testament figures do not officially bear the title of saint. This omission on the part of the Roman Church can be considered as a reflection of the dubious criteria used for conferring the title. Holy Scripture pointedly declares that there is no doubt of the holiness of Job, Moses, Elijah, and others after their earthly demise. However, we must "put the best construction" on the peculiarity and conclude that Rome was assuming their obvious sainthood without the formality of a papal conference of title.

Tradition has done some other quirky things beyond the giving and retaining of titles. Not every figure in the Old Testament, for example, is given a feast day on the sanctoral calendar. Not every judge or prophet has a symbol, while others may have several. For our purposes, though, we will survey Old Testament figures and their symbols in the same manner as with Roman saints.

Aaron

FIGURE 432

The flowering, fruiting staff of Aaron is described in Numbers 17:5–8. It is important that the flower and fruit are almond, for different flowering staffs are used to identify other biblical characters, including Joseph, the earthly father of Jesus.

Abraham

FIGURE 433

Because he dwelled in a tent, one is often included in his symbol. What is more important, however, is the inclusion of stars, which symbolize the offspring promised to the patriarch from the Lord in Genesis 15:5. Abraham is remembered on October 9.

Adam

FIGURE 434

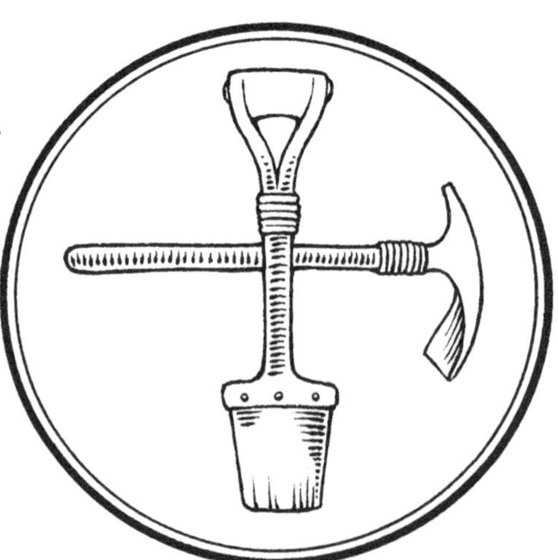

Most any agricultural hand tool may be used to symbolize Adam—especially after the fall, when God told him, "Cursed is the ground because of you; in pain you shall eat of it all the days of your life" (Genesis 3:17). But the symbol depicts hope in the conspicuous cruciform arrangement. Adam and Eve are both remembered on December 19.

Amos

FIGURE 435

One of the twelve minor prophets, Amos is symbolized by a shepherd's crook because he was among the shepherds when the word of the Lord came to him. (See Amos 1:1.)

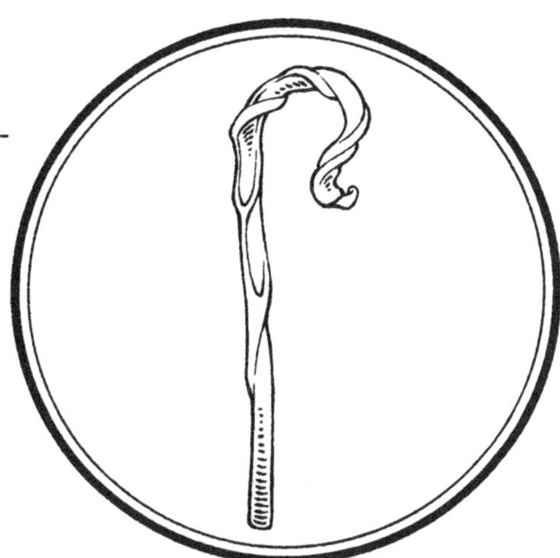

Daniel

FIGURE 436

One of the four major prophets, Daniel may be symbolized by a ram with four horns. Daniel is remembered on December 17, together with the three young men who were in the fiery furnace. (See Daniel 8:1–27 and 3:23–30.)

David

FIGURE 437

This biblical patriarch has been variously symbolized by a lion, a horn of oil, a sling with stones, a turreted castle, and even by the head of his adversary, Goliath. It is also acceptable to identify David by his star, which is a relatively new symbol, dating from the seventeenth century. It is important, however, that the star is composed of two interwoven, equilateral triangles. David is commemorated on December 29.

Elijah

FIGURE 438

July 20 is the commemoration day of this prophet. A fiery chariot, a sign of heavenly might and power mentioned in 2 Kings 2:11, may be used to symbolize him.

Elisha

FIGURES 439, 440

The prophet Elisha may be alternately symbolized by a she-bear (2 Kings 2:23–25) or by the rolled-up cloak of his predecessor, Elijah, parting water (2 Kings 2:13). Elisha is remembered on June 14.

Esther

FIGURE 441

Remembered on May 24, Esther was the Jewish queen to Persian King Ahasuerus. The fabricated symbol shown includes a stylized crown of the period with embellishments of a Star of David and a menorah-like tree to indicate the faith of her people.

Eve

FIGURE 442

Celebrated together with her husband, Adam, on December 19, Eve's symbol is a spindle and distaff to reflect her life of painful labor outside the garden (Genesis 3:16 and Proverbs 31:19).

Ezekiel

FIGURE 443

One of the four major prophets, Ezekiel can be symbolized by a closed gate—shown here with a conspicuous cross—because images of gates loomed large in the visions revealed the prophet throughout his book (Ezekiel 11, 40, 44). He is remembered on July 21.

Gideon

FIGURES 444, 445

One of the sixteen Old Testament judges and chosen by God to deliver the Israelites from the Midianites, Gideon is alternately symbolized by a broken jug containing a flaming torch (Judges 7) or a bowl and fleece (Judges 6).

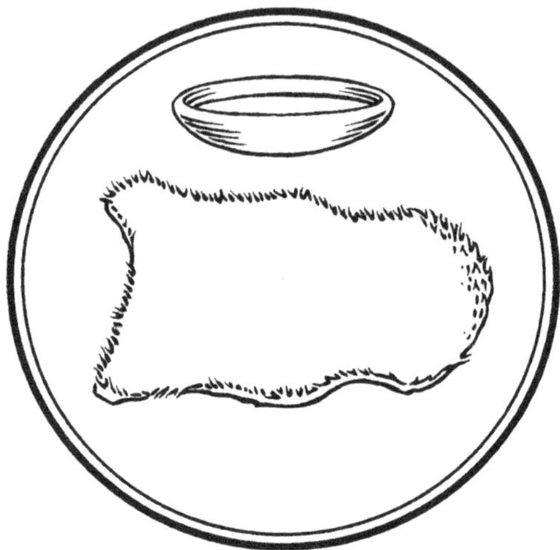

Habakkuk

FIGURE 446

Despite the woeful prophecies of Habakkuk, his symbol of the temple reflects one of his words of hope: "But the Lord is in His holy temple; let all the earth keep silence before Him" (Habakkuk 2:20). This prophet calls us to persistent faith amidst suffering.

Haggai

FIGURE 447

Haggai—one of the twelve minor prophets—is symbolized by a temple under construction because of his support of Zerubbabel and the rebuilding of the temple where the people would come together to hear God's Word. His commemoration day is December 29.

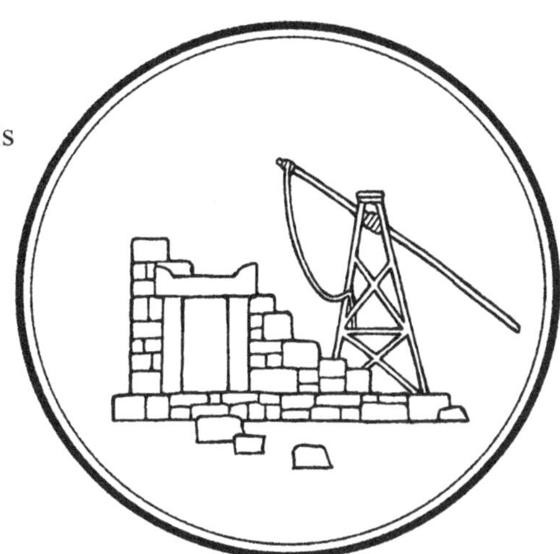

Hannah

FIGURE 448

The mother of Samuel is commemorated on September 2. Hannah's contrived symbol reflects her "speaking in her heart" (1 Samuel 1:13) and the meaning of her Hebrew name, "favor" or "grace," which ultimately was given to her by God in the answering of her petition for a son.

Hosea

FIGURE 449

One of the twelve minor prophets, Hosea is symbolized by a cast-off garment used in pointing to the infidelity of his wife, Gomer, and the entire house of Israel. His book reminds us of God's faithfulness to us, His unfaithful people. Hosea is commemorated on October 17.

Isaac

FIGURE 450

One of three patriarchs of the Israelites (the others being Abraham and Jacob), Isaac was a miracle child who was the forebearer of another miracle child: Christ Jesus. Because of his near-sacrifice at his father's hand, Isaac's prophetic symbol is a bundle of wood, a knife, and a rope placed in a cross configuration. Isaac is remembered on August 16.

Isaiah

FIGURE 451

This oft-quoted prophet and evangelist pointed to God's judgment and to redemption through the Messiah. Commemorated on July 6, Isaiah is symbolized by tongs holding a burning coal, reflecting his remission of sins as described in Isaiah 6:6.

Jacob

FIGURE 452

The father of the twelve tribes of Israel, Jacob dreamed of a ladder, a divine connection, to heaven on which angels descended and ascended. This patriarch's symbol is a ladder, which may or may not have angels, but should be in a "heavenward" position.

Jeremiah

FIGURE 453

One of the four major prophets, Jeremiah is often symbolized by the stones with which, by tradition, he was martyred. His lengthy book laments wickedness and the tumult that ensues, yet it reminds us of God's promise of salvation through the coming Messiah. Jeremiah is commemorated on June 26.

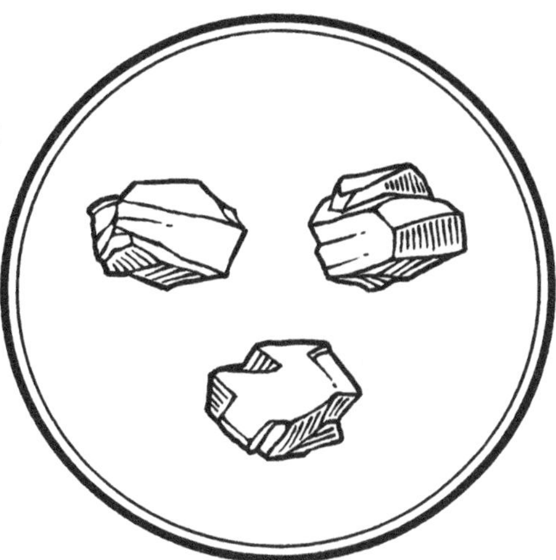

Jesse

FIGURE 454

The grandson of Boaz and Ruth and son of Obed, Jesse was the father of King David. Although this symbol is also prophetically applied to Christ Jesus, it may be used in proper context to symbolize Jesse himself. The symbol should show a vigorous shoot, in leaf and preferably in blossom, growing from the root of a very dead stump. Jesse's feast day is December 29.

Job

FIGURE 455

Tested by Satan and blessed by God, Job serves as a stellar example of life under suffering and is commemorated on May 9. His symbol is fabricated from two notions: First, the Lord did indeed place a "hedge" around Job—here in a cruciform shape—to protect him from Satan (see Job 1:10). Second, Job was blessed not only before his trial but also doubly so after it, which is indicated by the bursting pomegranate (see Job 42:10–17).

Joel

FIGURE 456

Not much is known about the life and times of this minor prophet, yet he was known to the apostles. Peter and Paul both quote him, and his call to repentance sounds loudly for us today. The blast of a trumpet is described in Joel 2:1, so a ram's horn—the temple's trumpet—is used for this minor prophet's symbol. His commemoration day is July 13.

Jonah

FIGURE 457

The minor prophet Jonah is the familiar subject of children's stories, but his story in Scripture is one of disobedience, punishment, repentance, and restoration. He is often symbolized by a whale, but it is probably best to follow Scripture and instead show a "great fish." This specificity adds emphasis to the peculiar history of the man, whose sacrifice is a clear foreshadowing of Christ. Jonah is remembered on September 21.

Joseph

FIGURES 458, 459, 460

One of the twelve patriarchs, Joseph is an example of faithfulness, patience, forgiveness, and God's sovereignty. He is variously symbolized by his famous coat of many colors or a sheaf of standing wheat (to which other sheaves bowed). He may also be symbolized by a great column with an Egyptian capital. Joseph is remembered on March 31.

Joshua

FIGURE 461

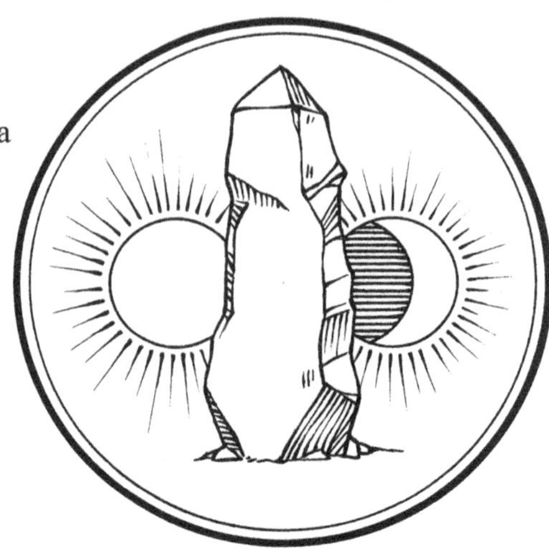

The leader of the Israelites after Moses, Joshua reminds us that God fulfills His promises and conquers His enemies. Commemorated on September 1, this biblical patriarch can be symbolized by a sun, a moon (Joshua 10), and a "witness stone" (Joshua 24).

Malachi

FIGURE 462

Malachi concludes the Old Testament by reiterating the failure of mankind to obey God's commands and by reinforcing that the great day of the Lord is coming. That awesome day of the Lord and His messenger are the basis for Malachi's symbol of an angel issuing from a cloud. He is commemorated on December 18, or January 3 in the Roman Catholic Church.

Micah

FIGURE 463

The opening verses of Micah 1 describe the foreboding image of the Lord coming down from His holy place, His temple. Thus, a temple perched on the peak of a mountain may symbolize this minor prophet. Micah also clearly prophesied the birth of Christ (Micah 5:2) and what peace in His kingdom will be like. Micah is commemorated on July 31.

Moses

FIGURES 464, 465, 466

Moses is mentioned more in the New Testament than any other Old Testament figure. Moses is the symbol of God's Law for us, of deliverance, and of eternity. Therefore, several symbols are used for the patriarch. A flaming bush may be used, but it is important that its foliage be unaffected by the flames. Alternately, a staff with a bronze serpent may be used, although this same symbol may be used for our Lord and Savior, Jesus Christ.

A third device—two rays emanating from his head—may also be used to distinguish Moses. While this helps to differentiate the man from the tri-radiant nimbus applied to the Persons of the Holy Trinity, it is poorly translated when applied to sculpture. Early translations from Hebrew manuscripts described Moses as being "horned," but a better translation leans heavily toward "gloried" or "shining." Moses is commemorated on September 4.

Nahum

FIGURE 467

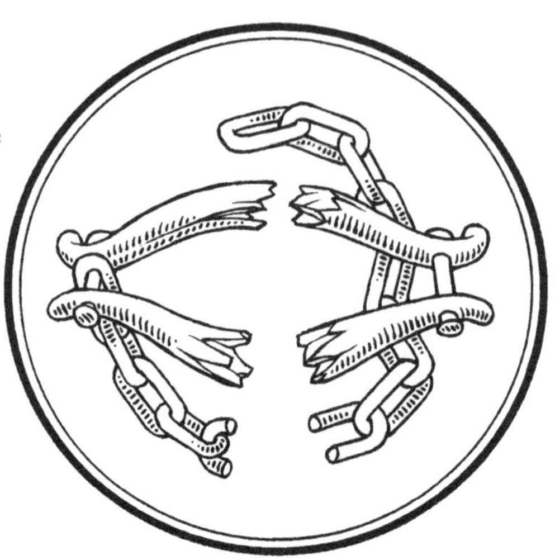

Whether his book was written as prophecy before the downfall of Nineveh or as history afterward, Nahum's message is one of God's grace for sinful people. Nahum may have been a contemporary of Isaiah, about a hundred years after Jonah. The symbol for this minor prophet is taken from Nahum 1:13, "And now I will break his yoke from off you and will burst your bonds apart." He is commemorated on December 1.

Noah

FIGURES 468, 469

One of the twelve patriarchs, Noah may be symbolized by various objects, including the ark, which may or may not have a rainbow, depending on context. He may also be symbolized by a dove carrying an olive sprig, but it is important that the dove not have a nimbus of any kind. Noah is commemorated on November 29.

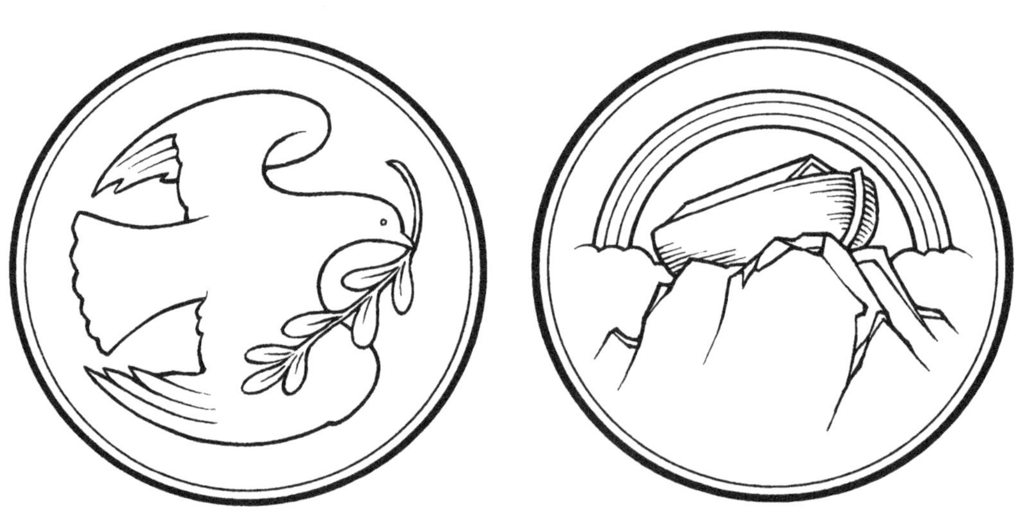

Obadiah

FIGURE 470

One of twelve minor prophets, Obadiah (perhaps a contemporary of the prophet Jeremiah) warned the people that Yahweh would completely wipe out the house of Esau for his arrogance and crime against his brother, Jacob. Oddly, the symbol for Obadiah comes not from his prophetic book but from 1 Kings 18:4, where the prophet hid one hundred fellow prophets from Jezebel and fed them with bread and water. A jar of water and loaves of bread are his symbol. His feast day is November 19.

Ruth

FIGURE 471

Ruth's story in the Bible is one of exile and return, of redemption and provision. A descendant of Lot, she was the great-grandmother of King David. Remembered on July 16, she is symbolized by a single strand of wheat. This alludes to her humbly gleaning in the fields after the harvesters had gathered the grain. She was not, however, slack in her labor, and gathered nearly twenty-nine pounds of barley by the end of the day.

Samson

FIGURES 472, 473

One of the judges of Israel, Samson was famous for his strength, which is shown in alternate symbols for him. He was also famous for his ego, violation of his Nazirite vows, and hair. The jawbone of an ass points to his slaughter of one thousand Philistines. A pair of misaligned columns may also be used to symbolize Samson, indicating the manner in which he died while destroying thousands of Philistine lords and their guests. His commemoration day is July 28.

Samuel

FIGURE 474

The son of faithful Hannah, Samuel is included in the "hall of faith" in Hebrews 11 for his life of service and obedience to God. Remembered on August 20, he served as the last of the judges and first of the prophets. Because he anointed Israel's first king, Saul, an oil-filled horn is the symbol for Samuel.

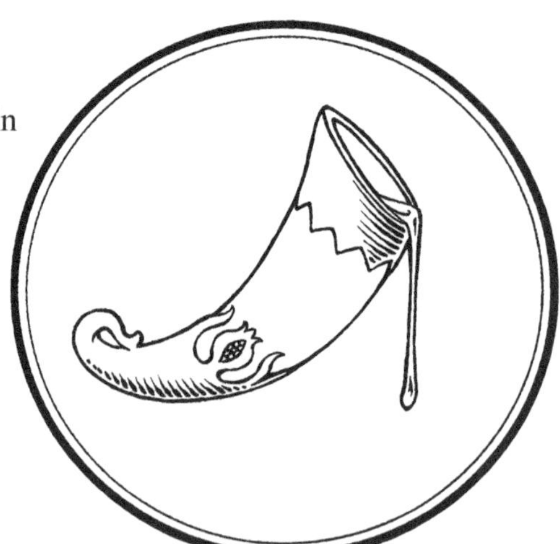

Sarah

FIGURE 475

Because she was the wife of Abraham, her contrived symbol of a crowned headdress gives homage to the tent and stars of her husband's symbol. Her Hebrew name underscores the visual. Sarah's life stands in contrast to Abraham's, however. Her doubt juxtaposed against Abraham's abiding trust in God was nevertheless rewarded by God's faithfulness. Sarah is remembered on January 20.

Solomon

FIGURE 476

The descendant of David bears not only his father's star but also his own sword. That same sword showed his great wisdom in judging between the caring mother and her callous imposter. The third and last king of an undivided Israel, Solomon asked God for wisdom and received it. God also gave him vast riches, peace, and a large family. When Solomon turned away from God though, his successes came to an end. Solomon is remembered on December 11.

Zechariah and Elizabeth

FIGURE 477

Being well advanced in years, this couple was the least likely to become parents since Abraham and Sarah. Yet the angel Gabriel came to Zechariah with a message similar to the one he would give Mary in a few months: the impossible would happen; they would have a child. Well aware of the messianic prophecy and the distinction of an angelic visit, they understood that their son was a miracle of God and praised Him. The aged parents of St. John the Baptist are commemorated on September 5. Their Hebrew names appear left and right of a table of incense, indicating their prayers to the Lord for a son. The meanings of the names help convey the story: "Remember Yahweh" and "My God has sworn."

Zechariah

FIGURES 478, 479

A contemporary of Haggai, this minor prophet wrote after the fall of Jerusalem in anticipation of the end of the world. Zechariah can be variously symbolized by a flying scroll (Zechariah 5:1–2) or by a donkey, which points to the familiar prophecy, "Rejoice greatly, O daughter of Zion! Shout aloud, O daughter of Jerusalem! Behold, your king is coming to you; righteous and having salvation is he, humble and mounted on a donkey, on a colt, the foal of a donkey" (Zechariah 9:9). Zechariah is commemorated on September 5.

Zephaniah

FIGURE 480

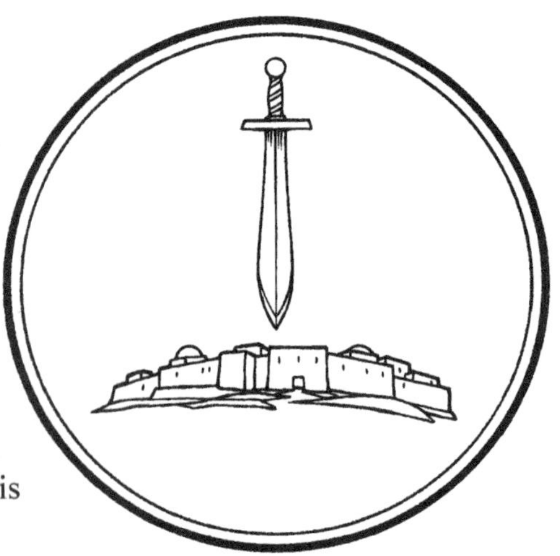

Believed by some to be the great-great grandson of King Hezekiah and, therefore, a cousin of King Josiah, Zephaniah's prophecies were about "the day of the Lord," that is, God's wrath over sin and deliverance from its consequences. A contemporary of Josiah, he may have influenced the young king to read the Scriptures and restore the temple. This minor prophet is symbolized by a great sword hovering above a walled city, indicating the looming judgment of the Lord, which figures so largely in the words of his prophecy. Zephaniah is remembered on July 31.

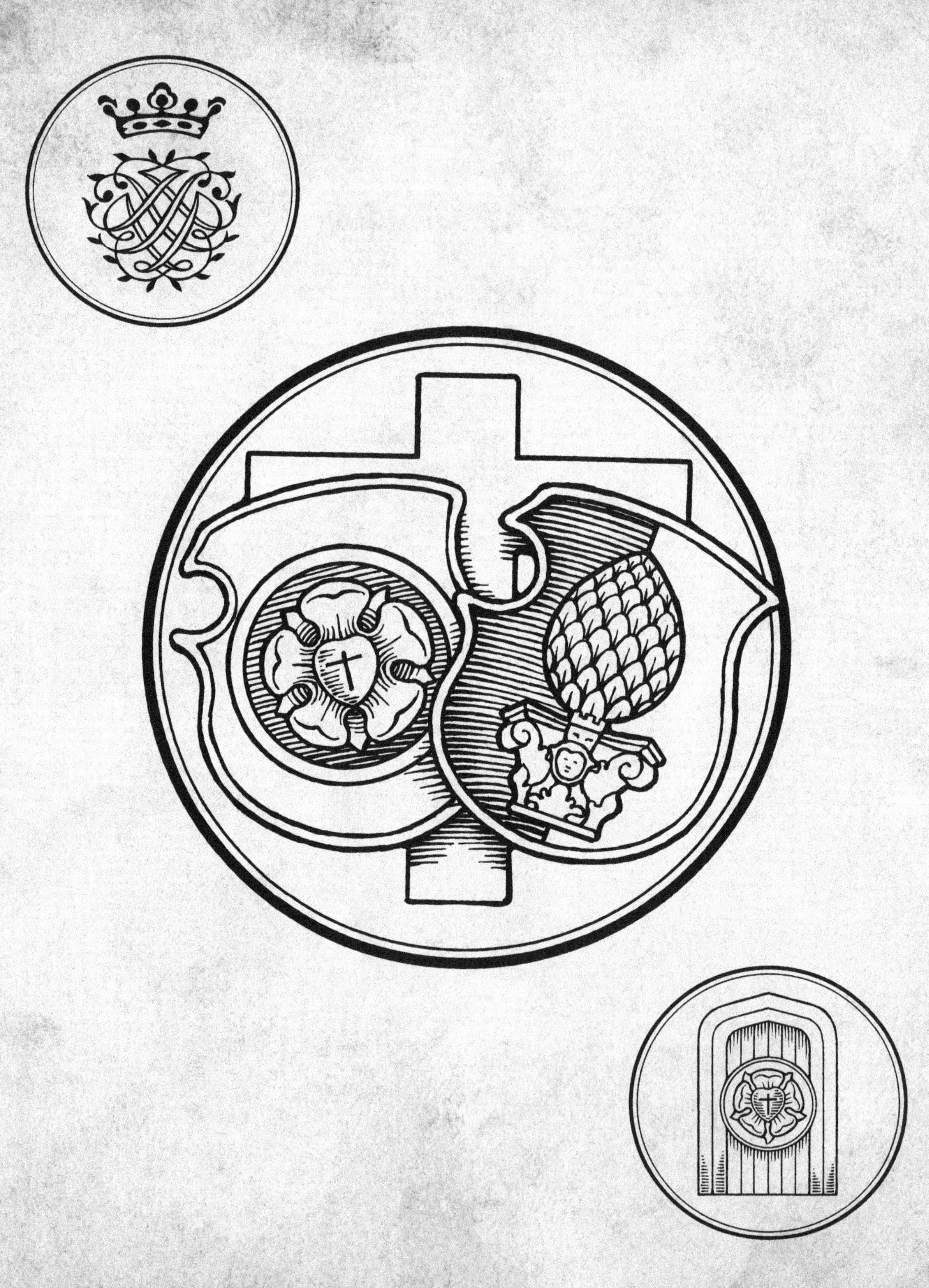

Lutherans and Their Time

It is important to include this segment of Christendom because the reformers arguably had more influence on the doctrine of the church than many other so-called saints. Not only are Reformation-era individuals commemorated throughout the sanctoral calendar, but the events and activities that surrounded them are as well. Some have their own symbols, usually coats of arms, which they either possessed by right or even designed on their own accord. For those who lacked a symbol—or whose coat of arms evaded research—one was fabricated for them. In those cases, each person was given the coat of arms from a town that had some significance in their life, along with their initials and some visual indication of vocation. While these symbols might never adorn a banner or stone embellishment, they do give credibility and remembrance to those who upheld Holy Scripture for the sake of the church and who confessed the same through the Lutheran Confessions.

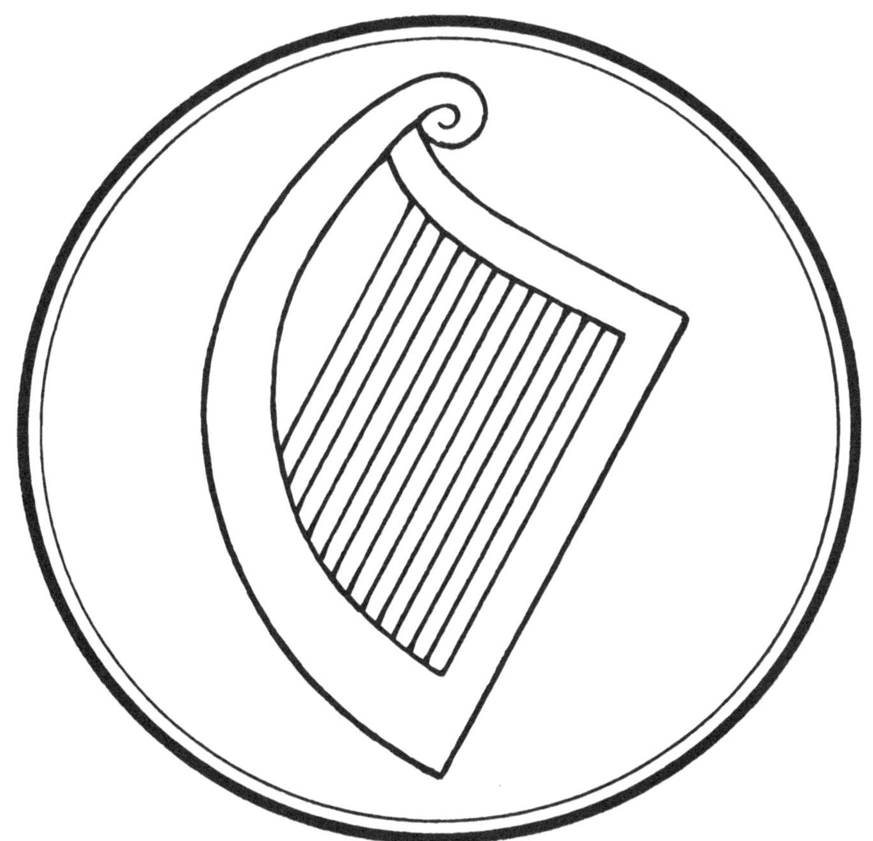

The Presentation of the Augsburg Confession

FIGURE 481

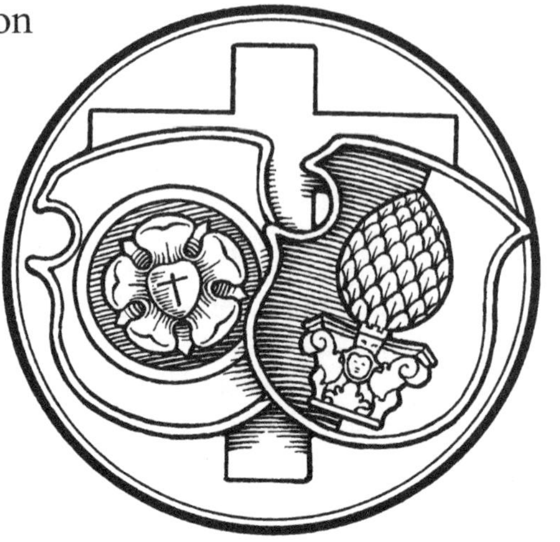

Commemorated on June 25, the document spelling out what the reformers confessed was presented in both German and Latin to the Holy Roman Emperor Charles V. To the chagrin of the emperor, the entire German text was read aloud in the assembly so that it was clearly heard by those standing outside the small chambers. The symbol combines a cross with Luther's seal and the coat of arms of the city of Augsburg.

Johann Sebastian Bach

FIGURE 482

A contemporary of Vivaldi and Handel, J. S. Bach was born in Eisenach into a respected and successful family of musicians. He attended the same school in Eisenach that Martin Luther had 265 years earlier. His father, uncles, and brothers were composers and performers, and Bach was known during his lifetime as a gifted organist. He composed over a thousand pieces, though many have been lost to the ages. His contribution to the Lutheran chorale is unmatched. J. S. Bach is commemorated on July 28 in the Lutheran Church. His seal was used during the kantor's stay in Leipzig and contains Bach's initials in a mirrored design.

Robert Barnes

FIGURE 483

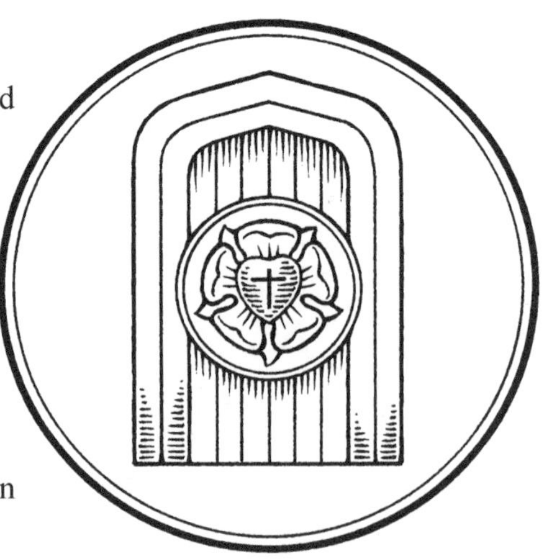

A confessor of Lutheran doctrine in England and a close friend of Martin Luther, Barnes encouraged Henry VIII to adopt Lutheranism. He did not support Henry's efforts to get his marriage to Anne of Cleaves annulled, however, and Henry did not convert to Lutheranism. Consequently, Barnes lost favor with the court and, along with several other Protestant and Catholic clergymen who disagreed with Henry's marital transitions, he was burned at the stake on July 30, the date on which the martyr is commemorated. His contrived symbol is Luther's seal superimposed on a Tudor door.

Johannes Bugenhagen

FIGURE 484

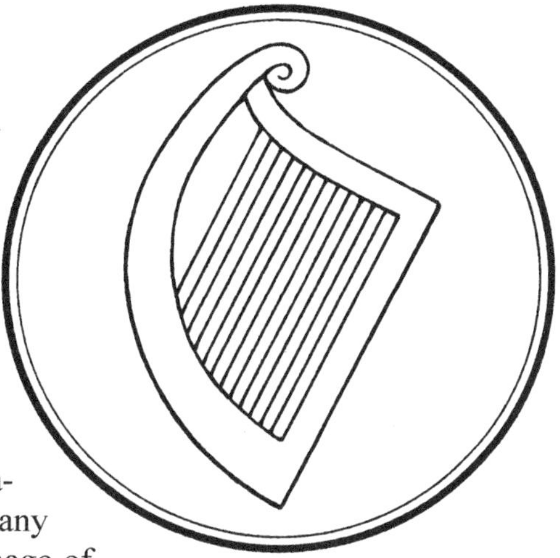

Here we see an example of the power of theological writings. Johannes Bugenhagen read Martin Luther's *Prelude on the Babylonian Captivity* and embraced Lutheran theology and doctrine, eventually becoming one of the first doctors of theology at the University of Wittenberg. He was Luther's pastor and helped translate the Bible into German. After Luther's death, Bugenhagen provided support for Katie and her children. Sometimes called the second apostle of the north for his work to establish the Lutheran Church, Bugenhagen served as a pastor with influence in northern Germany and Scandinavia. Because of his love for music, an image of a harp became his family coat of arms. He is commemorated on April 20.

Martin Chemnitz

FIGURE 485

A student of both Martin Luther and Philip Melanchthon, Chemnitz eventually became a professor of theology at the University of Wittenberg. Among his work as pastor and reformer, Chemnitz was part of a group of Lutheran theologians who composed the Formula of Concord and worked to get the Book of Concord published. His defense of the doctrine of the real presence of Christ in the Eucharist and the two natures of Christ are foundational to Lutheran studies to this day. The "second Martin," as he is sometimes called, is commemorated on November 9. His coat of arms appears in several portraits.

Lucas Cranach the Elder

FIGURE 486

More than any other artist, Cranach put a face on the Reformation. A vast portrait collection of Lutheran movers and shakers was created by his hand, his workshop, and the hands of his artistic progeny, including his son, Lucas the Younger. In addition to portraiture, he painted sacred and secular themes and created engravings and woodcuts. Lucas Cranach also ran a print shop (which was frequently used by Martin Luther) and an apothecary shop (which was in business until 1871). It was Frederick the Wise who bestowed the odd emblem—a winged, crowned snake carrying a ruby ring—on Cranach to use as a signature. He shares a commemoration date, April 6, with fellow artist Albrecht Dürer.

Albrecht Dürer

FIGURE 487

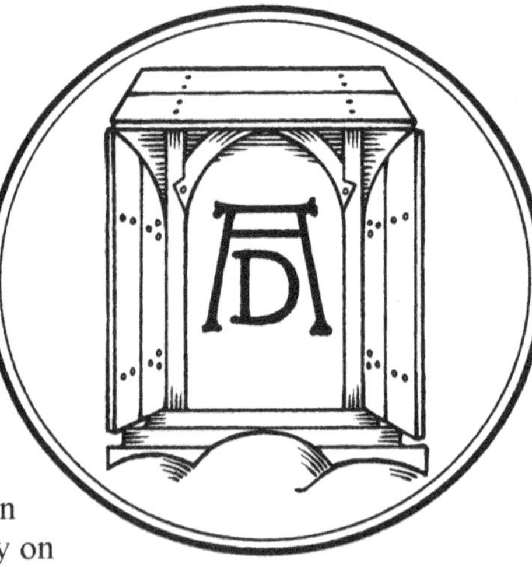

Another artist sympathetic to the Lutheran cause, Dürer was a contemporary of Raphael, da Vinci, and Bellini and corresponded with reformers, including Erasmus, Zwingli, Melanchthon, and Luther. He produced a vast amount of work and became well known as a young man for his woodcuts, engravings, portraits, and religious paintings. Among his most famous works is the image of praying hands. A true Renaissance man, Dürer also authored several scholarly books, including two volumes on geometry. Dürer used his distinctive initials when signing his work. In this example, the artist created a coat of arms with a play on words using his own name, hence the inclusion of a door. Dürer's commemoration date is April 6 and is shared with Lucas Cranach the Elder.

Frederick the Wise

FIGURE 488

Frederick III, elector of Saxony, became the patron and protector of Martin Luther. A founder of the University of Wittenberg, Frederick was a candidate for Holy Roman Emperor at about the same time that Luther was becoming widely known for his writings on reforming the church. The position went to Charles V instead. In his efforts to protect Martin Luther from assassination, Frederick orchestrated Luther's abduction and captivity at the Wartburg Castle. Officially a lifelong Roman Catholic, Frederick is said to have possessed nearly twenty thousand relics, including a twig from Moses' burning bush and hay from Jesus' manger. He is commemorated on May 5, the anniversary of his death. His royal coat of arms is used to symbolize the ruler.

Johann Gerhard

FIGURE 489

The Lutheran theologian is commemorated on August 17. Considered to be one of the major theologians of Protestant Germany, Gerhard wrote prodigiously on logic, theology, exegesis, and dogmatics, and authored commentaries on the Augsburg Confessions and on Genesis and Deuteronomy. His symbol is contrived of his initials flanking the coat of arms of Bad Colberg-Heldburg, the modern name of the town in which he did most of his work.

Paul Gerhardt

FIGURE 490

Coming a hundred years after Martin Luther, this educator and pastor is best known for writing more than five hundred hymns. Johann Sebastian Bach used many of Gerhardt's hymns with his compositions. Lutherans today still count his hymns among their most beloved, hymns such as "O Sacred Head, Now Wounded," "Awake My Heart, with Gladness," and "Rejoice, My Heart, Be Glad, and Sing." He shares the commemoration day of October 26 with fellow hymnwriters Philipp Nicolai and Johann Heermann. His contrived symbol is composed of his initials, the coat of arms of his birth place in Gräfenhainichen, and a harp.

Johann Heermann

FIGURE 491

A poet, educator, and pastor, Heermann suffered physically from a variety of illnesses throughout his life and lost all his possessions during the Thirty Years' War, yet he managed to live until the age of 62. His poetry and his hymns were based on Scripture and writings of the church fathers. Heermann's initials flank a hymnwriter's pen in this contrived symbol. He is commemorated on October 26.

Johann Konrad Wilhelm Loehe

FIGURE 492

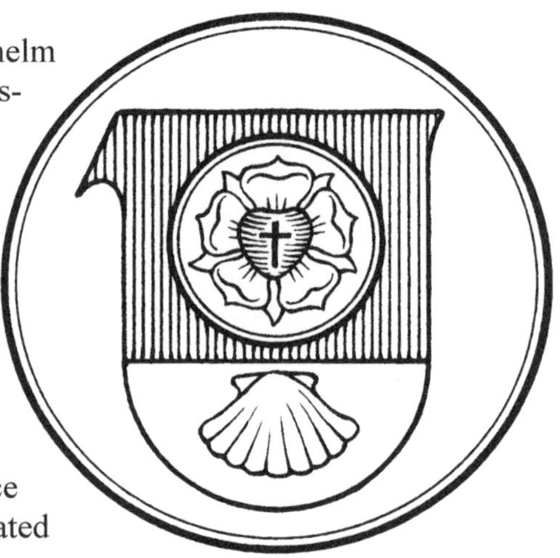

An avid student of the Lutheran Confessions, Wilhelm Loehe was a staunch advocate of German Lutheran missionary efforts. Although he never left Germany, he directly influenced the growth of Lutheranism in the United States by sending pastors to found congregations and schools there and by tirelessly raising funds to support them. His influence helped to establish The Lutheran Church—Missouri Synod. Loehe's death is commemorated on January 2. The coat of arms is that of the small German town of Neuendettelsau, from whence the pastor sent fellow pastors to far-flung areas of the world. Incidentally, such was Lutheran influence in Germany by Loehe's day that many towns incorporated Luther's seal into their civil coats of arms.

Martin Luther

FIGURE 493

More than five hundred years after he went public with concerns about how the Roman Church was misleading the people, Martin Luther remains one of the most significant figures in world history. Dr. Luther made good use of improved printing technology, arguably the birth of mass communication, to share his doctrine at a time when the world was ripe for change. Luther's symbol is a seal of his own design. He described it in a letter to his friend Lazarus Spengler: "a red heart representing the love of God, a black cross indicating the depravity of man, a white rose meaning joy, these on a blue field representing heaven and all surrounded by golden ring to show that the blessing of heaven is eternal." It should be noted that, while the background and outer ring are sometimes omitted, they should be included. The commemoration of Martin Luther's death is February 18.

Katharina von Bora Luther

FIGURE 494

Well-educated and courageous, Katharina von Bora was the wife of Martin Luther. She helped create the model of a minister's wife, was the devoted mother of six, and deftly managed a complex household. Her industriousness allowed Luther to focus on his writing and ministry. Katharina's symbol contains Martin Luther's seal and her own family's crest of a rampant lion. Her death is commemorated on December 20.

The Lutheran Martyrs of Florida

FIGURE 495

It may seem an odd to have martyrs commemorated in "the land of the free," but religious freedom on our shores did not always exist. In 1565, Huguenots (French Lutherans) were sent by the king of France to colonize Florida as a Protestant settlement, arriving near the Spanish settlement at St. Augustine. The Spanish colonists did not take this infringement on their territory lightly and cut down every man who refused to convert to Roman Catholicism. Their contrived symbol is Luther's seal flanked by palm trees.

Philip Melanchthon

FIGURE 496

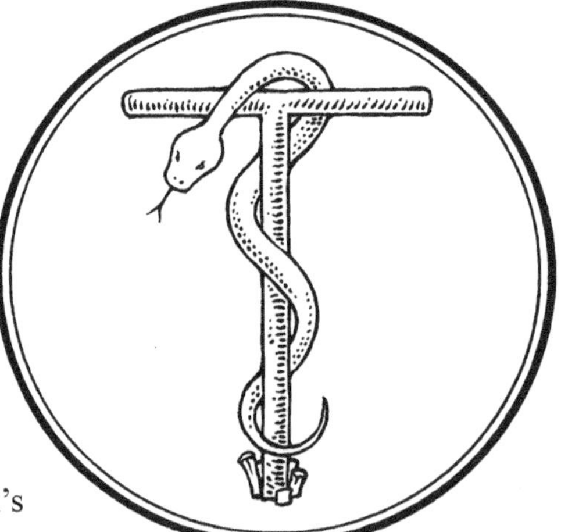

Friend of Martin Luther, Philip Melanchthon wrote authoritatively on such topics as original sin, grace, and justification; wrote commentaries on the New Testament; and was the author of the Augsburg Confession, the Apology of the Confession of Augsburg, and the Treatise on the Power and Primacy of the Pope. Melanchthon himself adopted the symbol of a brazen snake atop a pole in reference to the prophetic serpent Moses made, which ultimately pointed to the crucifixion of Jesus Christ. The Lutheran theologian's birth is commemorated on February 16.

Henry Melchior Muhlenberg

FIGURE 497

This pastor is credited with creating the first Lutheran synod in the United States in 1748—the Ministerium of Pennsylvania—and helping lead Lutheran churches from New York to Maryland. The patriarch of a distinguished colonial family, several of his sons and grandsons were also pastors in the new country. His oldest child, John Peter, was a brigadier general in the Continental Army, a commander at the battle of Yorktown, a US congressman, and (briefly) a US senator. Frederick Muhlenberg, Henry's second son, was also a member of the Continental Congress and the first Speaker of the House. Henry's symbol is taken from the seal of the Ministerium of Pennsylvania, and it shows a vineyard being tended. Muhlenberg is commemorated on October 7.

Philipp Nicolai

FIGURE 498

Commemorated with two other hymnwriters (Johann Heermann and Paul Gerhardt) on the anniversary of his death, October 26, this Lutheran pastor, poet, and composer created hymns that influenced Johann Sebastian Bach. Among his hymns are the beloved "O Morning Star, How Fair and Bright" and "Wake, Awake, for Night Is Flying." His symbol is his personal seal.

Michael Praetorius

FIGURE 499

Although he does not appear in the Lutheran sanctoral calendar, this musical great was the son of a Lutheran pastor and, among other things, composed a vast collection of work for the Lutheran Church. As an author, Praetorius generated three volumes that are important sources of information on music history, theory, instruments, and composition. His contrived symbol contains the initials of his given name, a harp, and the coat of arms of Wolfenbüttel, in which court he served as Kapellmeister.

Samuel Scheidt

FIGURE 500

This German composer and organist served as Kapellmeister to the Margrave of Brandenburg. Writer of sacred vocal and keyboard music, he influenced the Baroque style and contributed greatly to liturgical music, including congregational singing. His contrived symbol is composed of his initials, a rank of pipes, and the coat of arms for Brandenburg.

Johann Hermann Schein

FIGURE 501

An acquaintance of Samuel Scheidt and Heinrich Schütz, Schein was a German composer whose work has trickled down to us in the form of alternate settings of Lutheran hymns. He is known for generating a considerable collection of both sacred and secular vocal pieces. A contrived symbol contains his initials, a harp, and the coat of arms of Leipzig, where he died.

Heinrich Schütz

FIGURE 502

Considered by some to be the most important German composer before Johann Sebastian Bach, Schütz began his career as a choirboy. He studied music in Venice before returning to Germany as an organist and composer. While not commemorated in the sanctoral calendar of the Missouri Synod, he is celebrated in other Lutheran synods along with Bach and Handel on July 28. His symbol is composed of his initials, a rank of pipes, and the coat of arms for Weißenfels, where Schütz lived as a child.

Johann von Staupitz

FIGURE 503

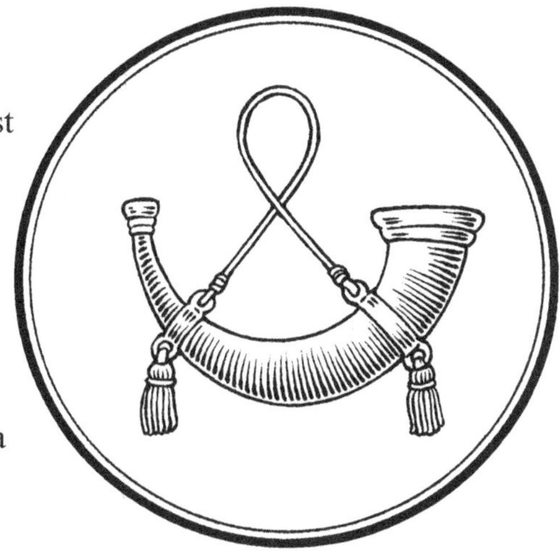

It may seem curious that this Roman Catholic priest is commemorated on November 8 in the Lutheran sanctoral calendar. However, Luther commented that "if it had not been for Dr. Staupitz, I should have sunk in hell." Staupitz was Luther's professor and confessor at the University of Wittenberg, pointing Luther to the means of grace. He was an early supporter of Luther's views, but he eventually distanced himself from the reformer. His family coat of arms, a hunting horn, is Staupitz's symbol.

Johann Walter

FIGURE 504

This Lutheran poet and composer served as kantor—and eventually director—for the chapel of Frederick the Wise. As an advisor to Martin Luther on liturgical music and its importance in catechesis, Walter helped shape the German Mass that was used for many years following the Reformation. His symbol is contrived of his initials, a harp, and the royal arms of Frederick the Wise. He is commemorated on April 24.

C. F. W. Walther

FIGURE 505

This German pastor, theologian, and author was born in Langenchursdorf, Germany, immigrated to America in 1838, and became the first president of The Lutheran Church—Missouri Synod and the first president of Concordia Seminary. After an intense study of Martin Luther's writings, Carl Ferdinand Wilhelm Walther became a champion of orthodox Lutheranism. His contrived symbol is composed of the coat of arms of Langenchursdorf, Luther's seal, and the coat of arms of St. Louis, Missouri, where the theologian died. Walther's death is commemorated on May 9.

F. C. D. Wyneken

FIGURE 506

A Germany-born pastor and a traveling missionary in Pennsylvania and midwestern states, Friedrich Conrad Dietrich Wyneken was a tireless advocate for Lutheran mission work in the United States in the mid-1800s. At his prompting, Lutheran pastors came to America to minister to the German settlers there. Wyneken was the second president of the LCMS, and he helped found and was the first president of Concordia Theological Seminary. His contrived symbol contains the coat of arms of his birth town, Verden an der Aller, and a portion of the seal of Baltimore, where he first worked in the United States. Wyneken's death is commemorated on May 4.

Doctrinal Symbols

From antiquity, symbols have been used to communicate a concept, idea, action, or notion in a simple and direct way. Symbols help us make sense of complex things and point to something that has a deeper meaning. The symbols here are among the most used in the church and will be familiar to many. Because these symbols include rites and sacraments supported by various teachings, they vary in use between church bodies. Also included in this group are a few miscellaneous but necessary symbols that defy categorization.

The Office of the Holy Ministry

FIGURE 507

Some have used crossed keys alone to signify the office, but because that same symbol is used to signify the Office of the Keys and also an alternative to symbolize St. Peter, expanding the symbolism as in our example gives it a clearer definition. In addition to crossed keys, a shepherd's crook is included to point to the pastoral aspect of holy ministry. A stole is also present in this example, symbolizing the yoke placed on the pastor's shoulders. While this stole is emblazoned with three crosses, a single cross may be used at the neck. It is customary for pastors to kiss the neck cross before donning the stole.

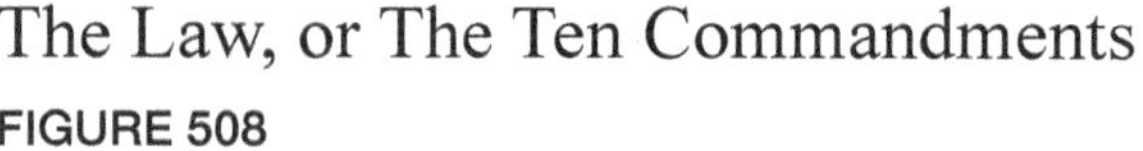

The Law, or The Ten Commandments

FIGURE 508

Among the various ways to symbolize the tablets, most take an abbreviated approach and do not include the entire text, but consistency ends there. Many use roman numerals, putting five on one tablet and five on another. Those of Calvinist or Eastern Orthodox persuasion often put four on the first tablet and six on the second. Lutherans and Roman Catholics most often put three on the first tablet and seven on the second. A twist is added in our example: Hebrew numbers are used, but because Hebrew is read from right to left, the first (right) tablet has the first three numbers and the second (left) tablet has seven.

Holy Scripture, or The Word of God

FIGURE 509

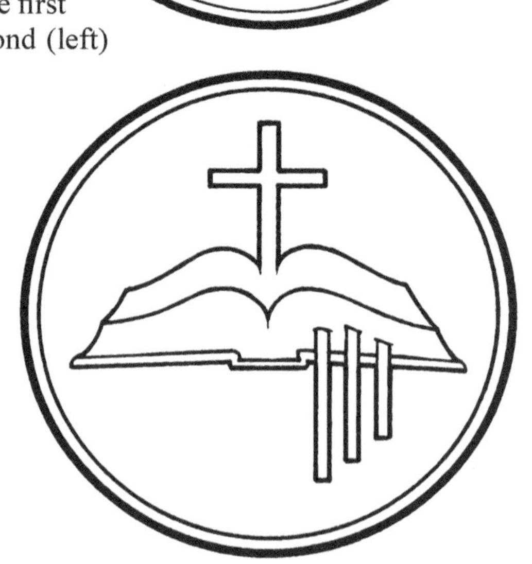

Because sacred artwork may depict various writers and writings, it's best to give some hint as to what writing is being shown. The example here not only has a cross emerging from its pages, but it also has three bookmarks, which give a strong nod to the Holy Trinity.

Holy Baptism

FIGURES 510, 511, 512

There are variations used in symbolizing the Sacrament of Holy Baptism. Strangely, the oldest symbol is not visual—it is numerical. The number eight has long been associated with the resurrection of our Lord and, by extension, Holy Baptism. Eight-sided baptismal fonts are common enough to make it the rule rather than the exception.

Although there is no biblical mention that the scallop shell was ever used as an impromptu vessel for applying water—indeed, such invertebrates were considered unclean—it has nevertheless come down to us as a visual symbol for Holy Baptism. Previously, the scallop shell was used as a symbol for a pilgrim, and because, by tradition, St. James is said to have traveled as far as Spain to spread the Gospel, it is also the apostle's identifying symbol.

It is important to add three drops of water when using a scallop to symbolize Holy Baptism. This signifies that we baptize in the name of the Father, and of the Son, and of the Holy Spirit. A Chi-Rho may be added to signify that we are baptized into Christ's death and resurrection, and the symbol of the Holy Spirit may also be added.

Holy Eucharist

FIGURE 513

A fancy cup by itself is not enough to symbolize the Sacrament of the Altar. A host must be placed above a chalice and, to visually confess what we believe, a monogram—such as a Chi-Rho—should be imprinted on both the host and the chalice. This confesses that the consecrated bread and wine *are* the body and blood of Jesus Christ.

Rite of Confirmation

FIGURE 514

Because the Rite of Confirmation is a reaffirmation of our Baptism and because it is usually linked with our first Holy Communion, it is common to include symbols for both of those sacraments. The rite takes place on Pentecost Sunday in many Lutheran congregations, and this example is reflective of that. A symbol of the Holy Spirit is fused with a cross and emits seven flames—signifying the seven gifts of the Spirit (1 Corinthians 12:4–11).

Office of the Keys

FIGURE 515

Context is important when using this symbol, for it is sometimes used to symbolize St. Peter and the office of the holy ministry. The common thread in all these symbolic uses is that the command was given by Jesus to forgive sins and bind the same (see John 20:22–23), hence, the two crossed keys. One key indicates the authority given to the servants of the church to forgive the repentant, and the other represents the power to withhold forgiveness from the unrepentant.

Rite of Marriage

FIGURES 516, 517, 518, 519

It is nearly impossible to consider anything other than interlocking rings when it comes to symbols for marriage. Things take a turn, however, when such a symbol is used in the context of a Christian wedding. The examples here show not only interlaced rings but also rings interlaced with a cross. A leafy cross may be used to signify that a Christian marriage exists under and within the living Word and to symbolize that the vocations of husband and wife are branches connected to the vine that is Jesus Christ. Symbols for marriage may be expanded by having a cross emerge from an open book—the Bible. A cord of three strands may also be worked into the symbol.

Holy Orders

FIGURE 520

This sacrament, observed in the Roman Catholic Church, is centered around the vows of men who are intent on becoming priests. The Lutheran equivalent is the Rite of Ordination, and the names of each share a common origin. For our purposes, the example shown leans a bit toward the Roman tradition. The open Bible is superimposed by a chalice and host. A maniple is placed over the open Bible. While Lutherans may certainly use this to symbolize the Rite of Ordination, some might be reluctant to use the maniple, which is not universally worn by Lutheran pastors.

Anointing the Sick

FIGURE 521

Considered a sacrament among Roman Catholics, anointing the sick may be symbolized by a cross-topped container of holy oil. Because only a small amount of oil is used, the container should be accordingly small.

Foot Washing

FIGURE 522

While this ceremony is more commonly used among the Anabaptists, it is also used in the Roman Catholic Church and Eastern Orthodox Church on Maundy Thursday. A ewer, basin, and towel are used to symbolize the underlying humility shown by our Lord when He washed the feet of His disciples.

Prayer, or The Lord's Prayer

FIGURE 523

Although the act of prayer may be illustrated by folded hands or a kneeling human form, we use Psalm 141:2 here because it connects prayer to the image of incense: "Let my prayer be counted as incense before You." The censer or thurible issuing a wisp of incense smoke is reminiscent of symbols used in ancient times to represent our faithful prayers rising to God. It may also specifically represent the Lord's Prayer.

The Church

FIGURE 524

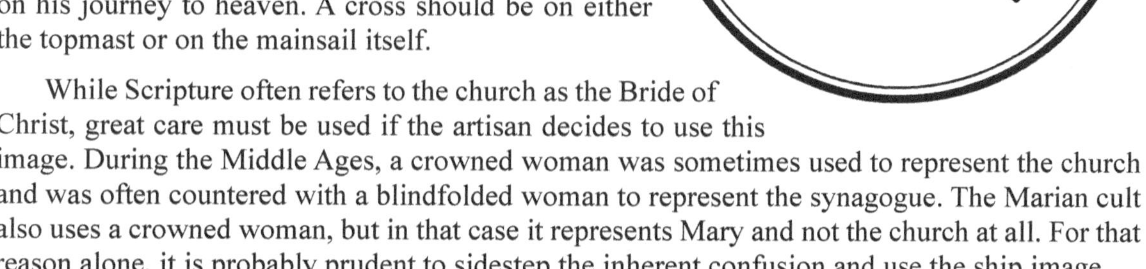

A ship has been used since antiquity to symbolize the church. Variations exist on the form of the ship, but in general it is shown as a sailing vessel in full sail on less-than-calm seas, representing the faithful protected by the church amid the stormy waves of the world. Additionally, a ship set on a course for a particular destination represents the life of the Christian on his journey to heaven. A cross should be on either the topmast or on the mainsail itself.

While Scripture often refers to the church as the Bride of Christ, great care must be used if the artisan decides to use this image. During the Middle Ages, a crowned woman was sometimes used to represent the church and was often countered with a blindfolded woman to represent the synagogue. The Marian cult also uses a crowned woman, but in that case it represents Mary and not the church at all. For that reason alone, it is probably prudent to sidestep the inherent confusion and use the ship image.

The Ecumenical Council of Nicaea

FIGURE 525

The event, celebrated on June 12, commemorates the gathering of Eastern and Western bishops in 325 under the Roman Emperor Constantine I. Among the many issues the council addressed were uniform observances of Easter, the formulation of canon law, investigation into the Arian controversy, and the formulation of the Nicene Creed. The symbol represents the Eastern and Western Churches by way of their respective miters, flanking the crown of Constantine I. Above the headgear is a symbol for the Holy Trinity, which the Nicene Creed confesses.

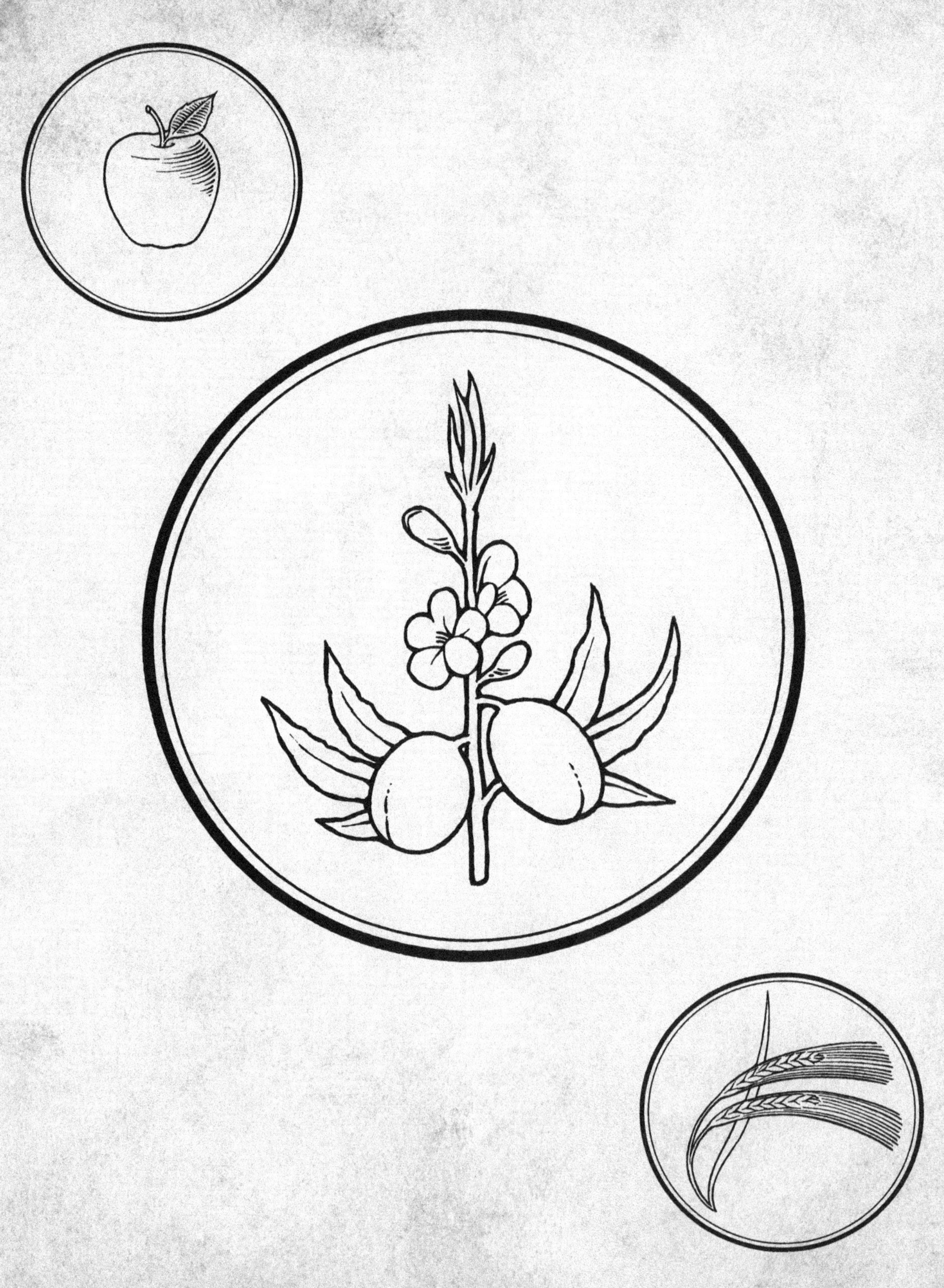

Flora

While the animal kingdom is well represented in Christian symbolism, most are either associated with the person of Jesus Christ, the Holy Spirit, or specific saints. Some species of the plant kingdom are closely associated with certain saints, but they otherwise often carry a more general meaning and are therefore included in this category.

The symbolism of some plants gained meaning during the Middle Ages while that of others has biblical origins. Symbols may appear woven into decoration, but simply add depth of meaning by their presence.

Almond

FIGURE 526

This is usually shown as a branch with buds, flowers, and ripe almonds. The golden lampstand in the temple had almond flowers worked into its design (Exodus 25:31–35). The staff of Aaron also budded and bore almond flowers (Numbers 17:8). This symbol conveys divine approval.

Apple

FIGURE 527

For unknown reason, the apple was unofficially chosen as the fruit forbidden in the Garden of Eden, though Scripture does not specify. At any rate, the poor fruit has come to symbolize sin, discord, and the fall of man. Strangely, it occasionally represents the (sinless) virgin Mary.

Barley

FIGURE 528

This grain was generally considered the lesser cousin of wheat and often was used as fodder for livestock. Bread made from barley was usually intended for the poor. It therefore carries an association with humility.

Bulrush

FIGURE 529

These marshy plants are usually used in reference to Egypt, and specifically the baby Moses. By extension, they are sometimes used to symbolize hope.

Cedar

FIGURE 530

Cedar was used as building material for the temple and as a fragrant ingredient in a cleansing offering for a leper. When mentioned as a tree, it is always associated with strength and longevity and therefore symbolizes faithfulness.

Clover

FIGURE 531

This humble plant is used to symbolize the Holy Trinity because of its three-lobed leaf. The leaf itself—often referred to as a shamrock and associated with St. Patrick—is frequently shown without its flower. The three lobes are also said to stand for faith, hope, and love.

Daisy

FIGURE 532

A member of the aster family, this flower's symbolism dates from the Middle Ages when it was used to denote innocence, simplicity, humility, and the new day.

Fig

FIGURE 533

The fruit of the fig tree was used to express fruitfulness, especially when relating to a land blessed by the Lord. Its leaves, on the other hand, sometimes symbolize fidelity, modesty, or even shame, as fully expressed in the aprons that Adam and Eve made for themselves after the fall.

Grafted Branch

FIGURE 534

This image is always used to express blessings of Gentile Christians' adoption as children of God, not by lineage or merit, but by the grace of God through the suffering, death, and resurrection of His Son and our Lord, Jesus Christ. Jesus used this imagery in John 15:1–5.

Grape

FIGURE 535

A grape cluster may, on its own, symbolize blessing, fruitfulness, or the Promised Land. When combined with wheat, however, it points to the Eucharist.

Holly

FIGURE 536

Despite its inclusion in Christmas decorations and motifs, holly was historically used to symbolize the Passion of our Lord. Even the lyrics of "The Holly and the Ivy" spell out visual clues of the holly's connection to the crucifixion of Jesus Christ.

Hyssop

FIGURE 537

Although there is debate whether the biblical hyssop is the same plant we now know, hyssop was used for purification and cleansing, and therefore symbolizes absolution and humility. A perennial evergreen, it is part of the mint family and classified as an herb. It may also be used as flavoring for foods or brewed for tea.

Ivy

FIGURE 538

Because it remains green throughout the year, ivy symbolizes eternal life. When used in weddings, it is said to stand for devotion and loyalty. When woven into a crown, it is said to stand for fertility.

Laurel

FIGURE 539

Branches of this aromatic evergreen plant were likely used to create the wreaths awarded to Roman and Greek athletes as described by St. Paul in 1 Corinthians 9:24, 25. In both classical and Christian artwork, the laurel symbolizes triumph or victory.

Lily

FIGURE 540

Depending on context, the lily can symbolize the virgin Mary, Joseph, or even the archangel Gabriel. In any of these cases, the flower itself should be white, which is why its underlying meaning is purity. It may also be used at funerals and at Easter to symbolize the resurrection of Christ Jesus.

Oak

FIGURE 541

Usually only the leaf and acorn of an oak are used. The oak symbolizes strength and virtue, protection and stability. Its use dates to ancient civilizations. In Scripture, it is used in reference to specific places that convey safety.

Olive

FIGURE 542

The olive may symbolize many things, including prosperity, friendship, and reconciliation. Its oil is used to signify the Lord's favor and blessing, as when anointing a king, or it may symbolize mercy and healing, as when anointing wounds. When used in the context of Noah, it symbolizes peace. Commonly used in ancient Roman and Greek cultures, the flowering olive in the Psalms, for example, stands for beauty and abundance.

Pomegranate

FIGURE 543

Symbolism of the pomegranate may go in one of two directions: it may symbolize the Lord's abundant blessings by the many seeds the fruiting body contains, or it may symbolize the resurrection when the ripe fruiting body erupts. Its use in mythology notwithstanding, it is listed as one of seven fruits and grains in the Old Testament and is one of the oldest fruits that still grows in the Middle East.

Thistle

FIGURE 544

Although bearing a conspicuous and beautiful flower, the thistle has come to symbolize sin, sorrow, and the fall because of God's words in Genesis 3:18. Its use suggests inconvenience, difficulties, and tribulation.

Thorn

FIGURE 545

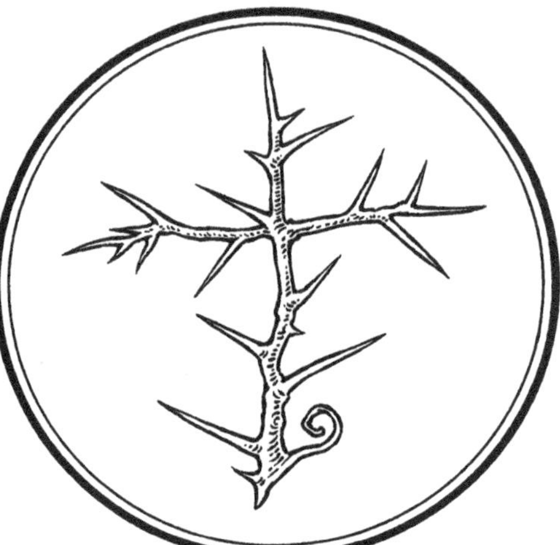

Any species of thorny, woody plant may be used to symbolize the Passion of our Lord. Typically no leaves or flowers are included. Thorns in the Bible refer to the state of the earth after the fall of mankind (Genesis 3:18; Matthew 7:16; Matthew 13:22) and are a reminder of our sin (2 Corinthians 12:7).

The Tree of Life

FIGURE 546

Care should be taken in using this symbol, as it has been absorbed into the teachings of groups as far afield as the Shakers, Mormons, and Kabbalah. It is best if it gives a visual nod to the cross and is shown bearing fruit. Mentioned in the first and last books of the Bible, the tree of life is a symbol of sustenance here and life in the world to come by the work of Christ for us.

The Tree of the Knowledge of Good and Evil

FIGURE 547

There may not be much use for such a symbol, but it works best when including overt themes of sin and death, as in this example. Its use may represent God's desire that we have a right relationship with Him as we exercise faith and obedience.

Wheat

FIGURE 548

Because it was a food staple for the people of Israel, wheat symbolizes bounty when used alone or in a sheaf. It may also be used to represent those who believe in Christ (see Matthew 13:24–30) and Christ Himself (John 12:24).

Wheat and Grapes

FIGURE 549

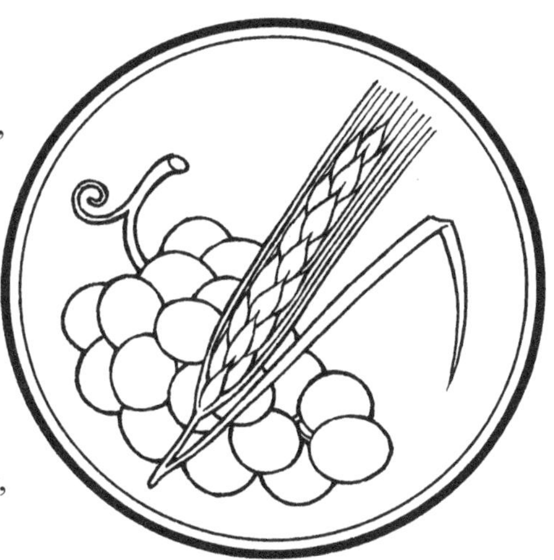

Considered to be the oldest known cultivated plants, both grow well in the Middle Eastern climate. A bountiful harvest would be a sign of God's provision and pleasure, while a failed harvest would be a sign of God's displeasure. As elements in the Lord's Supper, wheat and grapes represent the abundance of Christ's forgiveness for those who are grafted into Him and who receive the bread of life. While this pair symbolizes the Eucharist, it's best to confess Christ's body and blood by adding to it some identifier of Jesus Christ, such as a Chi-Rho.

Wheat and Tares

FIGURE 550

This combination is used to represent the church and the world or believers and unbelievers because, although they look very similar, one is meant to be enjoyed as a blessing from the Lord and the other is only meant to be burned. Jesus' parable in Matthew 13:24–42 points to the final judgment.

Miscellany

Some symbols refuse to be categorized, so they ended up in this section. At first glance, these entries may seem out of place in a collection of Christian symbols, but in reality only one—the old evil foe—may claim such distinction.

The Dragon

FIGURE 551

Satan may be symbolized as either a dragon or a serpent. It's important for the artist to stay within these bounds, taking cues from Holy Scripture, rather than skipping down the visual lanes that lead to the occult. It doesn't matter if Satan is depicted as menacing or coy, for we know he is the father of lies.

Skull

FIGURE 552

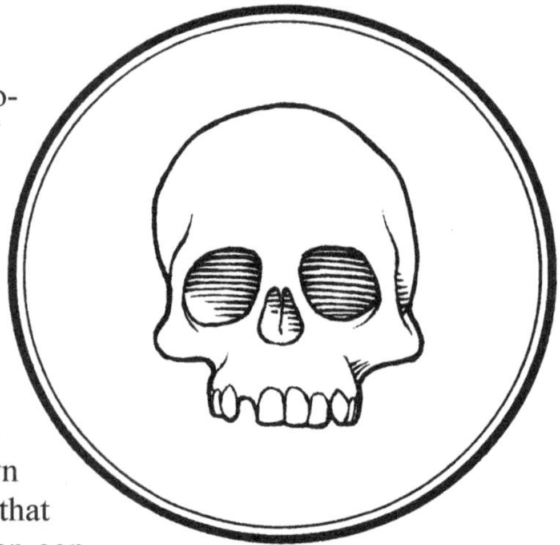

Skull motifs are sometimes depicted in Hindu, Korean, Mesoamerican, and popular art as reminders of the inevitability of death. And some Christian folks do not like images of skulls and avoid the symbolic use of them. It is probable that sanitized denominations lump the symbol with anything "of the devil," never mind that everyone has a skull in their own head and it was the Creator who placed it there.

Yet, in Christian art, context is the key to understanding what the skull is meant to convey. When shown with or held by a sainted figure, the skull often denotes that person as being a hermit. The idea is that hermits often contemplated their own mortality while in seclusion.

When placed at the foot of the cross, a skull has a far different range of meaning. It might be a nod to the name of the place where our Savior died—"the place of the skull." Or it may point to Christ Jesus' victory over death by His own death. Its meaning is also punctuated by a tradition that places the site of Jesus' crucifixion over the grave of Adam or to represent the death of the old Adam himself.

Four-Pointed Star

FIGURE 553

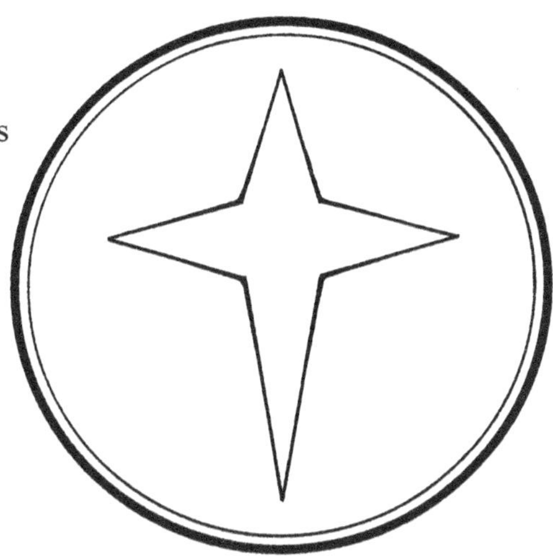

There are a near-infinite number of meaningful stars with varying numbers of points, but they have been reined in considerably for our purposes in this collection. The four-pointed star gives an obvious nod to the cross, which comes in handy when tempering images of an otherwise cute image of baby Jesus.

Five-Pointed Star

FIGURE 554

In older books on Christian symbolism, this star is associated with Epiphany. This may be one case in which a symbol has become anachronistic, for the vast majority of times one sees this star is on civil and national flags and emblems. Given other star options as well as its appropriation for anti-Christian use, it might be best to leave this one out of the religious realm.

Six-Pointed Star

FIGURE 555

Not to be confused with the Star of David, this symbol is known as the Creator's Star because it points to the six days of creation. The Star of David, on the other hand, is composed of two interwoven triangles and is used to identify the Jewish secular nation in general, as well as the Old Testament children of God and King David in particular.

Seven-Pointed Star

FIGURE 556

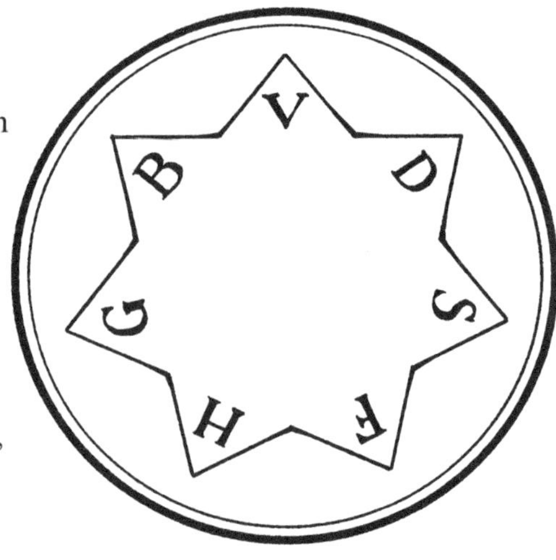

Used on the flags of Australia, Jordan, the nation of Georgia, Native American tribes, and law enforcement agencies, Christian tradition links this symbol to the Holy Spirit. The seven points correspond to the seven gifts of the Spirit and the initials represent either the Old Testament list from the prophet Isaiah or the list found in the book of Revelation, given in Latin. Our example follows the latter, and its initials represent *Virtus*, *Divinitas*, *Sapientia*, *Fortitudo*, *Honor*, *Gloria*, and *Benedicio.*

Eight-Pointed Star

FIGURE 557

The number eight is always connected to regeneration or the resurrection. It is for this reason that baptismal fonts typically have eight sides. This star is a wonderful choice for depictions of the Incarnation of our Lord (where the Bethlehem star is often depicted) or in images relating to the epiphany of our Lord. The reason for this is that the bottom arm may be extended to form a tail, and in so doing evokes not only an image of the cross but also that of a resurrection cross. In this, it points to Jesus' birth, death, and resurrection in a single confessional symbol.

Nine-Pointed Star

FIGURE 558

Said to symbolize unity, this is a counterpart to the seven-pointed star and represents the nine fruits of the Spirit. Taken from a list in Galatians 5:22, the Latin initials correspond to *Charitas*, *Gaudium*, *Pax*, *Longanimitas*, *Benignitas*, *Bonitas*, *Fides*, *Mansuetudo*, and *Continentia.* Because it is frequently seen on designs used by the Baha'i faith, it is best to avoid incorporating it into designs for Christian settings.

Vestments

Garments worn by clergy can be most curious. Their origins are often steeped in history, with regional and cultural overtones. The word itself is used in reference to an outer garment worn in ceremonial roles, and the practice of wearing vestments began as early as the fourth century and was well established by the ninth century. Without brocade and satin and every sort of handwork, some vestments would be indistinguishable from the everyday garments of ancient Romans, medieval Europeans, or other historical peoples. By the Middle Ages, it was common practice for clergy to don special garments for worship and to wear highly designed gloves, shoes, stockings, and more. After a time, they slowly settled into common use and, for the most part, little variance occurred thereafter.

As history progressed, vestments' context in the sanctuary offered opportunities to add meaning beyond mere "tradition." Eventually, church hierarchy dictated garment and color and ornamentation as subdivisions of basic vestments. Visually, it was logical. A novice in the church wore the simplest vestments, while patriarchal figures were adorned similar to their royal, secular counterparts. In some circles, those wearing "soft" caps were overseen by those wearing stiff headgear. All this was to reflect God's order in creation and underscore rank in the apostolic church.

Of course, it must be stated that vestments are not meant to show the undershepherd's prominence or status. Neither are they used to show the depth of church pockets. Rather, vestments symbolize that the grace of God covers all—yes, even sinful pastors.

What follows is a collection of some of the more recognizable vestments. As with symbols in general, it is nearly impossible to address every article of clothing, given the number of denominations in Christendom, not to mention variations based on region, culture, and monastic connection.

Alb

FIGURE 559

One of the simplest vestments, the white alb originated with the first-century Roman tunic but is ankle length. The alb is an outer vestment. It symbolizes the innocence of our Lord and His prophetic office. It is often tied at the waist with a belt-like cincture.

Anteri

FIGURE 560

Used in the Eastern Orthodox Church, the anteri is an inner vestment that may be of any color but is often black. Its use is similar to the Roman cassock. Instead of buttons, however, it is wrapped and tied much like a bathrobe.

Biretta

FIGURE 561

A stiff cap with three or four ridges and surmounted by a decorative tuft is typically worn by Roman Catholic clergy—except the pope—outside the sanctuary as a symbol of station. Specific colors of birettas designate rank.

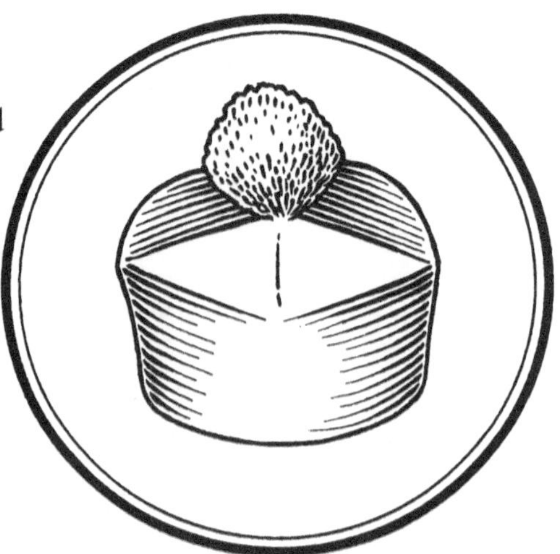

Cappello Romano

FIGURE 562

Worn outside the sanctuary, this wide-brimmed hat may be used by any member of the Roman Church and is primarily used to fend off sun and rain.

Cassock

FIGURE 563

This black inner vestment is worn by clergy in the Western Church and symbolizes man's sin. It has buttons down the entire front and a notched collar typical of many Middle Eastern tunics.

Chasuble, Fiddle-Back

FIGURE 564

There are several styles of chasubles worn by celebrants during a worship service. Their color follows the liturgical colors of the Church Year and is not indicative of rank. The fiddle-back style is shorter and has a distinctive hemline that resembles a violin's body—hence, the name. The word *chasuble* means "little house" and was originally ordinary Roman outerwear to protect the wearer from the elements while traveling. It is worn over the alb and stole.

Chasuble, Roman

FIGURE 565

The cross-like decoration of the longer Roman chasuble has rather unimpressive origins. Because loomed fabric was originally quite narrow, tailors had to piece this large vestment together. The unsightly seams were then covered by ornate "orphreys"—highly decorative bands of material—giving the vestment its final appearance.

Cincture

FIGURE 566

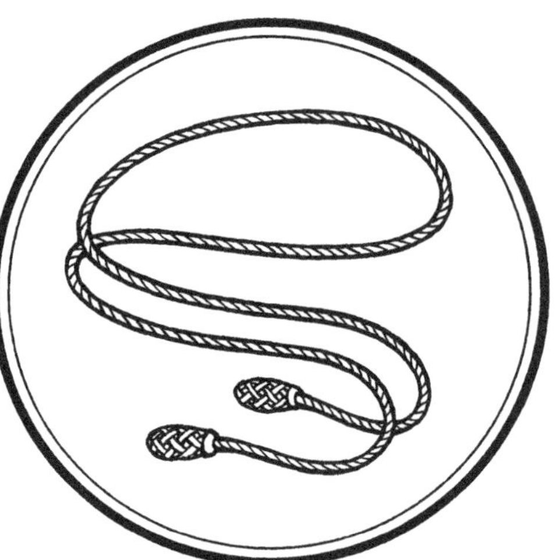

This item basically serves as a belt, though it is either of rope or constructed much like a stole. The ends may have decorative knots or be tasseled, and its color may either signify the church season or the wearer's rank.

Cope

FIGURE 567

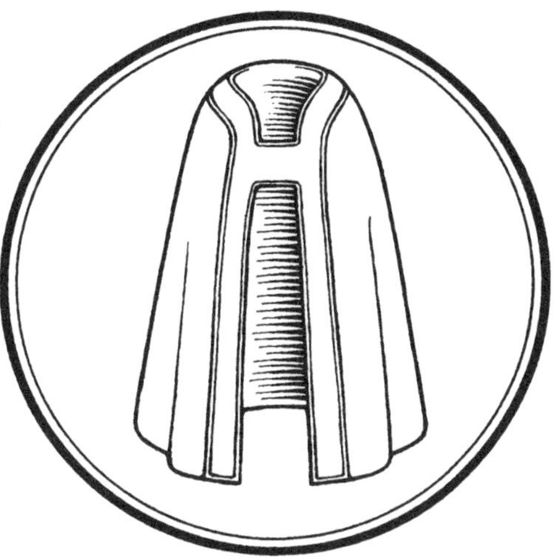

This outer garment is sometimes used in a similar fashion as a chasuble, or it may simply be used out in the elements and for processions. It may have an integral frontal band or may use a decorative chain to hold it in place. Similar to a cloak, it has not changed in style or use in hundreds of years. The cope may follow the colors of the liturgical calendar or may be black.

Cowl

FIGURE 568

A cowl is a long, hooded vestment with long sleeves. It is worn over the habit of a monk and signifies that he has taken his lifetime vows. The color of a particular cowl indicates the order to which the person belongs.

Crozier

FIGURES 569, 570, 571, 572

There are many types of crosiers, only some of which follow denominational lines. The word is derived from Latin and Old French, meaning "cross-bearer," and the staff is a symbol of rank in both the Eastern and Western Churches. Strangely, the rarest form is that of a staff topped with a crucifix. Most often a shepherd's crook is used as the model in the Western Church, although it may be hard to detect the shape within its ornamentation. In the Eastern Church, a tau cross is the basis, with downward-sloping arms and a second, smaller, Greek cross topping it. Alternately, the Eastern Church also uses a crozier topped with facing serpents and, again, topped with a small Greek cross. This latter form may seem a bit odd, but it is based on the serpent-topped staff of Moses. The crozier is often used in processionals.

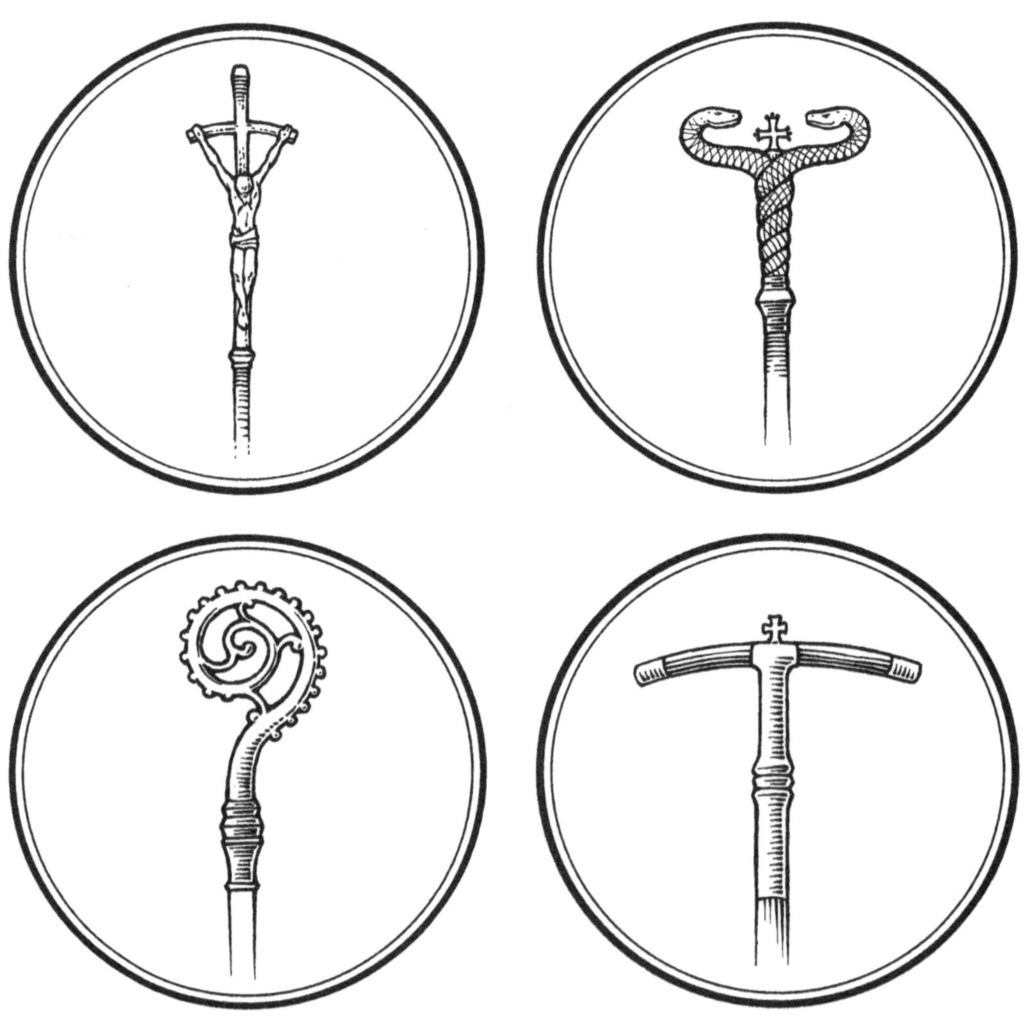

Dalmatic

FIGURE 573

This vestment is worn by deacons and, while slightly less ornate, usually matches the chasuble worn by the celebrant. There are a few deviations in its use, but it can usually be identified by its horizontal orphrey ornamentation. It dates to ancient Rome and was originally worn by women in the upper class.

Devotional Scapular

FIGURE 574

These small items are more likely to be worn by devout Roman Catholic parishioners than clergy. Typically, they are small rectangular images worn over the chest and back and connected by cords worn around the neck on the shoulders. They may have images or symbols of Mary or the Passion of our Lord and are worn to signify devotion or penance.

Encolpion, or Engolpion

FIGURES 575, 576, 577

Worn by Eastern Orthodox bishops, this chest ornamentation probably originated from the pagan practice of wearing amulets. In an effort to rectify this superstition, bishops in the Middle Ages began wearing small icons as medallions. There are several forms—some depict crucifixes, some depict Christ Jesus in blessing, and others depict Madonna and Child. The medallions are typically gold-plated, bejeweled, topped with a small crown, and suspended on gold chains.

Epigonation

FIGURE 578

This vestment article is typically worn when the bearer has been awarded for service in defense of the church. Its name literally means "over the knee," and it hangs over one shoulder to one side of the body. It is a square, stiff, decorative element the size of a small napkin and, by its placement, is meant to represent "the sword of the Spirit."

Epimanika, or Epimanikia

FIGURE 579

Said to represent the bindings of Jesus' hands upon His arrest, these are decorative cuffs worn over simple vestment sleeves during Eastern Orthodox Divine Liturgy. They are made of the same fabric and liturgical color as the rest of the vestments.

Epitrachelion

FIGURE 580

A type of stole worn by Eastern Orthodox priests, this decorative piece of fabric hangs "around the neck," as its name implies. Unlike the stole of the Western Church, however, the two ends are connected, and the piece may even be of single construction. Like the stole, it symbolizes the yoke of burden.

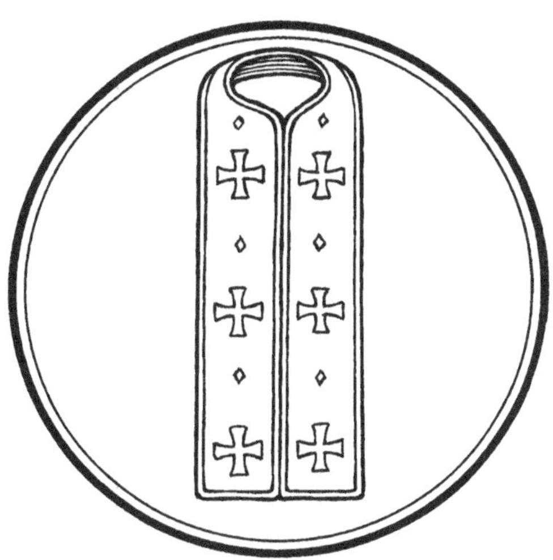

Exorasson

FIGURE 581

This is a vestment worn over the anteri in the Eastern Orthodox Church. It is usually black and may have a contrasting border on the sleeve. This piece of clothing is plain and is usually only seen during informal settings. In the Orthodox tradition, it is worn by married clergy.

Fascia

FIGURE 582

This is a specific type of cincture worn above the waist in the Western Catholic Church. Its color indicates rank. It is typically worn for everyday church business and not during worship services.

Ferraiuolo, or Ferraiolo

FIGURE 583

This cape can be worn by any clergy in the Roman Catholic Church, with the exception of the pope. Again, its color indicates rank. It is ankle-length and may be firmly fastened in front or hang casually from the shoulders.

Kamilavka

FIGURE 584

This head covering is generally worn in the Eastern Orthodox Church by ordained priests during the liturgy. There are a few regional variations in its use and color. There are also variations in its appearance, especially between Greek and Russian counterparts, but the kamilavka is always of stiff construction.

Koukoulion

FIGURE 585

This vestment piece is the Eastern Orthodox counterpart to the cowl worn in the Western Church. It is a peaked hood with two lappets and is worn by monks and certain patriarchs. As is often the case, there are marked variations between regional monasteries and patriarchal koukoulions. The helmet-like example is surmounted by a cross, indicating that the wearer is a patriarch of the church.

Maniple

FIGURE 586

With origins in a simple handkerchief used to wipe tears, this article has become much more ornate. The maniple is used in a worship service and usually matches the liturgical color and design of the chasuble. Common in the traditional mass of the Roman Catholic Church, it may also be occasionally found in the Lutheran Church. There are various suggestions regarding its symbolism. These include penance, the burden of sin, and that the wearer is a servant of servants.

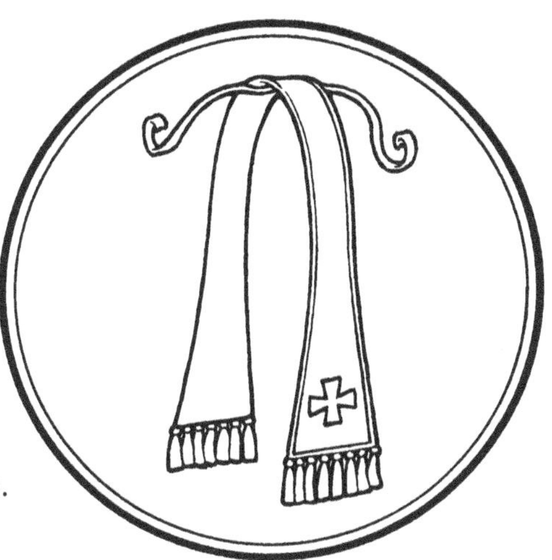

Mantiya

FIGURE 587

The mantiya is a cape-like outer vestment worn by Eastern Orthodox clergy during processions that do not lead to a worship service. Today it is distinguished by its length—which can include a sizable train—and by ornamentation, but it was originally a plain, simple garment. Its use is documented in 2 Kings when Elijah passes his mantle to Elisha to indicate the passing of authority.

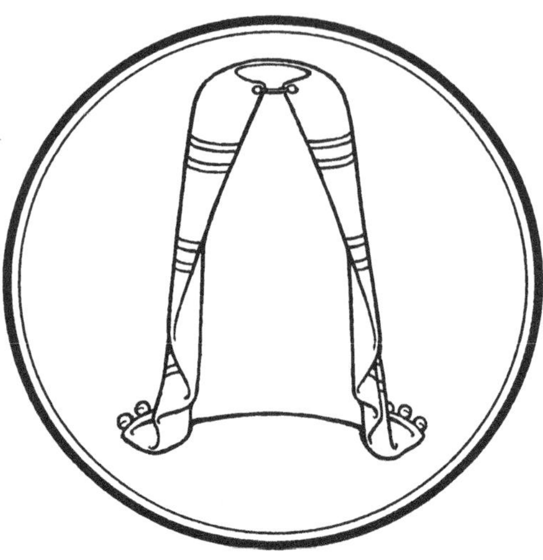

Miter, Eastern Orthodox

FIGURE 588

Miters are worn in both the Eastern Orthodox and Western Church, though there are marked differences in appearance. The miter represents the holiness of the office and is often white but may reflect seasonal colors. The Eastern Orthodox Church miter follows the pattern of imperial, secular crowns. Priests may wear a miter lacking a top cross.

Miter, Western Church

FIGURE 589

The Western miter is of cloth-covered, stiff construction. Two tapelets are attached at the base of the back of the miter. It comes to a tall point in the front and back, with a deep cleft between. Common in the Roman Catholic Church, this miter may also be worn by some Anglican bishops. As with its Eastern Orthodox counterpart, the miter is worn by bishops and those of rank.

Nabedrennik

FIGURE 590

This item is used exclusively in the Russian Orthodox tradition. Its Greek Orthodox equivalent is the epigonation. Both hang over a thigh, and both are service awards for priests who have defended the faith. Unlike the diamond-shaped epigonation, the nabedrennick is rectangular. It may be fashioned out of rich brocade and embroidered.

Omophorion

FIGURE 591

Similar to a long, wide stole, this vestment is worn by Eastern Orthodox bishops during worship services. Said to represent the lost sheep carried on the Good Shepherd's shoulders, the omophorion indicates the pastoral function of the bishop. It may be arranged around both shoulders or sewn together to mimic the arrangement. Its Western counterpart is the Roman Catholic pallium.

Orarion

FIGURE 592

Narrower than an omophorion, this is the distinguishing vestment worn by Eastern Orthodox deacons and subdeacons. It is worn over one shoulder and under the other. Often constructed from brocade, it may be adorned with crosses and may be of varying lengths depending on the wearer's rank and the occasion.

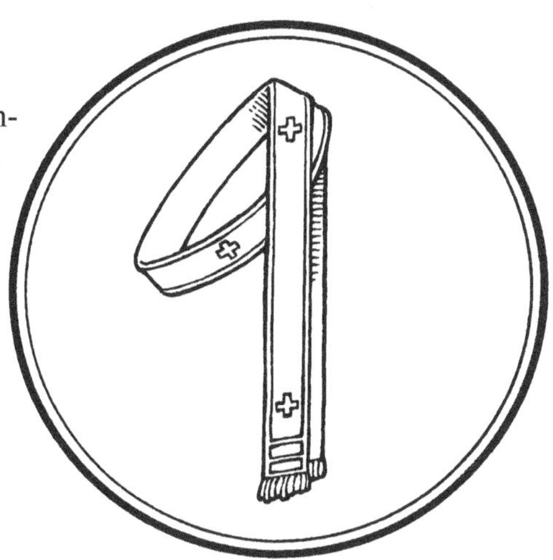

Papal Fanon

FIGURE 593

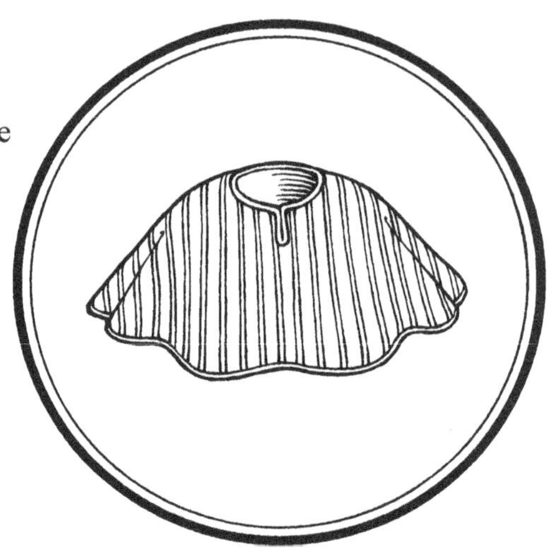

This small double cape is worn exclusively by the pope when he celebrates the mass. Its construction is similar to a tree skirt one might put around a Christmas tree. It is made of white silk and has conspicuous gold stripes running front to back. Although commonly used for centuries, it is seldom seen in contemporary times.

Papal Pallium

FIGURE 594

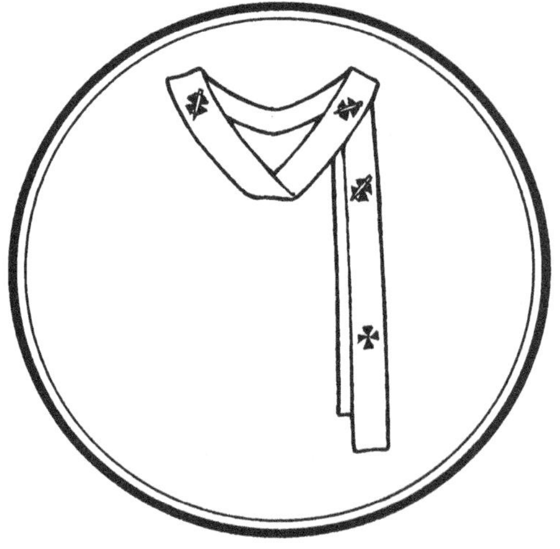

Derived—in name only—from the Roman pallium, this was originally an outer cloak. Now it is a narrow, woolen band worn by the pope in similar fashion as the Eastern Orthodox omophorion. It is white with six embroidered crosses and is usually pinned in three places by thick jeweled pins; it represents the plentitude of the pope's office.

Papal Shoes

FIGURE 595

The entire vestment set—including shoes—is unique for the pope. His shoes are of red leather and are often embroidered with crosses. They symbolize the martyrs, who walked in the bloody footsteps of Christ Jesus during His journey to the cross. Indoor shoes are made of silk or velvet and outdoor shoes are made of leather.

Papal Tiara, or Papal Crown

FIGURE 596

The papal tiara was last worn by a pope in 1963, and there is debate in the Roman Catholic Church to this day over its use or disuse. Strangely, its three tiers do not symbolize the Holy Trinity but point to papal one-upmanship during the reign of the Holy Roman Empire (962–1806) when the emperor wore—you guessed it—a double crown. The three tiers represent the three powers of the pope: the vicar of Christ, the governor of the world, and the patriarch of kings. They are also said to symbolize those who suffer, those engaged in warfare for the faith, and the church triumphant. Historical records show that popes wore a crown of some sort as far back as the early 700s. There are more than twenty such crowns in existence today.

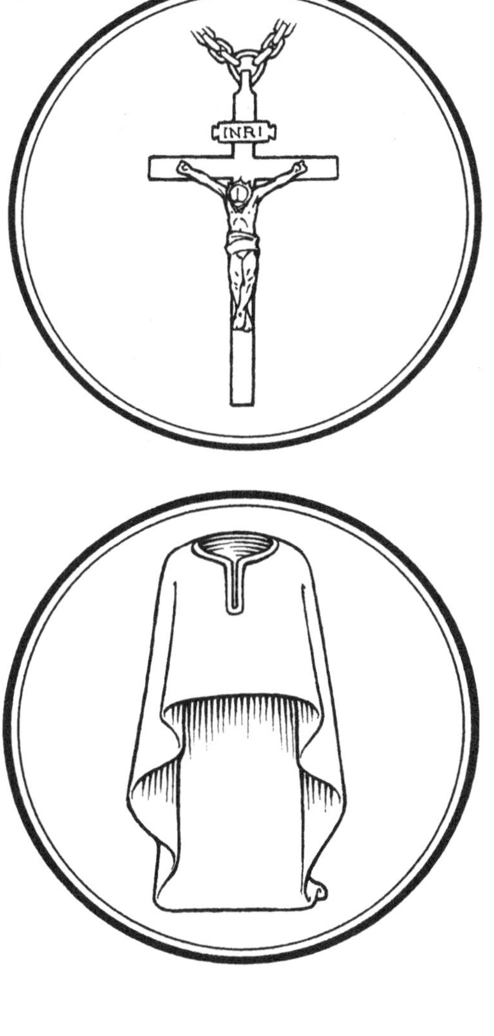

Pectoral Cross

FIGURE 597

The pectoral cross is worn by clergy in many denominations, although they are restricted to clergy of rank in both the Roman Catholic and Eastern Orthodox Churches. They are larger than those worn by laity as jewelry and are often made with precious metals and stones. Worn on the chest, they come in many sizes and styles, with and without the corpus.

Phelonion

FIGURE 598

Worn by Eastern Orthodox priests as far back as the fifth century, the phelonion is the equivalent of the chasuble worn in the Western Church, but its use is not limited to worship services. The distinguishing difference is that it is short in front and long in back.

Preaching Tabs

FIGURE 599

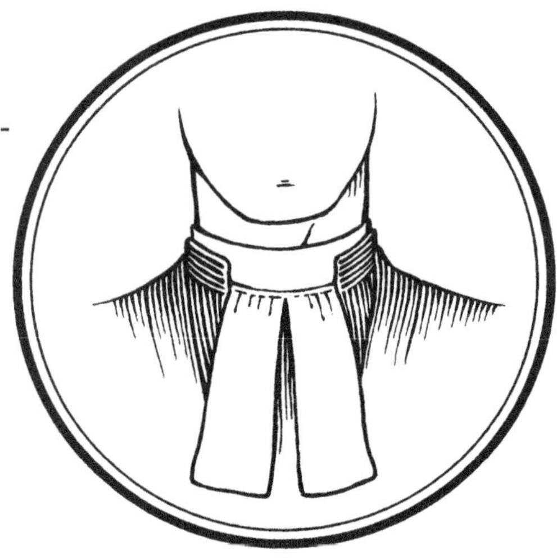

These latecomers to vestments are sometimes referred to as preaching bands (also called Geneva bands or barrister bands), are Calvinist in origin, and date to the 1600s. They are usually worn over a clerical collar and, according to some, symbolize the two tablets of the Law. This notion was likely imposed on the neckwear because it can also be worn by lawyers, judges, and professors. Length, width, color, and fabric vary.

Rationale, or Superhumerale

FIGURE 600

Rarely worn today (and when it is, it is worn exclusively by Roman Catholic bishops in Germany and France), these are said to symbolize a hoshen—the breastplate worn by the high priest in ancient Israel. It is worn over the chasuble and in somewhat the same manner as a devotional scapular.

Rosary Beads

FIGURE 601

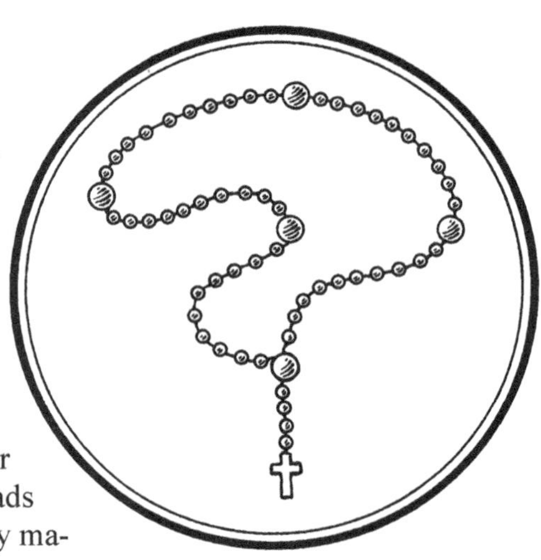

Prayer beads are used in both pagan and in Christian religions and date to at least the sixteenth century (knotted prayer ropes were used a thousand years before then). The rosary typically refers to a set of prayers, and the beads help to keep order while reciting those prayers. Variations are used in the Eastern Orthodox Church, Roman Catholic Church, and other denominational groups. Beginning with a crucifix, the rosary includes fifty-nine beads attached by cords or chains and divided into "decades" of ten smaller beads separated by larger beads. It may be made of nearly any material.

Sakkos

FIGURE 602

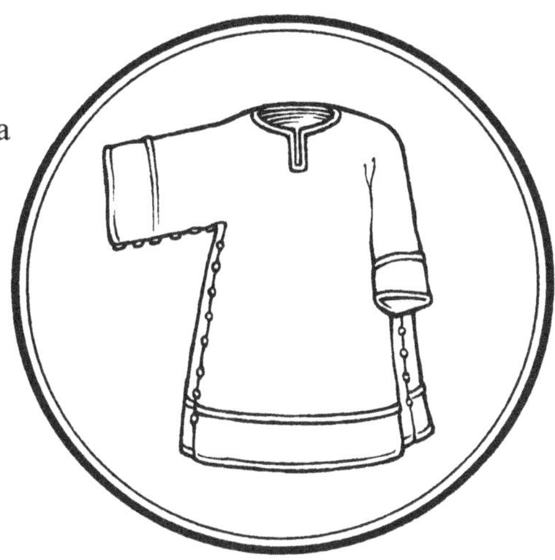

Worn by Eastern Orthodox bishops instead of a priest's phelonion, the sakkos is wide with sleeves. Typically fashioned from brocade and adorned with elaborate embroidery and bells, its use is traced to the eleventh century. It is fastened with a total of thirty-three buttons, symbolizing the number of years Christ Jesus lived on earth. The sakkos is worn when the bishop is fully vested for a worship service and for occasions such as Good Friday.

Scapular

FIGURE 603

Worn in the Western Church by monastic clergy, this vestment originated from an apron worn by monks and dates to the seventh century. It evolved into a long piece of fabric, worn over the shoulders, that covers the front and back of a habit. Open on the sides, it is the width of the shoulders and hangs to the ankles in both the front and the back. There are several styles and colors worn by both nuns and monks to help mark a particular order. Some Protestant denominations include the scapular with vestments for clergy or choirs.

Simar

FIGURE 604

This is a more elaborate version of a cassock that is worn exclusively by bishops in the Roman Catholic Church, including the bishop of Rome—the pope. In appearance it is more like an outer coat, with an integral shoulder cape, large cuffs, and sometimes double sleeves. The simar is black with red trim when worn by bishops and white when worn by the pope. It has thirty-three buttons to represent the thirty-three years of Jesus' life on earth.

Skufia

FIGURE 605

This soft, brimless cap is a softer equivalent of the kamilavka and is worn by monastics in the Eastern Orthodox Church. Clergy of higher rank will often wear a skufia with ornamentation.

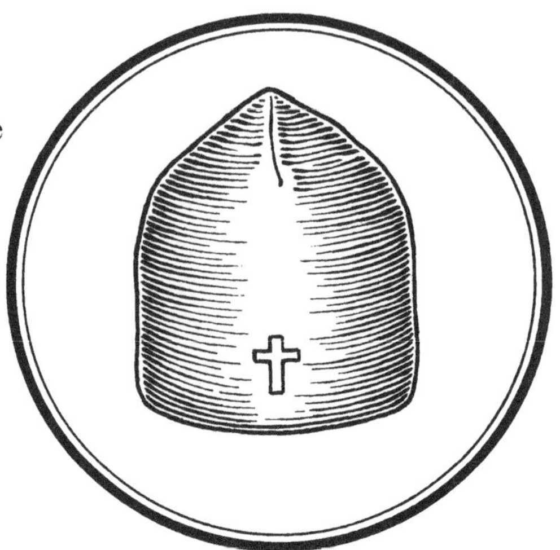

Sticharion

FIGURE 606

This is the Eastern Orthodox counterpart of the Western alb. As an outer vestment, it can be more elaborate and of liturgical colors other than white; as an inner vestment, it is white or gold. It is worn by all levels of priests and those who serve in the mass.

Stole

FIGURE 607

Worn in the Western Church, this is the equivalent of the Eastern Orthodox epitrachelion, omophorion, and orarion. Although its origin is not quite clear, it is associated with clerical use in the Roman Empire as far back as the time of Constantine I. The stole symbolizes the yoke of Christ and is worn by priests, pastors, and bishops. Stoles follow seasonal colors instead of clerical rank and are usually embellished with embroidery, braid, and fringe. A small cross is typically embroidered for placement on the back of the wearer's neck and at the lower edges. The celebrant sometimes kisses the stole while vesting.

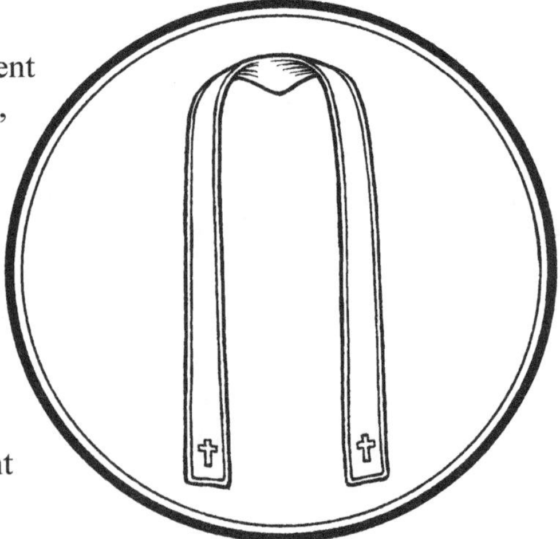

Sub-Cincture

FIGURE 608

Worn exclusively by the pope of the Roman Catholic Church and the Patriarch of Lisbon, this is a maniple-like band worn at the waist. An ornamental vestment, it comes in liturgical colors and often has an image of the Agnus Dei at one end.

Surplice

FIGURE 609

This white vestment is worn over the longer black cassock and is typical in the Western Church, except during the Divine Service. Documentation puts its use in the fifth century and possibly before then. It is symbolic of a baptismal garment and therefore covers the underlying sinful black. Surplices may be worn by pastors and acolytes.

Tab Collar

FIGURES 610, 611

More commonly referred to as a clerical collar, this recent addition to vestments was invented by a Presbyterian minister in the 1800s. There are a few variations, but all distinguish the wearer as a pastor or priest and reflect his office as one who proclaims the Word of God. Hence, white covers the wearer's throat. The white may be visible as a small square, a slightly wider rectangle, or as a white band that totally encircles the neck. It may be made of cotton, linen, or even plastic.

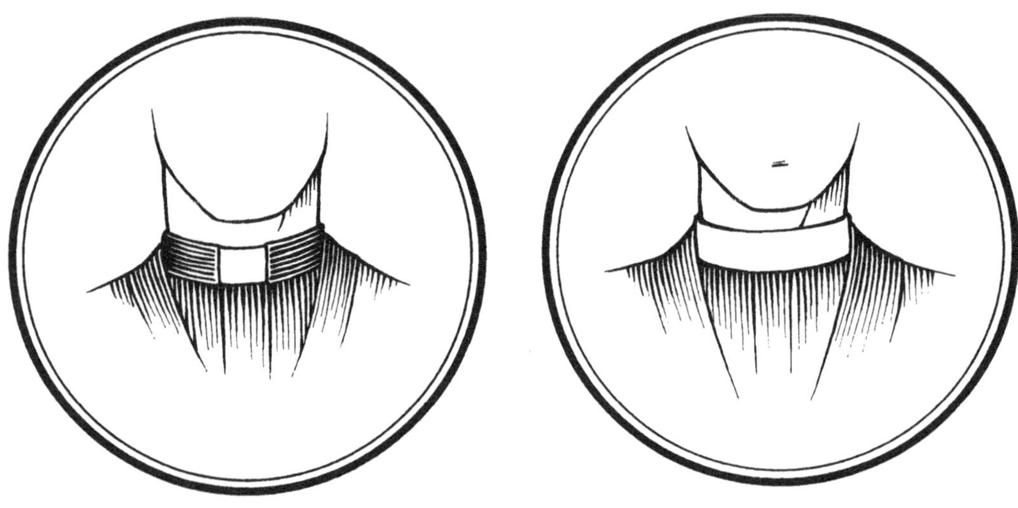

Zone

FIGURE 612

Similar to a cincture, a zone is worn at the waist by some elements of the Eastern Catholic, Eastern Orthodox, and Oriental Orthodox Churches during Matins or Vespers. It is not worn during the divine liturgy. Made from brocade in liturgical colors, it is adorned with crosses. The zone is symbolic of priestly power.

Zucchetto

FIGURE 613

These skullcaps may be worn by Roman Catholic, Anglican, and Syriac Orthodox clergy. It may be worn under a miter but is removed during the worship service. Its name derives, oddly, from the fact that it looks like the top of a pumpkin. Because its appearance is nearly identical to the Jewish yarmulke, some infer that we share a common heritage by adoption through Christ Jesus. With historical roots to the Middle Ages, the modern zucchetto is made of silk, and its color is indicative of ecclesiastical office.

Sanctuary Fixtures and Paraments

Although ecclesiastical architecture, design, and aesthetic styles have changed radically (especially in the past century), the fixtures found in today's church sanctuaries trace a lineage extending to Old Testament worship in the temple. There remain parallels between the temple's arrangement and layouts of traditional Christian churches. It should not be surprising, therefore, that much of the purpose is the same and that symbolism crosses both testaments, pointing from either side of history to Christ Jesus. That is, the design and arrangement of sanctuary fixtures is intended to direct the congregants' focus to the preaching of the Word and receiving the Sacraments. Whether the church building is a centuries-old Gothic cathedral or a repurposed storefront, fixtures and paraments are employed to gather the Body of Christ in the presence of God.

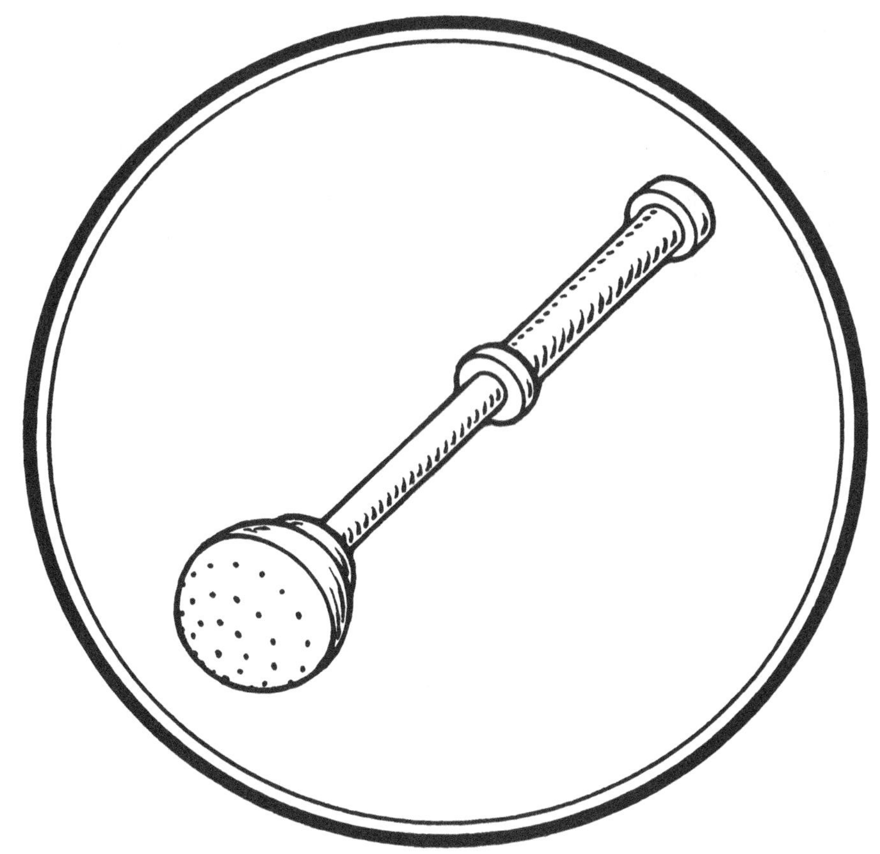

Altar

FIGURE 614

With a place of prominence in the sanctuary and centrally located, the altar is a raised table or block-like permanent structure (the word *altar* comes from a Latin word meaning "high"). The eyes of the congregants are drawn toward the altar, on which rest the elements of the Sacrament of the Altar, consecrated during worship. Many have five small crosses inlaid into the top, representing the five wounds of Christ, although these crosses are usually only visible on Good Friday when the altar cloths are absent.

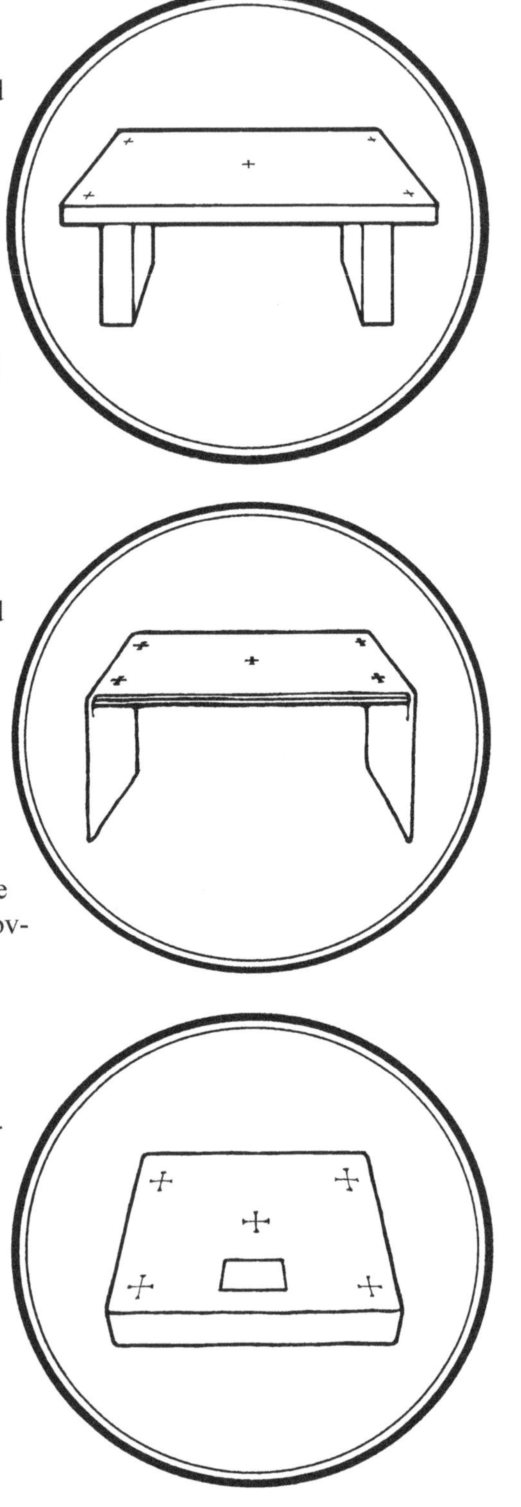

Altar Cloths (Cerecloth, Linen Cloth, and Fair Linen)

FIGURE 615

These white cloths, used in combination, derived from necessity in the early church to protect the altar and altar cloths and to show reverence. The wax-coated cerecloth was placed first as a barrier for any condensation on the altar itself. A linen cloth was laid over the cerecloth, and the nicest decorative fair linen was placed on top. In a tradition dating to the 300s, altar cloths are symbolic of the garments of Christ since the altar is a symbol of Christ Himself. It is therefore the church's tradition to strip the altar, removing all coverings, on Good Friday.

Altar Stone

FIGURE 616

To be properly observed, mass is said on a consecrated altar made of natural stone. Therefore, it became the practice for a traveling Roman Catholic priest to bring an altar stone with him. Often a small block of marble, it usually contained a small reliquary, and the stone itself would sometimes fit into a niche in the church's altar. Later these stones became more permanent affairs.

Antependium

FIGURE 617

This is an ornate parament that covers underlying altar cloths and hangs over the front of the altar, pulpit, and lectern. It is usually coordinated with the liturgical seasons and made from the same fabrics as the pastor's vestments. Such cloths have been in common use since the 400s, but the word *antependium* may also be used in reference to the front of the altar itself.

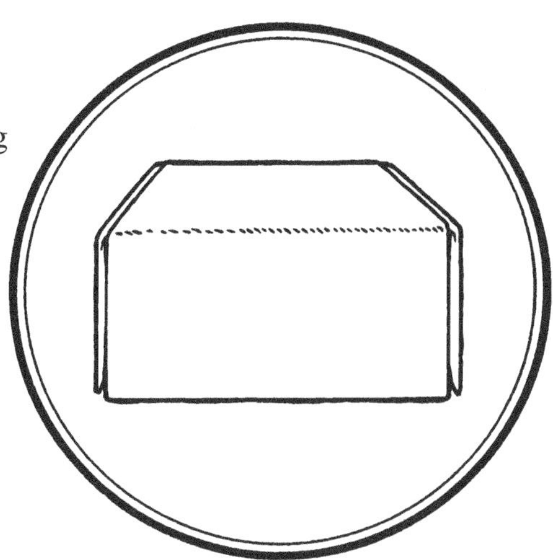

Aspergillum

FIGURES 618, 619

Used to sprinkle holy water, this is used in the Western Church with some exceptions in the East. It has a short handle and may be a solid metal instrument with a perforated head or have a broom-like end of stalks or hair. It may also include sprigs of basil or hyssop. In most of Eastern Orthodoxy, however, the priest uses his hand to accomplish the same. Holy water is sprinkled during the rite of Baptism, a funeral service, and on festival days such as Palm Sunday and Candlemas.

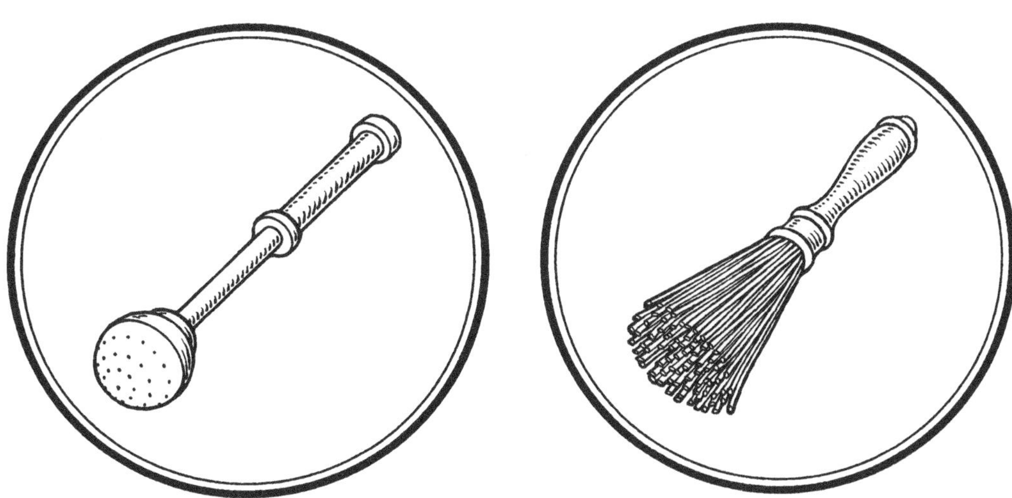

Baptismal Font

FIGURE 620

These vary greatly throughout Christendom, from large pools, similar to those found in antiquity, to small pieces of freestanding furniture. They may be made from carved wood, stone, marble, or metal. Fonts are often eight-sided to symbolize the resurrection of Christ, underscoring the fact that we are baptized into His death and resurrection. Their location may be just outside the sanctuary, anywhere on the central aisle of the sanctuary, near the altar, or in a room or separate structure of their own (a baptistry).

Burse

FIGURE 621

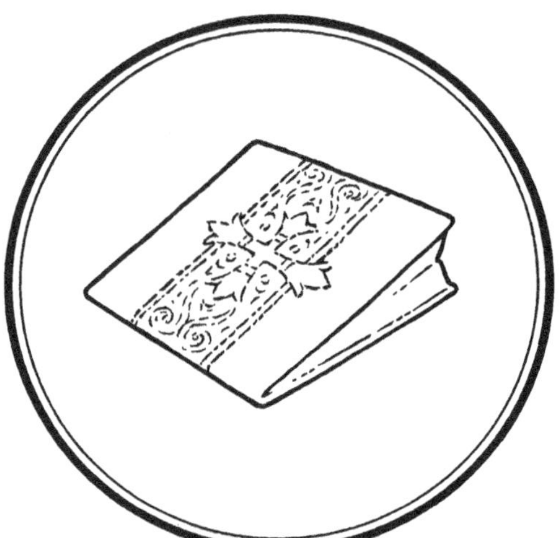

A stiff, cloth construction that resembles a square folder, the burse was historically used to reverently carry the corporal to the altar. It is usually heavily decorated and follows seasonal and liturgical colors. During a worship service, it is often displayed on the altar by setting it on its open end.

Candelabrum

FIGURE 622

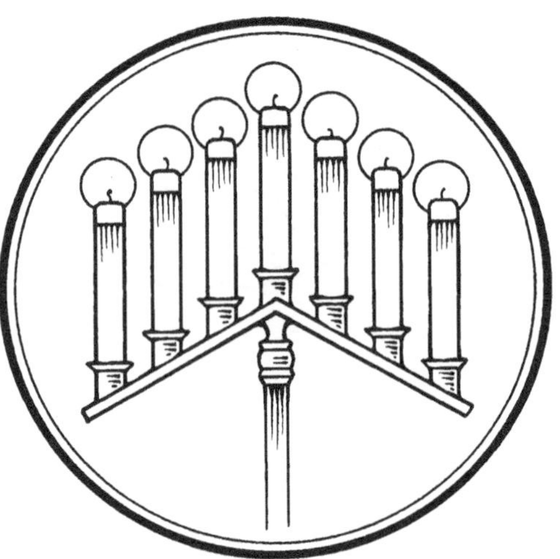

These candleholders were originally used to give sufficient light at the altar but now are used in a more decorative role. They symbolize that the service is taking place, being lit before and being extinguished afterward. They often hold seven candles—the biblical number for completeness—and are designed similarly to the Jewish menorah and, more pointedly, the lampstand of the tabernacle.

Cathedral

FIGURE 623

Some Roman Catholic church buildings have a conspicuous, ornate chair near the chancel that is often left unused. This is the *cathedra,* a Latin word for chair, which is a permanent piece of furniture reserved for bishops, including the pope. Churches that have this chair are referred to as cathedrals. It is from these chairs that official proclamations are made, and such edicts begin, *Ex cathedra,* or "From the chair." Synonymous with "elaborate church building," the word has been adopted to mean something large and important. Historical use of the term dates to Constantine, who chose Christianity as the official religion of Rome.

Chalice and Ciborium

FIGURE 624

Used for the same purpose as a chalice and paten, the ciborium is closer in form to a chalice and has a lid. These sacred vessels are often made of precious metals and treated with reverence and care as they are used for the Sacrament of the Altar.

Chalice and Paten

FIGURE 625

Vessels for containing and for distributing the consecrated wine and host, respectively, they may be simple earthenware or be made of bejeweled, precious metalwork. The paten is either a very shallow bowl or a plate without a cover. The chalice is mentioned specifically in all four Gospels in the account of the Last Supper.

Chalice Veil

FIGURE 626

Originating as a protective covering for the chalice and ciborium, the chalice veil is often highly decorative and may have symbols for Christ—such as a Chi-Rho—to identify what, and Who, is beneath the veil. Usually made from linen, the veil covers the sacred vessels until the Service of the Sacrament, when the pastor consecrates the wine and host prior to distribution.

Chrisom

FIGURE 627

In some churches, the tradition of clothing a newly Baptized infant makes use of a simple cloth that is tucked around the infant's head or body. It symbolizes—as does a funeral pall—that we are covered in Christ's perfect righteousness.

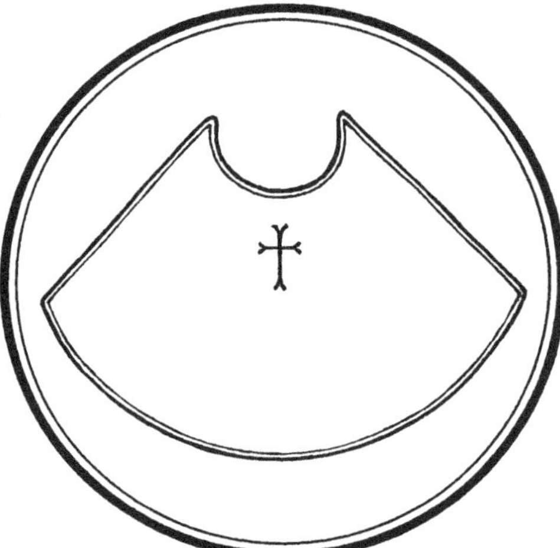

Corporal

FIGURE 628

There is some debate regarding this simple piece of cloth. Some traditions stipulate that it is spread out on the altar under the chalice and paten, while others make use of it to carry the host to the altar. Yet other traditions equate it with a purificator. Regardless, it has been in use during worship services since the 300s and is made from fine linen. This is to remind us of the linen cloth used to wrap the body of Christ when He was laid in the tomb.

Eucharistic Pallium, or Pall

FIGURE 629

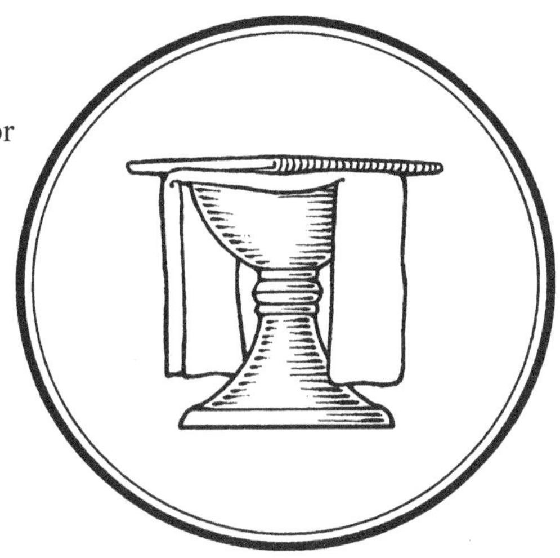

From humble beginnings as a protective cover for the chalice, this small, stiff article gives the chalice veil its square top. If a burse is not used to remove the corporal, then the corporal is folded and placed over the chalice. The pall is then placed on top of the folded corporal. The pall is often inserted into a linen sleeve, which may be embroidered with a cross.

Funeral Pall

FIGURE 630

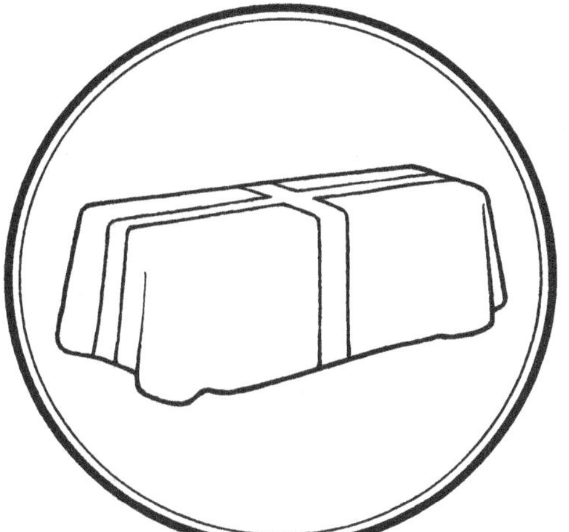

This covering symbolizes how Christ's perfect righteousness covers us in life and at our death. It should have a large cross. If a veteran's casket is flag-draped, the flag is removed before entering the sanctuary and the pall replaces it. The flag may then be redraped once the casket leaves the sanctuary.

Holy Oils

FIGURE 631

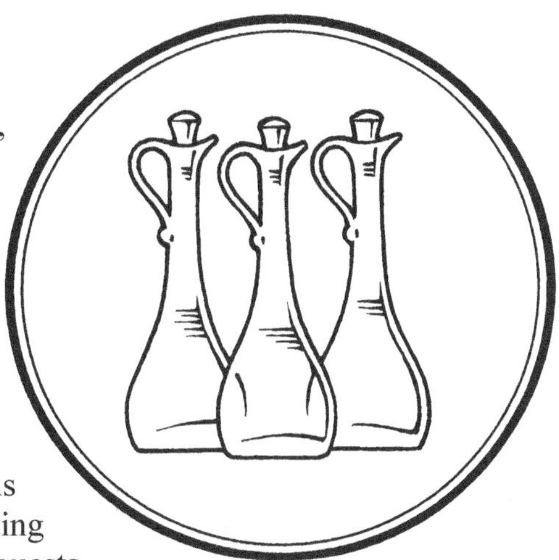

There are three types of holy oils—oil of the sick, oil of the catechumen, and oil of chrisms—and they are used in specific rites of the Roman Catholic and Eastern Orthodox Churches. All contain pure olive oil, but the oil of chrisms also has balsam. The anointing oil in Exodus 30:22–25 is made from olive oil blended with myrrh, cinnamon, cassia, and calamus. This was the oil used in Jesus' anointing. The use of oil dates to Old Testament anointing of kings and treating of the wounded, and those former applications undergird the symbolism of their modern use. Anointing with oil was also used as a way to welcome and honor guests.

Iconostasis

FIGURE 632

Based directly on the temple curtain, these ornate partitions separate the chancel and its high altar from the rest of the sanctuary and its congregants within Eastern Orthodox Church buildings. The wooden partition always has icons placed in a specific order, and one or more doors may offer access for priests. Rare peeks at the altar are the only thing offered to the worshiper in this unfortunate hand-me-down from antiquity.

Orlets

FIGURE 633

One of the more odd paraments is the special rug on which a Russian Orthodox bishop stands while preaching. It always has an image of an eagle flying over a city, which symbolizes the bishop's overseeing of his jurisdiction.

Ostensorium, or Monstrance

FIGURE 634

Used almost exclusively by the Roman Catholic Church, this container is for displaying a consecrated host during times other than the liturgy. While meant for devotion and adoration, it clearly ignores Holy Scripture's command to "take and eat." The ostensorium may be carried during processions or, when not in use, placed in a locked cabinet called a tabernacle. Typically made of gold or silver, it may also be used as a reliquary.

Paschal Candle

FIGURE 635

This large white candle is used in the Western Church to symbolize the risen Christ and represent Him as the light of the world. The name derives from "Passover" but is used synonymously with "Easter." A new candle is lit every Easter and used throughout the Easter season and on special occasions thereafter. It is usually adorned with symbols, such as the cross or the Alpha and Omega symbols.

Prie-dieu

FIGURES 636, 637, 638

Literally "pray God," this piece of furniture is intended for personal use. It is not often seen in church sanctuaries but may be found in clerical antechambers or private homes. They all have kneelers and a place to rest one's arms, but designs vary from elaborate Gothic constructions to odd, chair-like pieces. The prie-dieu may be used for the bride and groom in the wedding ceremony.

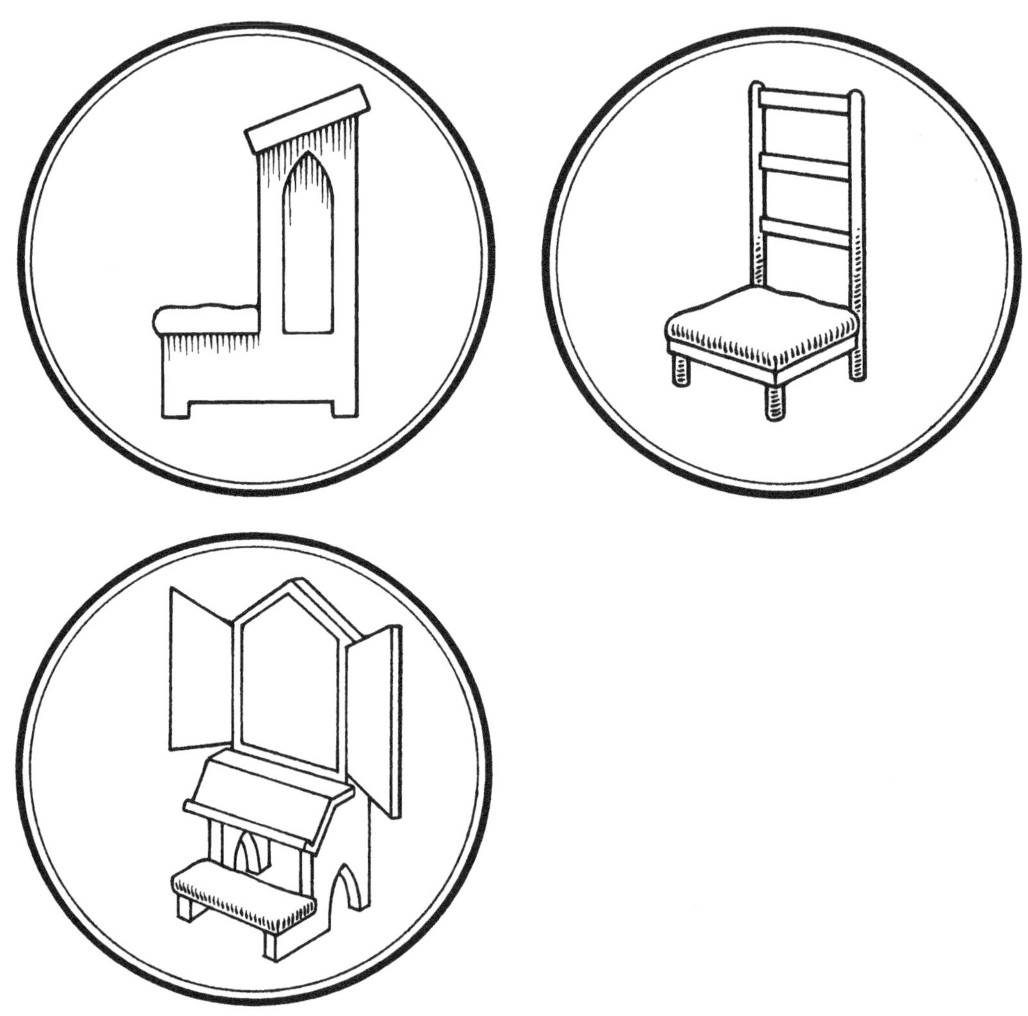

Processional Cross

FIGURE 639

Simply put, the processional cross is a cross or crucifix on a pole that is carried at the fore of processions. Long used in the church, they may be placed in a stand or, in some cases, detached from the pole and placed on the altar. Contrary to the notion of an elaborate parade, its entry into the sanctuary symbolizes that the Word is coming among those gathered. Its exit from the sanctuary reminds parishioners that Christ goes with them out into the world. As such, it has been customary to bow to the cross as it passes by.

Purificator

FIGURE 640

A simple napkin kept on the altar near the chalice and paten and used to wipe the chalice after use, it is typically made of white linen.

Reliquary

FIGURE 641

These are containers developed during the fourth century to contain holy relics, including such objects as pieces of the so-called "true cross" or anatomical pieces of saints. They often came with bragging rights for a given church, much to the chagrin of the reformer, Martin Luther. A reliquary may be set into a locket or ring, or it may be an ossuary. It may be constructed to resemble the thing it contains. It may be made of wood covered with precious metal, enamel, and gems, or it may be made of enamel, ivory, or glass. It is often portable.

Sanctuary Bells, or Altar Bells

FIGURE 642

Sanctuary bells are smaller bells used during the liturgy in Roman Catholic, Anglican, Methodist, and some Lutheran churches. They are usually handheld and may consist of several bells, although some are permanently mounted to chancel walls. They are rung as the Words of Institution are read and symbolize the miraculous event that is the Lord's Supper.

Sanctuary Light

FIGURE 643

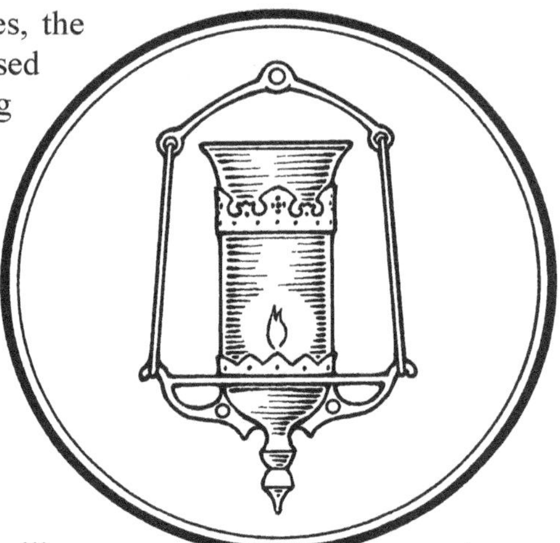

Seen in Jewish synagogues and Christian churches, the symbolism of sanctuary lights obviously differs based on context. In the Christian tradition, it is left burning to signify that Christ is the light of the world, which burns even in the darkness of sin. It is often an oil lamp shrouded by red glass. It may be mounted on the wall, sit on a dedicated stand, or hang suspended from a chain and positioned near the altar.

Tabernacle

FIGURE 644

From the book of Exodus, the tabernacle is the dwelling place of the Lord. Moses was charged with building the tabernacle and taking it along on the Israelite journey to the Promised Land. For Christians, Jesus is the true tabernacle. Some Bible translations use the word as a verb to make the point that Jesus dwells with us: "the Word . . . dwelt among us" (John 1:14). In a contemporary Christian context, this dwelling is a container for the consecrated elements of worship services. It is large enough to hold the chalice, ciborium, and ewers, is often a permanent fixture, on or behind the altar, and may be covered in precious metals and stones. While primarily used in Roman Catholicism and Eastern Orthodoxy, they can also be occasionally found in other denominations, including the Lutheran Church.

Tower Bells

FIGURE 645

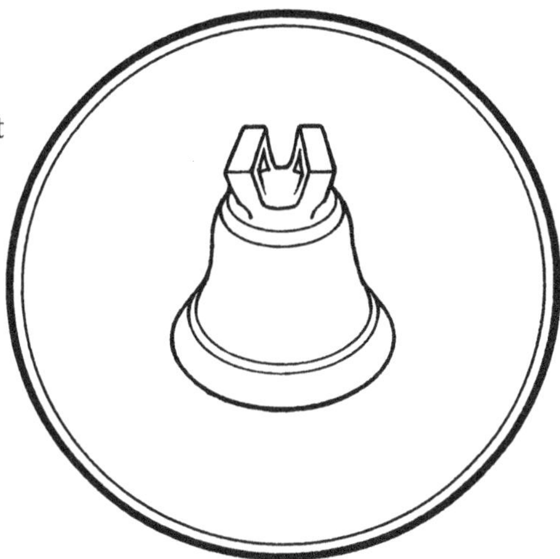

Hung within the bell tower, these are the largest found at a church and are used to call the faithful to worship, to celebrate a wedding, or to mark the passing of a congregation member. They may also toll on secular occasions, such as during royal coronations, and at the cessation of war. There may be one or more tower bells; note that a carillon must have a minimum of twenty-three bells.

Zimbelstern

FIGURE 646

This small mechanized bell chime is often constructed as part of a pipe organ. It is usually a star or wheel from which several small bells are suspended. Its gentle sound is used to accompany the Sanctus or doxological hymn stanzas and is meant to symbolize the heavenly hosts joining with the faithful in worship.

ACKNOWLEDGMENTS

I would like to thank Peggy Kuethe for fleshing out the leaner parts of this book and for reining me in when necessary. Gratitude is also due to the rest of the staff at Concordia Publishing House for seeing the worthiness and usefulness of this book. I owe a great deal of thanks to my artistic forebears, who not only created symbols for Christendom but also perpetuated their use through the ages. Finally, all glory to our Lord, who created these hands with which to praise Him and who is the infinite reality behind these finite symbols.